Britain's Black
Population

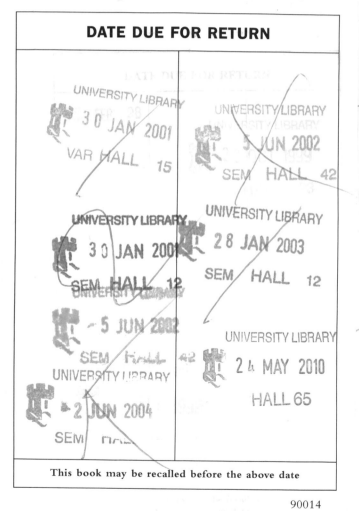

Dedicated to all the black youth in their
struggle for survival

Britain's Black Population

A New Perspective
2nd Edition

Edited by

Ashok Bhat
Roy Carr-Hill
Sushel Ohri

The Radical Statistics Race Group

Gower

Aldershot · Brookfield USA · Hong Kong · Singapore ·Sydney

Published by
Gower Publishing Company Limited
Gower House
Croft Road
Aldershot
Hants GU11 3HR
England

Gower Publishing Company
Old Post Road
Brookfield
Vermont 05036
USA

British Library Cataloguing in Publication Data

Britain's black population : a new perspective.
   —2nd ed.
   1. Great Britain. Coloured persons. Social
   conditions ·
   I. Bhat, Ashok   II. Carr-Hill, Roy
   III. Ohri, Sushel, *1951–*   IV. Radical
   Statistics Race Group
   305.8′00941

ISBN 0 566 05179 6
          0 566 05796 4 (Pbk)

Printed and bound in Great Britain by
Anchor Brendon Limited, Tiptree, Essex

Contents

Contents

Figures

Tables

Abbreviations

ASLEF	Associated Society of Locomotive Engineers and Firemen
CBI	Confederation of British Industry
CRC	Community Relations Council
CRE	Commission for Racial Equality
DES	Department of Education and Science
DHSS	Department of Health and Social Security
ECT	electroconvulsive therapy
EPA	Educational Priority Area
EPVT	English Picture Vocabulary Test
ESN	educationally subnormal
GHS	General Household Survey
GLC	Greater London Council
GREA	grant-related expenditure assessment
HIP	Housing (Strategy) Investment Programme
ICD	International Classification of Diseases and Causes of Death
ILEA	Inner London Education Authority
IMF	International Monetary Fund
LEA	local education authority
LFS	Labour Force Survey
MCE	multicultural education
MPD	Metropolitan Police Division
MRC	Medical Research Council

Abbreviations

MSC	Manpower Services Commission
NALGO	National Association of Local Government Offices
NCWP	New Commmonwealth and Pakistan
NUPE	National Union of Public Employees
NUR	National Union of Railwaymen
NUT	National Union of Teachers
OPCS	Office of Population Censuses and Surveys
PEP	Political and Economic Planning
PSI	Policy Studies Institute
RRB	Race Relations Board
SMR	standardised mortality ratio
TGWU	Transport and General Workers' Union
TIC	Total Indicative Cost (System)
TUC	Trades Union Congress
YOP	Youth Opportunities Programme
YTS	Youth Training Scheme

Biographical notes on the contributors

Ashok Bhat works at St George's Hospital Medical School where he is Honorary Lecturer in Biostatistics and a founder member of the Ethnic Study Group. He has published articles in the fields of mental health and race and is one of the Co-ordinating Group.

Heather Booth is a demographer. Now working for the South Pacific Commission in New Caledonia, she was previously with the forerunner of the Centre for Research in Ethnic Relations at Warwick. She played a prominent part in the first edition of this book and was instrumental in the genesis of this edition.

Roy Carr-Hill is a Senior Research Fellow in Medical Statistics in the Centre for Health Economics at the University of York. Previously employed as a Research Statistician at the MRC Medical Sociology Unit in Aberdeen, as Professor of Mathematics at Universidade Eduardo Mondlane in Maputo, Mozambique, and as an International Civil Servant at the Organization for Economic Co-operation and Development in Paris. Member of the Co-ordinating Group.

Harbajan Chadha-Boreham is presently a Lecturer in the Department of Computer Studies and Mathematics at Bristol Polytechnic.

David Drew is presently Senior Lecturer in Statistics in the Department of Statistics and Operational Research at Sheffield City Polytechnic. Previously Lecturer in Mathematics at the University of Sierra Leone. He played a prominent role in the first edition of this book. Specializes in social statistics and in particular the statistics of race relations.

Shaista Faruqi Senior Research Officer at the Commission for Racial Equality since 1985 and previously a Statistical Assistant at the Centre for Ethnic Relations in the University of Warwick.

Mike Grimsley is presently Senior Lecturer in the Department of Statistics and Operational Research at Sheffield City Polytechnic since 1976.

Mohan Luthera has held a number of posts in various inner city areas including that of Housing Aid Manager, Housing Research Officer and Community Liaison Officer. He is currently working as a Research Fellow at the Department of Government at Brunel University on secondment from the London Borough of Greenwich where he has been a Principal Race Relations Advisor.

Pam Nanda is a management consultant working on equal opportunities issues. She previously worked as Senior Race Relations Advisor at the GLC Ethnic Minorities Unit and has published in areas related to race.

Philip Roys is Principal Social Worker in the Department of Psychiatry at St George's Hospital, Tooting. He has previously worked in community social work, is an Executive Member of the Transcultural Psychiatry Society (UK) and has publications in the field of race and social work.

Sushel Ohri is presently the Equal Opportunities Policy Coordinator for Kirklees Metropolitan Council and was previously Recruitment and Equal Opportunities Manager with the London Fire and Civil Defence Authority. Member of the Co-ordinating Group. Over the years has worked for a number of local authorities initially as a Social Worker then specialized in race and community work, prior to working for the now abolished West Midlands County Council as their Ethnic and Race Relations Advisor.

Preface and acknowledgements

The first edition of *Britain's Black Population* edited by the Radical Statistics Race Group and the Runnymede Trust, was well received but, like all 'data books', it has rapidly become out of date and there have been many requests for a second edition. Because over seven years have elapsed, the material has been completely rewritten and the authorship has changed dramatically.

The decision to write this second edition was taken in 1982 by some of the authors of the first edition. Until her departure for New Caledonia in late 1984, the group was co-ordinated by Heather Booth. Since then, the present version has been co-ordinated by Ashok Bhat, Roy Carr-Hill and (more recently) Sushel Ohri.

We wish to thank the Centre for Research in Ethnic Relations (University of Warwick and in particular John Wrench) for their helpful comments on all the chapters. We could not have completed our task without the sterling efforts of Jenny Hardy in transforming a dozen manuscripts into typescript, and without the permanent encouragement and patience of Jane Anthony of Gower Publishing Company.

But the main debt must be to the black population of Britain without whom the book would simply not be written. (We, unapologetically, use the term black to describe all the residents of the United Kingdom who are non-white. The majority of the group is often labelled euphemistically by the British State as originating from the New Commonwealth or Pakistan (NCWP) – that is, those people who were born in, or whose families came from, the ex-colonies of Africa, Asia and the West Indies.)

1

Introduction

Ashok Bhat and Sushel Ohri

The first edition of *Britain's Black Population* was published in 1980 with three main aims: to provide a statistical picture of the black population; to describe the official policy reponses by local and central government; and finally, to discuss the inadequacies of the available statistics and the problems in using them. However the first edition, once published, was seen, in the main, as an academic textbook and its use outside academic institutions, or by the black community, was limited.

In the intervening seven years since its publication, the black population has experienced a traumatic period. In spite of a long history of positive black contributions to British society, the state continues to exploit and use blacks as the scapegoat for much that is wrong in our society, whether it be the economic decline, the increase in crime, drug abuse and so on. The continuation of racial harassment of black people in the streets and their homes by right-wing organizations and the police has contributed to the well publicized rebellions in the inner cities during the 1980s. The state, along with its powerful institutions, has manipulated and abused statistical data on race to mislead the public and cover up their own inefficiencies. The 'numbers game' from the 1960s is still alive and prospering and is no longer concerned with just the influx (numbers) of immigrants entering this country, be it temporary or permanent, but with the numbers of black British resident in this country.

White people's responses to the presence of black people have

1

varied. Some have blamed the size of the black population as the cause of the socio-economic decline of Britain. There are those who blame the diversity of cultures, customs, religion and language and the fact that these 'immigrants' have not been totally assimilated into the British culture. Then there are those that recognize that there is racial discrimination – prejudice – which leads to black people being at the bottom of the heap in employment, housing and so on. But it is predominantly black people, whose daily encounters with the state (including local government) and its institutions, who come to the conclusion that the real problem is one of racism, not only at a personal level, but more importantly, at an institutional one. It is due to the inability, or unwillingness, to recognize the latter which has led to the lack of change in the position of blacks in our society.

Thus, in this climate, when considering the nature of this new edition, the present authors have decided to make several important changes. Though the three main aims of the old edition were laudable, that edition is out of date not only because its published statistics are dated, but also because it fails to give a clear perspective on the issues facing black people. This book, by authors from within and outside the Radical Statistics Race Group, is an attempt to remedy that deficit, and in doing so we have not just produced an updated book, but a different one.

Although covering similar subjects to the previous one, this edition is much closer to developing and promoting a black perspective both in assessing the current situation, and in moving towards solutions which have more support from the black communities themselves. It updates some of the relevant academic research related to the issues raised in the previous volume and goes on to examine critically the policies and practices as they affect black people: that is, the process of racism and the blatant direct and indirect discrimination which lies behind some of the statistics. In addition, the structure and the style of this book are very different from the first edition. The statistical information given is examined in a much broader context rather than the simplistic 'numbers game' approach and there are new chapters on crime and on how white attitudes are perceived in the black community. The chapter on demography, however, has been omitted and will be published separately.

In many ways the general theme of the book is outlined in Chapter 2 which examines the politics of race statistics and the recent history of the subject. The ongoing debate from the first book on the 'numbers game' is developed and in particular the actual merits and demerits of 'ethnic data' are examined. The use and abuse of statistics at a national and local level is analysed and an attempt made to put forward a black perspective on the whole issue. Chapter 3 not only portrays the way the police abuse race statistics on crime, but also describes the relationship between blacks and the police. Reference is made to the treatment blacks receive from the penal institutions, and attention is drawn to the underexposed issue of blacks as the victims of crime.

Chapter 4, on employment, looks at the experience of black people, and young blacks in particular, in the employment market before going on to analyse the impact of the recession upon the black community and some of the explanations for the over-representation of blacks on the unemployment register. The responses by the state, local authorities and trade unions to the racial discrimination existing in employment is then examined. The chapter further draws attention to the black community's own response to the employment crisis, including its own attempts to create jobs and the development of a political lobby to promote equal opportunity policies. Finally it suggests how more positive strategies for change in the field of employment might be attempted by the government and other bodies. Chapter 5, on housing, develops an overview of the history of race and housing in the UK. The central focus of the chapter is the role of the local and central state in supporting the gatekeepers and professionals who protect what the author describes as 'white interests'. This protection of interests has contributed to the development of quantitative imbalances in the allocation of housing, acquisition of low-quality and low-value equity held by blacks and their increasing racial harassment in the inner city areas. The author emphasizes the need to develop a direct dialogue between the black community and central government in order to remove the race and housing debate from the increasing ideological crossfire between central and local government. There is emphasis too on the urgency to increase and maintain the equity of black people in housing, in particular that of young blacks with a view to alleviate the increasing feeling of disenfranchisement.

Chapter 6 examines the important area of education. It describes the different ways racism is expressed through power, practice and prejudice. It then goes on to show how the curriculum is permeated with racism, how teachers - whilst rarely explicitly racist – are often ignorant about their pupils, and to describe the second-class treatment of the problems faced by pupils 'needing' to learn English as a second language. Against this background, any complete assessment of 'achievement' is very difficult, although, on balance, blacks of West Indian origin do less well out of the educational system than others. A thorough-going move towards anti-racist practice is the only answer. Chapter 7 on social services exemplifies how departmental services continue to fail in serving the black communities appropriately. The chapter argues that, generally, only lip-service is being paid to black clients, as outlined by examples in relation to services provided to children and the elderly. Although some progress has been made on 'training', the chapter goes on to argue that it is not only through anti-racist training, but also through a greater political say for black people and the employment of more black staff that the structure and delivery of services will be more appropriately geared to meet the needs of the black community. Chapter 8 on health shows that black people do not have equality of health or health care. It outlines how the National Health Service is failing to provide adequate health care to black people by focusing on indicators of health and specific areas such as obstetric care and mental health. Reference is made to the inability of current health structures to deal with illnesses specific to black people, such as sickle-cell anaemia and rickets, and some suggestions are put forward as to what changes should be made.

Chapter 9 places ethnic data collection in a political context and details a black response. The author analyses how the resistance to the census question is related to suspicion of central government and the Home Office, and the lack of any evidence that such statistics would be used in the interests of the black population. The chapter also mentions how statistics are rarely being used in the context of claiming Section 11 funding so as to be directly beneficial to blacks. Finally the last chapter shows how, in many ways, black Britons perceive the attitudes of Britain's white population, and draws some analogies between the experiences in South

Africa and the situation here. The chapter portrays the black response to the kinds of racism and inequality outlined in previous chapters and attention is drawn to the continuing bias of the media and the need to develop and promote a black perspective.

It has taken a great deal of time to complete this new edition. There have been long debates about the independence of individual authors and the need for stronger editorial influence to allow more consistency throughout the book, particularly by moving towards a black perspective. Our main concern has been to produce a book which would be of use to the wider black community and we are aware that, in so doing, we may not satisfy some of the more specialized and narrow requirements of the academic community. We recognize too that in the present volume there is either an absence or little reference made to certain important race issue-areas such as legislation and immigration, black youth, inner city rebellion, black women and the state's response to the issue of race. Some of these topics have been written about in more depth elsewhere and we hope that, where there are gaps in our book, these issues will be taken up by members of the black community.

We also hope the book has succeeded in developing further the issues raised in the first edition. By moving towards a black perspective on the issues covered, it is our intention that not only academics, local authority officers, administrators and politicians would find this compulsory reading, but that more black people would also use it as a basis for further dialogue with the individuals and institutions which affect their everyday lives. If we achieve the latter, only then will it have been worthwhile.

PART I
RACISM AND SOCIETY

2

The politics of racism, statistics and equal opportunity: towards a black perspective

Sushel Ohri

INTRODUCTION

The object of this chapter* is to explore the question of the wider political and policy context in which the racialization of statistics has taken place in the post-war period. It is not intended as a complete analysis of this question since a number of other chapters in this volume will touch upon this issue as well. The main objective is to suggest the need for taking a broader political view of the whole question of 'race statistics', particularly when thinking about how to challenge prevailing racist conceptions of the position of black people in contemporary Britain. In addition it will be suggested that there is a need to develop a specifically black perspective on the collection and use of 'race statistics', since it is black people who are most immediately affected by the collection of such data.

The chapter will be structured around three broad themes. First, the historical and political background against which the

* The ideas developed in this paper are partly based on my experience of working as Race Relations and Equal Opportunities Adviser at West Midlands County Council 1984–86. I wish to thank John Solomos for his encouragement and critical comments on this paper.

racialization of statistics has taken place over the last forty years. Second, the use of race statistics to legitimise the pursuit of specific kinds of state policies. Third, the ways in which the development of a critical black perspective can help us to break out of the current impasse, in which more and more statistics on 'race' are being collected while little or no change can be detected in the economic, social, political and other everyday problems which confront black communities.

THE RACIALIZATION OF STATISTICS AND STATE POLICIES

Robert Miles has argued that the idea of 'race' is not a universal ideal, but emerges out of specific social and political circumstances. He defines this as a process of 'racialization', which he takes in its broadest sense to refer to 'any process or situation wherein the idea of 'race' is introduced to define and give meaning to some particular population, its characteristics and actions.[1]

A good example of how this process works is the history of the racialization of statistics. There is by now a long history of the collection of 'race statistics' by various agencies of the state, notably by the Home Office and the Departments of Employment, Education and Science and the Environment.[2] There is also a panoply of research studies by the government, local authorities, professional bodies and academics which show the extent, depth and structural nature of racial inequality in British society.[3] This is not the place to describe and discuss the findings of this wealth of material, something which other chapters in this volume attempt to do, but it is important to analyse the impact of such statistics on political debates and policy. To what use have such statistics been put by the state and its various agencies? What possibilities exist for using the collection of relevant data to help the development of anti-racist and other equal opportunity policies?

The first point to make is that there has been no shortage of attempts to use the 'numbers game' as an ideological symbol to mobilize racist support and bolster racist attitudes against blacks. From the infamous election campaign in Smethwick in 1964 numerous politicians have returned to the theme that blacks are essentially to blame for a wide variety of social problems, whether these be housing shortages, unemployment, crime, youth delinquency, urban decay or a 'fall in moral standards'.[4] The history of racism over the past thirty years shows the ways in which the 'numbers game' has been a central issue in political and ideological debates from the very early stages of black migration in the post–1945 period.[5] It is thus impossible to see the collection of statistics on race as anything but a political issue, even when it is legitimized as simply a technical one, or as a necessary prerequisite for the implementation of equal opportunity policies. The recent experience of the use of 'race statistics' by the Metropolitan Police, the Department of Employment, and in relation to the popular protests of 1980–81 and 1985, shows that such statistics can never be neutral. It is therefore important to develop a critical analysis of how this racialization of statistical data has developed, its consequences, and the possibilities for using such data to achieve anti-racist objectives.

The following account will attempt to do this through an analysis of three aspects of the racialization of statistics: immigration controls and the 'numbers game'; anti-discrimination legislation and social policy; race, crime and statistics. It will then suggest some ways in which more positive use of statistics can be made, from a black perspective. By way of a general overview of the main issues, however, some comments on the historical context of state intervention in this field are necessary.

HISTORICAL BACKGROUND OF 'RACE' STATISTICS

The wider social context of the last four decades provides the basic background against which we have to locate the racialization of statistics on such issues as employment, housing, crime, unemployment and 'riots'.[6] The history of concern over the number of black people living in the United Kingdom is, in some ways, centuries old and dates back certainly to before the period of growth in black immigration.[7] The 'numbers game' as it is called has been a central concern of official thinking and policy over the last four decades – it has had an important impact on the various forms of immigration legislation, race relations legislation and nationality legislation. The collection of race statistics has inevitably become a part of this

11

process, and this explains the deep suspicion which surrounds any claim that the collection of such statistics is a neutral tool of policy-making. Robert Moore has expressed this point with some cogency in his evidence to the Home Affairs Committee's investigation on *Ethnic and Racial Questions in the Census*. He argues forcefully that the history of political interventions in relation to immigration controls undermines claims that the collection of race statistics is neutral and will help produce 'better' policies:

> There is no technical reason why answers should not be obtained on questions of race, ethnicity and colour but two conditions are necessary for this to be done successfully:
>
> (1)   That the political circumstances are appropriate – crucially that the whole population has the confidence to collaborate.
> (2)   That the Minister responsible for the Census tells OPCS exactly what he wants them to do. Prior to the 1981 Census OPCS probably thought they knew what was required: to ask a general purpose question on race which could meet a wide range of needs in tackling a broad range of policy issues. This was an impossible task.

He goes on:

> One important possible justification for an ethnic or racial question in the census would be its contribution to the monitoring of a programme of racial equality. No British Government has been seriously committed to such a programme. It is this which makes comparisons with the USA largely irrelevant to the present discussion.
>
> It has been the policy of successive Governments to strip Commonwealth citizens of their citizenship rights. This has been done on a *de facto* racial basis and no pretence has been made since 1968 that it is otherwise. Black citizens have been harassed as a result of legislation and (less publicly) through the harsh administration of immigration rules. The increasing number of tragic cases reported in the press suggest that a covert repatriation policy is already under way. Blacks have also been subject to discriminatory treatment by the police, abuse by the Courts, and

to increasing surveillance from the police, health and educational services, operating as agents in the control process, on behalf of the Government.[8]

The harshness of Moore's comments is also reflected in the criticisms which are increasingly being voiced from within the black community about the role of statistics and research on race in the construction of stereotypes of the black communities.[9] These voices are asking: what are all these statistics supposed to achieve for black people? What evidence exists that they have helped to influence the development of anti-racist social policies?

To return briefly to Miles' definition of racialization as a sociopolitical context which gives meaning to the idea of 'race', it is important to note that what we are analysing here is an actual process which affects the life chances of black people in relation to their present and future status in British society. The racialization of statistics has a direct impact on the conditions which confront black people in every aspect of their lives – from the point of entry to this country, to their entry into schools, employment, housing and welfare services. No issue reflects this more clearly than the development of immigration controls which are legitimized on a 'racial' basis.

← see p11

IMMIGRATION CONTROLS, THE STATE AND INSTITUTIONALIZED RACISM

In the 1950s and early 1960s people from the Caribbean and Asia responded to the government's call by coming to this country in order to play a positive role in its re-building. Nevertheless, it soon became apparent that they were not necessarily welcomed, even in the worst jobs and in an inferior social position. The 1962, 1968 and 1971 Immigration Acts were used to restrict immigration to this country. In order to legitimize these controls over immigration, the collection of immigration statistics was used to monitor the operation of controls and to convince the white electorate that the government was doing its best to control the number of 'New Commonwealth' (that is black) migrants to Britain.[10] By 1965 a strong cross-party consensus between the Conservative and Labour

13

Parties emerged in favour of a dual strategy of immigration controls and measures to reduce the numbers of black immigrants and to integrate migrants already here into British society. In the now famous words of Roy Hattersley: 'Integration without control is impossible, but control without integration is indefensible.' In other words, there was a need to control the number of immigrants, otherwise there would be 'too many', and their integration into British society could not then be guaranteed. This rationale dominated the thinking of both the Conservative and Labour Parties throughout the 1960s and 1970s and had a direct impact on policy in the form of the Immigration and Race Relations Acts passed from 1962 onwards, and the 1981 Nationality Act passed by the Thatcher Government.

From the mid–1960s the 'numbers game' became the focus of political propaganda. Enoch Powell's 1968 'Rivers of Blood' speech was but one example of the kind of images which politicians, the popular media, and the actively racist groups began to construct of Britain being taken over or destroyed from within by people from a different ethnic and cultural background. These images relied, for their legitimacy, on the use of statistics about the number of black immigrants coming to Britain. This is exemplified by Reginald Maudling's defence of the 1971 Act:

> The main purpose of immigration policy . . . is a contribution to . . . peace and harmony . . . If we are to get progress in community relations, we must give reassurance to the people, who were already here before immigration, that this will be the end and that there will be no further large-scale immigration. Unless we can give that assurance we cannot effectively set about . . . improving community relations.[11]

The key message was that by reducing the number of immigrants one would enhance good race relations in this country and protect the dominant 'English' cultural values. This was a theme taken up by Margaret Thatcher in 1978 prior to the 1979 General Election in her famous 'swamping' statement, which took up similar themes to those articulated by Powell, among others, during the 1960s:

> People are really rather afraid that this country might be rather

swamped by people with a different culture . . . the British character has done so much for democracy, for law, and done so much throughout the world, that if there is any fear that it might be swamped, people are going to react and be rather hostile to those coming in.[12]

During the recession of the 1970s and 1980s the 'numbers game' has continued to play an active role in much of the political debate about 'race' and has taken on new meanings in relation to issues such as unemployment, crime, riots and social conflict. For example, right-wing groups have been suggesting a direct link between the number of blacks in this country and high levels of unemployment – implying that a solution to unemployment can be found in the repatriation of blacks.

At a more general level the prevalence of the 'numbers game' and 'immigration' in relation to 'race' issues can be observed in the expressions of concern about the relatively high birthrate of the black population, the number of black children in schools and the number of black people who are using welfare services etc. But the 'fears' which have been articulated around the immigration issue underpin all these other themes, since the central dilemma which underpins other versions of the 'numbers game' is the number of 'immigrants' who are entering Britain or who could come at some point in the future.

In the current context, the 'numbers game' is usually only associated with blacks. The now pending hand-over of Hong Kong to China in 1997 and the potential 'influx' of Chinese who may wish to exercise their right to enter Britain may change this situation, and one should not at all be surprised if further legislation is introduced (as in the case of the Asians who were expelled from East Africa) to ensure that only a limited number of 'orientals' arrive in the UK. After all, during the late nineteenth century, fears about immigration centred on the numbers of Jewish and Chinese immigrants, and the restrictions on immigration introduced in the early twentieth century were largely aimed at these groups.

The 1981 Nationality Act was introduced to reduce even further the potential number of blacks entering this country, but enough loopholes have been left to allow white people from the Commonwealth and other countries to enter without too much difficulty.

15

What is interesting, of course, is that there seems to be little official or popular concern about the number of white people who could potentially come to settle here, for example, from South Africa. As if legislation was not enough, the present government has introduced even more stringent administrative procedures to restrict the entry of blacks. Such procedures have been deemed to be racist by many blacks, and the formal investigation by the Commission for Racial Equality seems to confirm this.[13]

Although the statements of successive governments have attempted to legitimize the development of immigration controls and nationality legislation as 'non-racial', there is in fact little doubt that the primary concern since 1962 has been with the numbers (or potential numbers) of 'black' migrants. This has recently been shown by the CRE in its investigation of the immigration control procedures, which concluded among other things that:

> The way in which the (immigration) controls developed and all the surrounding debate and controversy made the issue as much one of race as of immigration *per se*, and there have been several opposing views about what are acceptable objectives of immigration control policies. At one extreme has been the view that the efficiency and effectiveness of the controls can be judged almost solely on their success in reducing and restricting the numbers of black people admitted for settlement. At the other has been the view that the legislation has been racist and that the governments responsible have pandered to racist attitudes in society, even encouraging and exacerbating them, rather than seeking to eradicate them.[14]

The administrative mechanisms set up to operate the immigration control procedures have been dominated, according to the CRE, not by 'non-racial' criteria but by the mythology that the United Kingdom may be 'swamped' by the number of people from the New Commonwealth, Pakistan and other Third World countries who are under 'pressure to migrate'.

The history of immigration controls and the use of the 'numbers game' explains the way in which black opponents of the ethnic component of the 1981 Census perceived the issue. While the government and official opinion saw this as a largely technical issue, which was essential for social policy planning, the history of immigration controls and state racism meant that most black people could not see the question of 'numbers' as separate from the racist use of statistics for the purposes of social control.

ANTI-DISCRIMINATION LEGISLATION AND SOCIAL POLICY

Apart from the use of the 'numbers game' to justify successive Immigration Acts from 1962 onwards, there has been a massive use of statistics in the pursuit of policies aimed at social 'integration', 'assimilation' and 'equal opportunity'. It is clear, for example, that since the 1965 Race Relations Act the need for legislative measures to help 'improve' race relations has been legitimized through arguments which imply that, without state intervention in relation to housing, employment and social welfare, the presence of 'too many' black people in Britain will cause social problems.[15] From the 1965 White Paper on Commonwealth Immigration successive governments have relied on the commonsense notion that immigration control and race relations legislation were complementary to promote racial harmony, and have used this notion to give legitimacy to both racist immigration controls and supposedly liberal race relations legislation.[16]

In broad outline, successive governments have argued that there is a need for more statistical information on the social position of black people in order to (a) allow for the effective formulation of the most effective policies to tackle racial discrimination and (b) to monitor the effectiveness of such policies in fulfilling their stated objective of increasing equality of opportunity for blacks in various fields. In addition, they have developed quasi-state institutions to implement 'race relations' policies and provide them with regular information on how their policies on 'race' are working - the Race Relations Board, the Community Relations Commission and, since 1977, the Commission for Racial Equality. In large measure it is these quasi-state bodies which have fostered much of the data collection on black communities, with the stated objective of helping them to achieve more equality of opportunity in fields such as employment, housing youth provision and social services.[17] In

17

addition, other government agencies have fostered a massive expansion of data collection on 'race' issues over the last decade.

What a number of black commentators are increasingly arguing, however, is that the statements made by the government and the CRE in favour of 'race statistics' evade the fact that, despite the massive weight of evidence which shows that discrimination and institutionalized racialism are pervasive at all levels of British society, the achievements of successive governments in reducing levels of racial inequality are minimal and relatively marginal.[18] This is an argument which recent research by the Policy Studies Institute (PSI) on the impact of the race relations legislation in the field of employment seems to bear out. The PSI researchers show that, since 1965, the levels of discrimination in recruitment to employment have remained largely the same and in some areas may have actually worsened.[19]

The weight of evidence against the effectiveness of measures against discrimination, and the use of statistical data to support racist immigration controls, have contributed to the high levels of distrust among black communities about why statistics are collected and the possible uses to which they may be put. Such distrust has been recently exhibited in relation to the debate about an ethnic and racial question in the 1981 Census, the collection of race-specific statistics on unemployment by the Department of Employment, and the use of race statistics by the police.[20] More recently the unwillingness of the Home Office to allow the CRE to investigate possible racist practices in the immigration control service confirmed fears in the black community that the state was only interested in collecting certain types of statistics, and not ones which may reveal its own racist practices and the possible misuse of statistics to exclude blacks from entry or to create exaggerated fears about the numbers waiting to enter this country. Although the CRE was eventually able to go ahead and carry out its investigation, the opposition from the Home Office seemed to confirm some of the black community's worst fears about the political manipulation of racialized statistics.

The CRE has argued consistently that such fears are an expression of largely unwarranted misperceptions, since the collection of data on 'race' is intended both to help the implementation of the 1976 Race Relations Act and to convince those who are not yet convinced of the levels and extent of racial discrimination. Arguing in favour of the inclusion of an ethnic and racial question in the 1981 Census, the CRE was moved to warn that:

> Strategic planning by local and central government departments to reflect the changing demographic, geographic, social and economic circumstances of the population over the next decade or so will be seriously impaired unless the 1981 Census contained the full range of the usual sorts of information as well as an ethnic question which would enable policy makers and others to identify the extent to which important sectors of British society, such as ethnic minorities, are integrated into the fabric of our social and political life.[21]

The CRE has attempted to use similar arguments in favour of race data by employers and other institutions in the form of 'ethnic monitoring'. Over the last few years, the whole concept of 'ethnic monitoring' has indeed become a catch-all phrase to describe the whole process by which various bodies, including local and central government, keep records on the composition of their labour force, on the use of public services, and on access to public goods such as housing by various ethnic groups.[22]

The CRE has argued forcefully that the implementation of equal opportunity policies is only feasible when adequate data is collected by employers, local authorities, central government and other institutions, which show how their policies are working in practice. They argue that it is only via such a process that organizations can measure how successfully racism is being tackled. Statistical data can help organizations keep their policy objectives under regular review, tackle problems that arise in implementing them, and overcome internal opposition to change.[23]

But what such arguments fail to confront directly are the kind of doubts which black people are beginning to express with increasing stridency. First, why are more statistics necessary when there is a wealth of official, academic and local government research which documents both the extent of racial inequality and the processes which produce it? Second, why has 'ethnic monitoring', in all its various forms over the last two decades, failed to bring about the

19

effective implementation of existing policies and to remedy the historic consequences of racial discrimination?

To confront these questions requires a move away from the search for more technocratic solutions to the issue of racial inequality, in the form of calls for more 'strategic planning'. It requires more adequate answers to the question of why the limited reforms proposed by successive governments have not worked. 'Ethnic monotoring', if it is to be at all meaningful, needs to be merely one aspect of a strategy for tackling the roots of institutionalized racialism. Beyond that, it calls for a shift in emphasis towards meeting the demands of the black community for more detailed programmes of action to tackle racism by developing more specific channels for consultation and discussion with the black groups at both central and local government levels.

The GLC experience from 1981 onwards shows the possibilities for more positive actions, and the importance of the full involvement of black groups in formulating and developing anti-discrimination policies – including 'ethnic monitoring'. The significance of the comprehensive policy in relation to ethnic minorities which the GLC introduced was its emphasis on the need not just to collect statistics, but to set 'targets' in order to measure how far its policies were actually influencing both its employment practices and its delivery of services. Indeed the GLC doubled the number of its black staff from 6 per cent to 12 per cent during 1982–84. In addition, towards the end of its existence, the GLC linked the equal opportunity policy objectives to a contract compliance policy in order to ensure that all those companies that relied on GLC contracts took account of their equal opportunity profile.[24]

The London Boroughs of Hackney and Lambeth are also interesting from this angle. Hackney developed a detailed five-year targeted programme for racial equality, and used monitoring and information on equal opportunity to succeed in these objectives. As a result, the borough increased its percentage of black employees from nearly 14 per cent in 1981 to 22 per cent at the end of 1984. Lambeth progressed from having 6 per cent black staff in 1979 to 24 per cent at the end of 1984. Hence, with the aid of ethnic monitoring and the political support of black groups, very positive results have been achieved by these authorities. However, the reality for the vast majority of local authorites and central government departments is that they have equal opportunity declarations in theory rather than in practice. As far as 'monitoring' is concerned, even fewer authorities are committed to its use as part of an integrated programme of action. Various excuses are used by employers and trade unions alike to ensure that no effective monitoring system is used, so that their racist policies can never be 'proven' to be discriminatory. Even local authorities which boast about the high status of their race advisers and the comprehensive consultations they have with the ethnic minorities are adamantly against effective ethnic monitoring and equality targets. A recent survey of 40 local authorities by the Labour Research Department found that, of the 26 that replied, 24 had adopted an equal opportunities policy and only 10 of these monitored its operation. Therefore it is quite apparent that ethnic record-keeping by local authorities is at best very piecemeal and open to abuse, and full of loopholes.

However, as the GLC and a few other progressive boroughs in London have only had a fairly limited impact upon other local authorities, the problem of tackling racism remains. This experience therefore only reinforces Ouseley's argument that there is a strong need for central government to take adequate account of the importance of targets which measure how its policies help black people achieve equality of opportunity and access; but the present administration (like its predecessors) shows little sign of taking this issue more seriously.[25]

RACE, CRIME AND STATISTICS

The use of 'crime statistics' is perhaps the most important aspect of the political use of statistics to the detriment of black people's interests.[26] In fact, the supposed association of young blacks with certain forms of crime, particularly mugging, has been a constant theme of the popular media and the police ever since the early 1970s.[27] While not wanting to reproduce the arguments developed elsewhere in this volume, there are some aspects of the use of crime statistics which need to be mentioned here.

The first point to be made is that the experience of the police's manipulation of race data since the early 1970s calls into question the whole idea that 'ethnic monitoring' is, by itself, a neutral technical process. According to Stuart Hall's critique of the use of statistics on mugging to criminalize whole sections of black youth in inner city areas, the social processes which allow for such data to be collected point to the pervasive racism which links the 'numbers game' in relation to immigration to the decline of inner city areas.[28] Hence the common and frequently-made argument that an area has declined because 'there are too many blacks' provides the backcloth against which racist stereotypes are developed and manipulated around notions of crime and 'race'.

The second point is that the increasing use of such data to characterize all forms of street crime, urban violence and riots as 'race' issues has tended to provide the basis of a wider social and political construction of black people as an 'enemy within' which is threatening to destroy the traditional values and institutions of British society. The ways in which the media and the police have represented the urban protests of 1980–81 and 1985 point to the complex ways in which black people are increasingly seen as an 'alien wedge' within British society. The misuse and amplification of 'race data' by both the police and the media has made a fundamental contribution to the popularization of this imagery, and helped to establish the popular image of black youth as muggers, rioters and as alien to 'British culture'. This presents a dilemma for all who are involved in ethnic monitoring or the collection of even the most banal 'race data'. According to Stuart Bentley, the police's misuse of 'race' statistics on crime has wider implications for social policies and anti-racist initiatives:

Starkly, in the case of crime figures in April 1981 and March 1982 statistics and data-gathering should be recognised in analysis as a political issue in a wider social setting. In my view, no credible argument can be put forward to maintain the notion that it is possible for uncontaminated, value-neutral data to exist in a class-stratified society where class power is a reality. This position, of course, throws into question the validity of using 'racialised' statistics to inform policy or its administration.[29]

Within the present climate of opinion the use of racialized statistics to support sterotypes about 'black criminals', the 'streets of fear' and the 'enemy within'. represents an obvious cause for concern.

The experience of the 1981 and 1985 urban protests has helped to create even stronger stereotypes along these lines, particularly because of the type of media coverage which they received. Throughout the recent events in Handsworth, Brixton and Tottenham it was all too common to see headlines which emphasized the role of 'drug barons', 'alienated' or 'criminalized' youth, the 'cultural' differences between young black and white people, the role of 'mugging' and so forth. All of these images rely on the use of statistics which are supposed to prove the drift of young blacks into crime and related activities.

Any rounded analysis of the politics of racialized statistics cannot ignore this wider political context and the role of policy statistics in constructing, amplifying and confirming popular stereotypes about the position of young blacks. The 'political side' of the collection of racialized statistics must be taken fully into account, and serious attempts made to tackle the problems which arise, because of the misuse of such statistics for political purposes which are detrimental to the interests of the black communities.

TOWARDS A BLACK PERSPECTIVE

A recent black-led review into black people's grievances in the Handsworth–Lozells area of Birmingham has warned that the pattern of state response to racism over the last two decades has tended to shore it up rather than break it down.

Over the past two decades pathetic attempts have been made by central government, and local government, to deal with the perceived threat posed by the Black presence in Britain. There have been discriminatory immigration legislation to stop black people's entry, race relations legislation with restrained enforcement provisions and the exemption of the Crown from all charges with racism, 'Section 11' funding for local authority posts intended to deal with 'new commonwealth immigrants' in their areas; the Urban Programme; Educational Priority Areas; MSC schemes; and the Inner City Partnership. Because none have

23

addressed the central issue of racism, these programmes have all had marginal benefits for Black people and in many cases have been discriminatory.[30]

As argued above, it is this failure to address racism which perhaps best explains growing dissatisfaction in black communities with the collection of statistics, with ethnic monitoring, and with central and local government policies. What is the point, it is asked, of collecting even more data when substantial evidence about the experience of discrimination and the processes of racial inequality is already available to those with the power to change things? What is the role of black people themselves in the decision-making process which influences how 'race data' is collected and how it is used?

As shown above, 'race' or 'ethnic data' has been collected for decades by both central and local government. There appear to have been times when such data has been collected without public knowledge, as confirmed by the Metropolitan Police episode in 1982[31] which pointed to the selective use of 'race data' to re-enforce negative stereotypes of the black community. This politicized use of statistics collated and used by the police force at their will, is further demonstrated by the way police have been harassing the black community after the recent urban protests of 1981 and 1985. The daily tabloids' reporting of such events only serves to 'legitimize' such data and to perpetuate the view that all blacks are criminals, muggers and 'drug barons'. Such ethnic data is then used by police forces to confirm their popular stereotypes of blacks.

Although the government's desire to have an ethnic question in the 1981 Census was resisted by the black community, as demonstrated by the short survey in Haringey, both national and local government have continued to collect ethnic data through other means. Central government departments have access to and indeed demand, statistical information upon black minorities prior to the allocation of financial resources to local authorities: for example in relation to funding under Section 11 of the 1966 Local Government Act and the allocation of Urban Programme funding to the decaying inner city areas.

Many local authorities, in times of great financial constraints, are happy to claim everything from central government and the use of

24

'race data' helps them to receive millions of pounds. The introduction of equal opportunity policies is supposed to assure the black community that the authorities are putting their own house in order. But the harsh reality of the situation is that blacks are generally 'bypassed' when it comes to allocation of resources.[32] Very little of Urban Programme funding goes directly to the benefit of the black community, and as for Section 11 funding, there is ample evidence of not only abuse of funding by local authorities but also that very few black staff are appointed to these types of jobs.[33]

It is not therefore surprising that the black community has so little faith in such data collection. If one is to persevere with the collection of such statistics then, for a start, *the black community must be directly involved in the decision-making processes which determine what data should be collected, how the data is to be collected, and by whom.* The issues of confidentiality of the data, who is going to use it, and what are likely to be the gains for the black community as a result of the exercise must be addressed. Black people must be involved in collecting and analysing the data, and placing a black perspective on them. All this will only happen if blacks form part of the decision-making process and can influence both central and local government. Local authority experience has demonstrated that it is only by setting goals and targets, with the appropriate political commitment, that ethnic monitoring can be justified and supported by the black community. But this involves recognition that not only is there no possibility of adequately tackling racism without black involvement, but that blacks can and should exercise some control over the types of policies which determine the collection and use of 'race data'.

Black people encounter racism, discrimination and prejudice every day of their lives. They want equality of opportunity and, if the collection of statistics will help to convince those in power to recognize that their policies are racist and discriminatory and that they are prepared to eliminate such policies and practices, then most black people would openly support 'ethnic monitoring' or other forms of collection of 'race data'.

The priorities which dominate the collection of racialized data at all levels of British society have been determined largely without consulting those who suffer from racism. It has to be recognized, therefore, that this has produced a bias in the types of statistics

25

collected, how they are legitimized and how they are used. A fundamental change in this situation can only come about when black communities themselves begin to determine the agenda on which data is to be collected and the uses to which such data is put. In addition, the collection of statics on issues which are of primary concern to the black communities themselves rather than to decision-makers and adminstrators has to become the primary concern. Examples of such issues are: racial attacks, racial harassment, the role of the police and the courts in relation to black people, the position of black pupils in schools, to name a few.

Quite apart from the definition of a black perspective on such issues, the first step should be a fundamental shift from the collection of statistics *for* black people to the collection of statistics *by* black people. Such a shift in emphasis needs to form part of the pressure which the black communities are exerting to transform the overall political agenda on 'race'.

CONCLUSION

In a prescient statement of the reality of the last forty years Robert Moore has argued:

> Statistics have seldom been used to the advantage of the black population, but have been the basis for abuse and for building a climate of opinion in which 'the numbers game' proclaims that blacks are intrinsically a problem.[34]

This is the basic reason why black people today are very angry at being constantly counted with no consultation and no black input into the decision-making processes. It seems that, daily, new research findings by the government, academics, the CRE and reputable voluntary organizations continually confirm that if you are black you are at the bottom in every sphere, and that 'they may be on the same boat as poor whites but on different decks'. It is only when those in power are forced to decide that they are going to tackle the racial inequalities in our society and demonstrate this through their actions and not just words, that the black communities will begin to believe that 'race data' will lead to a positive change. History has shown that, so far, 'race data' have been used for dubious political ends by both national and local government and by powerful institutions like the police. What have been the positive gains for black people? Increasing numbers of blacks are saying: 'Not very much!' Furthermore, they are deeply concerned by the constant misuse of data to confirm popular racist stereotypes. This is the reality which everyone concerned with the collection and use of 'racialized' statistics and the pursuit of greater racial equality needs to address.

Notes

1. R.Miles,'Racialization' in E. Ellis Cashmore, (ed.) *Dictionary of Race and Ethnic Relations*, London: Routledge and Kegan Paul, 1984.
2. D. Drew, 'The Politics of Statistics' in Runnymede Trust and Radical Statistics Race Group, *Britain's Black Population*, London: Heinemann, 1980; S. Bentley, 'A Bureaucratic Identity: A Note on the "Racialization" of Data', *New Community*, vol. X, no. 2, 1982 pp. 259–69; H. Booth, 'Ethnic and Racial Questions in the Census: the Home Affairs Committee Report', *New Community*, XI, 1/2, 1983, pp. 83–91.
3. C. Husband (ed.),'Race' in Britain*, London: Hutchinson, 1982.
4. CCCS Race and Politics Group, *The Empire Strikes Back: Race and Racism in 70s Britain*, London: Hutchinson, 1982; F. Reeves, *Brtitish Racial Discourse*, Cambridge: Cambridge University Press, 1983.
5. B. Carter, C. Harris and S. Joshi, 'The 1951–64 Conservative Government and the Racialization of Black Immigration', Coventry: Centre for Research in Ethnic Relations, University of Warwick, 1987, Policy paper in Ethnic Relations no. 11.
6. Drew, op. cit.; see also L. Killion, 'The Collection of Official Data on Ethnicity and Religion: The US Experience, *New Community*, vol. XI, nos. 1/2, 1983, pp. 73–82.
7. P. Fryer, *Staying Power: the History of Black People in Britain*, London: Plutopress, 1984.
8. Home Affairs Committee, Sub-Committee on Race Relations and Immigration, *Ethnic and Racial Questions in the Census*, vol. II, Minutes of Evidence, London: HMSO, 1983.
9. CCCS Race and Politics Group, op. cit.; see also H. Ouseley *et al.*, *A Different Reality: An Account of Black People's Experience and Their Grievances Before and After the Handsworth Rebellions of September 1985*, Birmingham: West Midlands County Council, 1986.
10. I.A. Macdonald,*Immigration Law and Practice in the United Kingdom*, London: Butterworths, 1983.
11. As quoted in ibid., pp. 16–17.
12. As quoted in *Daily Mail*, 31 January 1978.
13. Commission for Racial Equality, *Immigration Control Procedures: Report of a Formal Investigation*, London: Commission for Racial Equality, 1985.
14. Ibid., p. 126.

15. A. Sivanandan, *A Different Hunger*, London: Pluto Press, 1982.
16. R. Miles and A. Phizacklea, *White Man's Country: Racism in Britain Politics*, London: Pluto Press, 1984.
17. Bentley, op. cit., pp. 267–8,
18. H. Ouseley, 'Local Authority Race Initiatives' in M. Boddy and C. Fudge, (eds), *Local Socialism*, London: Macmillan, 1984.
19. C. Brown and P. Gray, *Racial Discrimination 17 Years After the Act*, London: Policy Studies Institute, 1984.
20. Booth, op. cit., pp. 83–4.
21. Commission for Racial Equality, *1981 Census: Why the Ethnic Question is Vital*, London: Commission for Racial Equality, 1980.
22. Ouseley, op. cit., pp. 133–45.
23. CRE. op. cit. 1980.
24. Ouseley, op. cit., pp. 155–6.
25 R. Miles and A. Phizacklea, op.cit., concluding chapter.
26. P. Gilroy, 'Police and Thieves' in CCCS Race and Politics Group, op. cit.; P. Gilroy and J. Sim, 'Law, Order and the State of the Left',*Capital and Class*, no. 25, 1985, pp. 15–55.
27. S. Hall *et al.*, *Policing the Crisis*, London: Macmillan, 1978.
28. Ibid., Chapter 10.
29. Bentley, op. cit., p. 268.
30. Ouseley *et al.*, op. cit., p. 18.
31. S. Smith, *Race and Crime Statistic*, London: Board of Social Responsibility, 1982.
32. Ibid., pp. 89–90.
33. Ouseley, op. cit., pp. 142–3.
34. Robert Moore in Home Affairs Committee, op. cit., p. 138.

3

Blacks, Police and Crime*

Roy Carr-Hill and David Drew

INTRODUCTION

> Britain faces the chilling spectre of an increase in the type of crime which plagues the ghettos of America. This was the blunt message from Scotland Yard yesterday as the extent of black involvement in violent crime was revealed for the first time.
> (*Daily Mail*, 11 March 1982)

This garish headline was prompted by a press release from New Scotland Yard which noted a particular concern with the increase of 34 per cent in the number of offences of robbery and other violent theft in 1981 as compared to 1980 and, for the first time, provided a racial breakdown of the presumed assailant, based on the 'Victims' Perception of the Appearance of the Assailant'.[1] This offence category of 'mugging' only constituted 3 per cent of all serious recorded offences [2] and a racial breakdown was not provided for other categories, yet the press focused on these statistics. Why? We need to understand the context. These figures were released

* This chapter is new to this edition and has a long and chequered history. Both the authors wish to record their thanks to Paul Gordon for permission to use his brief summary of the history of police–black relations and to the many people who have commented on this and earlier drafts: in particular Tony Jefferson, Ken Pease and Monica Walker. Dr Carr-Hill acknowledges the ESRC for their support and Mr Drew, Sheffield City Polytechnic. Finally both authors realize that, without the help of Sally Baker, this chapter would not have reached completion.

three months after the Scarman Report on the Brixton riots in April 1983. Amongst other things, the Report had argued that young police officers tended to be racist and recommended changes in recruitment and training.[3] Scarman had already been criticized at a Home Affairs Committee of Conservative MPs for transforming a 'straightforward issue of crime into one of race relations'.[4] A report by Sim concludes: 'the Yard were . . . using the crime figures . . . to confront Scarman's challenge to their power and autonomy.'[5]

There are all kinds of ways in which such statistics can be manipulated by those that produce them and those, like the press, that use them. This chapter does not dwell on the media and the crude and racist link made by the *Daily Mail* between black people and crime. But such distortions are the context for this chapter: for the amount of systematic information that is available is very sparse indeed, so that much of our so-called knowledge about black involvement in law and order is influenced by casual prejudiced observation, as well as by the media.

Given the focus of this book, we concentrate, of course, on how the black community are being represented in the (official) statistics and how those official statistics create or reinforce a certain image of black groups in the UK. But before examining the evidence, it is important to ask how criminal statistics should be interpreted in general.

This chapter is, therefore, organized as follows. In the first section we examine the problems of interpreting criminal statistics as being a reflection of the 'real' thing; and very briefly summarize the relations between black people and the police over the last quarter of a century.[6] The second section follows through the involvement of the black population with law and order first as potential 'offenders' then vis-à-vis the police 'on the streets' through arrests and prosecution to the courts and finally, to conviction and imprisonment. The third section considers the related issue of black people as victims – particularly of racial harassment.

WHAT DO CRIMINAL STATISTICS REPRESENT?

Crime could be defined as a transgression of legal, moral or social rules. The theoretical debate is often worthy of a monastic seminary.[7] But the cutting edge is really rather simple: whether or not we approve or disapprove, like or dislike what people do, recorded and publicized crime and criminality essentially depends on what is defined in the law and interpreted by the police as crime. Often there will be little disagreement with their judgement: for example, most of us disapprove of unwarranted violence and we are, on the whole, happy that someone is doing something about it. It would be difficult to reach this level of consensus for other types of offence. Thus, when police do act on offences against property they tend to concentrate on small-scale frauds by companies.[8] For whilst we might all agree in principle that all offences against property are equally heinous, the 'crimes of the powerful'[9] are less likely to be discovered, or even recognized, because the perpetrators are less exposed[10] and if discovered, less likely to be pursued because they are protected.

So, how do the police come to label an activity as criminal – or to put it another way, how does some event come to be counted as a criminal statistic? We have given part of the answer: it is a result of the particular laws which are in operation and the way in which these laws are applied and interpreted in a particular social context. But, more important in the context of this book, is the process by which official criminal statistics are generated. This process can be portrayed as a series of stages as follows:

Counting crime and the involvement of different groups

No realistic estimates can be made of the total volume of offences committed (Stage 1 in Figure 3.1) but the numbers are potentially very large indeed.[11] Surveys of victims provide estimates of the relative number at other stages. Most authors agree that the majority of those incidents recognized as offences are not in fact reported by the victims to the police (Stages 2 to 3). The authoritative British Crime Survey showed that only a third of incidents reported to them (itself affected by difficulties of recall) were also reported to the police and that this proportion had dropped between 1981 and 1983.[12]

Even among those incidents reported to the police, only a fraction are recorded by them as offences: the British Crime Survey

Stages	Statistics available or potentially available	Estimated numbers for 100 convictions
I N C I D E N T	1. Incidents which could potentially be offences	—	No estimate
	2. Recognition of an incident as potentially illegal	Victim Survey	8772
	3. Incidents reported to the police	(Reports to Police)	3158
B A S E D	4. Offences recorded by the police	Recorded Offences	794
	5. Police identification of possible actor	Clear Ups	203
P E R S O N	6. Person arrested or summonsed	Arrests	157
	7. Persons prosecuted etc.	Cases Prosecuted	117
B A S E D	8. Persons convicted etc.	Convictions and Disposals	100

Source: Stevens and Willis (1979): this version is adapted from their Figure 11, pp. 28–9.

Fig. 3.1   *The generation of criminal statistics from incidents to convictions*

showed that, even among those incidents classified by the researchers as offences, and reported to the police, only about two-thirds were actually recorded.[13] Consequently, a small change or distortion at any of the first three stages will dramatically alter the statistical picture of recorded crime (Stage 4).

This general argument can be illustrated by comparing police statistics with responses from questions asked in the General Household Survey (GHS) where a random sample survey of the whole population is asked whether or not they have been a victim of a crime. Thus, in 1980 in England and Wales, there were 2.36 million recorded 'serious' offences (defined as those which could be tried in the Crown Court before 1977).[14] These figures represented an apparent jump of 410,000 since 1972, but an analysis by the Home Office[15] of questions on burglary and theft in a dwelling included in the GHS of 1972, 1973, 1979 and 1980 in comparison with the official police statistics for the same years concludes:

The proportionate increase in the estimated number of such offences committed over the period 1972–80 at an average rate of 1% a year was not significant and was not as large as that for offences recorded by the police which increased at an average annual rate of 4% a year. *The larger increase in those offences recorded appeared to have been due mainly to an increase in the proportion of such offences committed which were recorded.* (Authors' italics)

They go on to remark that, although the public claimed to have reported the same proportion of burglaries to the police, the proportion recorded of those reported to the police has risen from two-thirds to three-quarters. A later analysis of the British Crime Survey findings comes to a similar conclusion.[16]

Obviously, these distortions could affect the relative likelihood of different social groups appearing in the criminal justice system. There have frequently[17] been suggestions that white victims would be more likely to report an offence to the police if they thought a black person was involved, and this has been confirmed in a secondary analysis of data from the *British Crime Survey*.[18] As Pease says, 'the first stage in making offenders available to the penal system is discriminatory'.

But the main 'problem' is that police have wide-ranging 'discretion' over how to react towards a report from the public.[19] The

33

accounts of two women giving evidence to the Review Panel after the Handsworth rebellion in 1985 speaks volumes:

..when they finally do arrive, they don't come to investigate the crime, they are more concerned about our immigrant status.

The police were hell-bent on getting their revenge. For weeks after the rebellion they were rounding-up people in search of those supposed to be involved in the rebellion.[20]

There is extensive evidence of this nature: the increase of 34 per cent in the number of offences of robbery and other violent theft reported in March 1982 – the issue of muggings with which this chapter began most likely reflects changes in the proportions of victims reporting an attack and especially the proportion of those recorded by police.

Comparing black and white offenders (Stages 5 to 8)

Linking an individual to an incident means yet more filtering, for less than half of recorded offences are actually related to an identified person (cleared up) and only a proportion of those lead to an arrest. Once again, a small change or distortion at the stage of recording or clearing-up would lead to large differences in the representation of different groups at the arrest stage as compared to any of the first three stages.

In fact, distortions can easily occur here through police procedures and routines which lead them to concentrate on some kinds of incident and some types of people as typically 'criminal' or through selective policing of certain areas and situations.[21] Whilst this only directly affects a restricted category of offences, any differential identification of a specific social group could lead to the creation of stereotypes. This could then have an indirect impact on police attitudes to those people involved in other kinds of incident.[22]

It should, therefore, be clear that arrest rates (or rates of prosecution or of conviction) do not necessarily bear any relation to the underlying 'criminal behaviour'; second, statistics collected in Britain cannot, by themselves, show whether there is any bias in arresting or charging suspects; and third, police statistics themselves are a product of a wide variety of factors including both public perception of 'crime' and public co-operation with the police.

Moreover, apart from these problems of interpretation, any apparent differences between population groups could arise from a combination of other relationships between variables. A relatively straightforward example is the differential arrest rates for black and white populations which can, in part at least, be explained by differences in the age structure of the two populations. For there are proportionately more young people in the black population, and young people are more likely to be arrested.[23] In principle, differences like these, which arise from dissimilar population structure, can be avoided in a carefully designed study. Differences between areas are important and need to be taken into account: indeed, it is important to emphasize that many of the studies reported in this chapter are for London and the results may not apply to other parts of Britain. More involved relationships controlling for area-specific and socio-economic factors require correspondingly complex statistical modelling.[24] The opportunity for the effective use of the powerful analytical techniques is unfortunately rare because of the lack of systematic data.

Statistics as propaganda

Criminal statistics have been used for decades as a way of getting at people.[25] During the 1950s and 1960s, when youth culture was at its height, the Home Office invented 'delinquent generations', and one spectacular publication managed to ascribe all burglaries to the demographic increase in the adolescent population;[26] since the mid- and late 1960s the black population have come in for their share of the stick. Similarly, in 1965, McClintock published an analysis of violent crimes in which he laid particular stress on the involvement of West Indians without any adjustment for the sex let alone age of the immigrant population.[27] The press release from New Scotland Yard was the latest statistical attack.

Of course, global statistics are complex to present and interpret but when official bodies, such as New Scotland Yard who should know better, make press releases without any caveats at all, one has to assume that their purpose was simply to distort and mislead. At least on the level of provoking media hysteria, they succeeded.

35

POLICE AND BLACK PEOPLE

This subject is endless and is continually being documented. There have been several very good articles and books on this history and up-to-date accounts of the most public incidents are reported in the Runnymede Trust *Bulletin*. This brief section does not pretend to summarize those but simply to highlight incidents which illustrate that history.

The steady deterioration

Allegations of police racism are considerable and have a long pedigree.[28] In 1966, the London Region of the West Indian Standing Conference cited numerous cases of racial abuse by police officers, lack of prosecution for black people, and a general tendency among police officers to stereotype black people as being crime-prone.[29] In 1970, John described relations between police and black people in Handsworth, Birmingham as 'one of warfare – and anything but cold'.[30] The Select Committee on Race Relations and Immigration inquiry into police/immigrant relations in 1970–71 heard similar allegations from all over the country.[31] The National Council for Civil Liberties warned that 'the worsening situation between the police and the black community is very serious indeed',[32] while the Institute of Race Relations concluded that 'police/black relations are deteriorating fast, to the point where violent solutions will soon be sought'.[33] Humphrey and John used case material to present an alarming account of how 'to many blacks in our inner cities, police harassment has become a way of life.'[34]

Such allegations continued throughout the 1970s. For example, a collection of interviews with young black people and their parents in Handsworth highlighted the concerns and complaints of previous reports – racial abuse, harassment, assault, and a feeling that the police were beyond any legal or community control.[35] Over one-third of those interviewed recounted at least one incident of harassment or brutality which they had experienced themselves, while nearly every other person interviewed knew of an incident involving a close friend. The following year, the Institute of Race Relations' evidence to the Royal Commission on Criminal Procedure (set up in 1978) documented a large number of cases illustrating various police malpractices including raids on black meeting places, over-policing of black areas such as Lambeth and black events such as the Notting Hill Carnival, arbitrary and violent arrest,[36] harassment and breaches of the Judges' Rules which are supposed to govern police questioning of suspects. Black people, the Institute argued, stood outside the general concept of police accountability to society and were treated as a community apart, requiring special 'liaison' measures to explain police ways to overcome the 'traditional mistrust' which black people felt towards the police. The police, it said, would have had no small part to play in the polarization of society if, as seemed was happening, Britain was moving towards 'two societies, one black, one white – separate, unequal'.[37]

The end of the decade saw the demonstration at Southall on 23 April 1979 against the National Front, when Blair Peach was killed by a blow from a police truncheon or similar implement and many others were seriously injured. Over 300 people were arrested. Demands for an independent public enquiry into police behaviour and the death of Blair Peach were rejected.[38]

Southall Rights, a local advice centre, concluded that police behaviour had

> . . . left a deep scar on the people of Southall that will take years to heal. The racial abuse that accompanied the violence, the wanton destruction of property . . . and the pursuit of persons running away and/or trying to seek shelter, all give the lie to any suggestion that the Police were merely defending themselves, and are consistent with Superintendent Hurd's comment early in the afternoon that Southall needed to be 'taught some discipline.'[39]

In the same year, Lambeth Borough Council, concerned at the heavy-handed policing methods of the Special Patrol Group in their locality, set up an enquiry into relations between the police and the public in the borough. The report of the working party consisted largely of extracts from evidence submitted and contained a large number of allegations of police misconduct, including intimidation, arbitrary arrest, misuse of police powers, harassment and failure to recognize the rights of suspects. Published in January 1981, it concluded that the state of relations between the police and the public in the borough was 'extremely grave', a situation created by the nature of the police force and basic policing methods.[40] Three months later, the borough was the scene of the Brixton riots and street-fighting between the police and black and white people – unprecedented in modern times.

The riots

The riots of 1981 in over 50 British towns and cities[41] were ascribed by many to police behaviour, particularly towards black people – the culmination of years of unheeded warnings and complaints, and there were numerous allegations that black people were arrested at random, that those arrested were assaulted by police, that people's homes were badly and unnecessarily damaged during police raids, and that black people were racially abused.[42] There were sporadic complaints of racial harassment during the next few years. One incident stood out: Mikkleson (believed to have been the only black Hell's Angel in Britain) was arrested in West London in July 1985. During a violent struggle, he was hit by a truncheon and died soon after. Seven police officers were suspended from duty in March 1986.[43]

Finally, in the autumn of 1985 there were again riots in urban areas starting with Handsworth in early September and then Brixton, Liverpool and Tottenham. The riots in Brixton followed the shooting of a black woman, Cherry Groce, by the police; in Liverpool after four defendants were refused bail; and those in Tottenham after the death of a black woman, Cynthia Jarrett.[44] In the latter, a police officer was killed and two journalists received shotgun wounds.

The police, at least in Handsworth, tried to blame drugs. As several youth organizations said:

> The police drug theory is a joke. Drug dealers cannot organise an uprising. There is no way that outsiders can come in and invite a riot, the conditions are perfect for rioting.[45]

Current research on police-black relations

This general picture of policing and black people at the time is supported by more specific research about police attitudes and about how people view the enforcement of particular laws against black people and on how black people are treated after arrest.

Statistical evidence about police attitudes is found in a detailed study of police attitudes, cognitive styles and personalities by Colman and Gorman in 1982.[46] They interviewed 48 recruit constables, 36 probationer constables and a control group of 30 non-university townspeople. On the basis of four psychometric and three open-ended questions, recruits and probationer constables scored significantly higher in the conservatism and authoritarianism scales and gave considerably more illiberal answers to questions concerning coloured immigration and mixed marriages. Colman and Gorman present a series of quotes from police constables in reponse to these questions and conclude that:

> Socialisation into the police sub-culture seems to foster hostile attitudes towards coloured immigration. The depth of prejudice towards black immigrants held by many experienced police officers can be gauged from the responses.[47]

The major study by the Policy Studies Institute in London[48] presents a considerable volume of qualities evidence – from a participant obversation study of a group of black youths and a study of police officers at work – to show racist attitudes, stereotypes and language used by the police. These reports give overwhelming support for a view that such attitudes do not represent isolated cases where individual officers have an unfortunate bias against black people but indicate a pervasive atmosphere of tolerance of racist attitudes.

The survey by the Policy Studies Institute in London also interviewed a representative sample of the black population in London.[49] Table 3.1 shows that a larger proportion of West Indians saw themselves as being stopped for almost any reason and very often for no reason at all.

Given this treatment, it would not be surprising to learn that black youths thought they were being singled out. A study by Gaskell confirmed that young blacks have a more negative attitude

Table 3.1
Foot stops: informant's behaviour and whether a reason was given for this stop, by ethnic group (column percentages)

	White N=305	West Indian N=153
Were you doing anything out of the ordinary?		
Yes	27	8
No	73	88
DK	—	4
If no, did the police officer(s) give a reason for approaching you?		
Yes	53	52
No	20	36

Source: Smith, *Police and People in London*, 1983, vol. I from their Table.

than young whites; but, importantly, this is not only because the police are seen as symbols of an oppressive white society but because of specific past policing strategies.[50]

That specific strategies are at issue highlights the fact that the majority of the studies of crime and policing have focused on London and the Metropolitan Police. The picture may well be different elsewhere.[51]

FROM THE STREET TO THE STATION

This and the following section follows the black population from incident to incarceration. This section looks at the direct contacts between black people and the police.

Street crime

There is no data on the participation of different groups in crime overall but sporadic data has been collected on interpersonal incidents. Note that the issue is *not* how criminogenic are the different ethnic groups.[52] Indeed, to ask the marginalized or the poor in any society the question 'why do they turn to crime' is simply to put the wrong question or, as Hall puts it 'a practical obscenity'.[53]

Unsurprisingly 'a fraction of the black labouring class [mainly the male youth] are engaged in the traditional activity of the wageless and the workless: doing nothing, filling out time and trying to survive'.[54] The point here is simply to present the little data available on interpersonal incidents.

Both Tuck and Southgate in Manchester[55] and the PSI survey in London[56] asked about the race of the offender as perceived by the victims. Among those victims who could remember their assailant – only 30 per cent in Tuck and Southgate's survey - the ethnic minorities were 'overrepresented' by a factor of between 2 to 1 and 3 to 1.[57] Both sets of authors attempt to explain this overrepresentation by pointing to the particular sociodemographic distribution of the ethnic minorities.

Table 3.2
Numbers and percentage distribution of 'skin colour' of offenders according to victims' reports

		Assault		Robbery	
	Population Distribution	Proportion of Assaults Attributed to each Group	Percentage of those Incidents Cleared-up	Proportion of Robberies Attributed to each Group	Percentage of those Incidents Cleared-up
White	86	71	74	31	16
Non-white	9	26	73	65	7
Mixed	5	2	59	2	14
Total where offender's skin colour known		11,608	74	16,750	10
Total where offender's skin colour unknown		5,766	13	2,502	5
Overall total		17,364	53	19,258	10

Note: Mixed, where there was more than one offender
Source: Home Office, 1983a, Tables 7 and 53

The Home Office figures[58] which were the subject of the *Daily Mail* headlines are given in Table 3.2. Non-white offenders are overrepresented in both assault and robbery cases but the variation in clear-up rates is instructive. Thus, about one-third of assault victims could not give the 'skin-colour' of the assailant and these had a very low clear-up rate, in contrast to the high clear-up rate (74 per cent) for cases where the victim reported a 'skin-colour'. Although the clear up rates are much lower in robbery cases, the same effect is observed.

The researchers tried to break down this picture by comparing the race of the victim to his/her perception of the race of the offender. Tuck and Southgate's data showed a slight tendency for attacks to be intraracial rather than interracial[59] which reflects early American findings[60] and the detailed breakdown of the MPD data.[61] The trouble with all this evidence is that very minor incidents might be reported and therefore recorded perhaps because of the race of the assailant.

The only detailed data on this issue comes from the study by Steven and Willis;[62] a selection of their results are given in Table 3.3.

Table 3.3
Degree of injury in relation to race of attackers and victims

Degree of Injury	White Attacker/ White Victim	White Attacker/ Coloured Victim	Coloured Attacker/ White Victim	Coloured Attacker/ Coloured Victim	All (including race unknown)
Fatal	3	3	0.5	2	1
Serious	9	8	4	12	7
Slight	66	68	46	63	61
None	22	21	50	23	31
n=100%	6,521	643	3,616	937	19,114

Source: Stevens and Willis, 1979, Table 7

These data show how there were fatal or serious injuries in 12 per cent of the cases identified as attacks by whites and in 6 per cent of those identified as attacks by non-whites. However these arise, whether through differential reporting by the public or differential recording by the police, these data provide a rather different view to that of the *Daily Mail*.First, some 80 per cent of all fatal incidents and 75 per cent of all serious incidents where the MPD felt able to assign an ethnic group code involved a white attacker; second, attacks by whites appear to be twice as serious as attacks by blacks or – more likely – incidents involving blacks are twice as likely to end up as a criminal statistic.

Stop and search

Throughout the 1960s and 1970s the police use of the 'sus' law was widely regarded as discriminating against black people.[63] One estimate was that blacks were 15 times more likely than whites to be arrested for 'sus'[64] and a Runnymede Trust study of 1976 data, which showed that 42 per cent of those arrested by the MPD for 'sus' were black even though only 12 per cent of all arrests were black, argued that the police used 'sus' to keep young black people off the streets.[65]

Evidence to the Royal Commission on Criminal Procedure[66] and the 'Scrap "Sus" Campaign'[67] led to an inquiry by the Parliamentary Home Affairs Committee and the repeal of that law, but its partial replacement by new offences with the Criminal Attempts Act, 1981.

Prior to the 1981 riots, in the four divisions around Toxteth, a total of 3,482 people were stopped and searched in the first seven months of 1981, yet only 179 were arrested.[68] The inquiry by the Merseyside Police Authority into the riots noted that 'harassment is the allegation expressed most vociferously and most often'.[69] The most reliable evidence (in the statistical sense) comes from the Policy Studies Institute study.[70]

They found that if someone was stopped at all, they tended to be stopped several times. The detail is presented in Table 3.4. West Indians were stopped in a vehicle slightly more than whites and more than twice as often as Asians. On foot, the differences are much more striking, West Indians being stopped more than three times as often as whites and more than five times as Asians. Among 15–24 year olds, whites and West Indians in a vehicle are equally likely to be stopped; but Asians less than half as often; whilst on foot, nearly half of all West Indian youth had been

Table 3.4
Stops by police of males

	Whites		West Indian		Asians	
	% Stopped	Mean No.* Stops	% Stopped	Mean No.* Stops	% Stopped	Mean No.* Stops
All Ages:						
In a vehicle	14	1.5	18	3.2	5	1.6
On foot	3	2.0	11	2.0	2	1.2
Aged 15–24:						
In a vehicle	35	2.2	34	4.7	15	2.1
On foot	18	2.4	45	2.2	7	1.3

*Among those who have been stopped.

Source: Smith, 1983, Tables IV.3, p. 96 and IV.6, p. 100.

stopped compared to less than 20 per cent of whites and less than 10 per cent of Asians. Such rates must mainly be interpreted in terms of stereotypes held by the police, rather than as reflecting any characteristics of the different groups.

Police officers were asked about the circumstances of 'stops' they had made during the last two weeks. Officers were asked about each 'stop' up to a maximum of three. Their survey results showed a close match between the proportions of people stopped and people arrested.[71] The officers were asked the reason for making the stop: Whilst Smith suggests that there is little difference between the ethnic groups, his results show 10 per cent of blacks (Police Identification Code 3) were stopped for unconventional appearance, but only 6 per cent of whites. Moreover, the officers said that 41 per cent of blacks were rather or very unco-operative as compared to 16 per cent of whites – although co-operativeness did not apparently influence the arrest rates.[72]

A study specifically designed to investigate 'stop and search' is reported in Willis.[73] The people stopped by police attached to four police stations were race-coded with the breakdown as detailed in Table 3.5. In every district, both for all black males and young black males, blacks are more than twice as likely to be stopped as whites. Willis goes on to point out that only a quarter of stops led

Table 3.5
Estimated annual stop rates (4 police stations 1981)

	Stope rate per 100 pop.	Stop rate per 100 males	Stop rate per 100 blacks	Stop rate per 100 males 16–24	Stop rate per 100 black males	Stop rate per 100 black males aged 16–24
Kensington	31	62	82	123	149	298
Peckham	14	27	29	70	60	147
Watford	5	9	18	27	32	88
Luton	1	3	5	8	10	29

Percentages of stops which lead to:

	Arrest	Prosecution
Kensington	13	9
Peckham	11	8
Watford	4	2
Luton	2	2

Source: Willis, 1983, Table 3.

to a search, and the final column shows how few actually led to an arrest, especially in Watford and Luton.

Another recent study by McConville[74] in Notting Hill was based on streets in two areas, people in every house being asked whether the house had been searched and if the occupants had been stopped and searched. Eleven of the 279 (4 per cent) white houses had been searched and eight of the 85 (9 per cent) Afro-Caribbean houses; 17 per cent of 340 whites and 32 per cent of 104 blacks had been stopped.

There have been only two systematic studies of complaints against the police where the ethnic group of the complainant has been identified. Stevens and Willis[75] studied complaints made in the MPD in 1973 and 1979, and the PSI survey also asked about complaints.[76] The difficulty is that, because only a very small proportion are ever substantiated,[77] it is difficult to interpret them either as evidence of discrimination or of lack of discrimination.

Arrest

There is an overrepresentation of the black population in arrest statistics (see Table 3.6). Data from Stevens' and Willis' 1975 study, PSI's 1974 and 1982 surveys[78] show an overrepresentation in proportion to numbers in the population by a factor of two or three and higher ratios for certain offence groups. Stevens and Willis showed that adjustment for differences in the age distributions of the two populations made little difference; they accounted for their results partly in terms of variations in social conditions (for example, unemployment) between areas [79] but they were unable to carry out a thorough statistical analysis. Given the considerable overrepresentation of black people in arrests for 'sus' where there was considerable scope for selective perception of potential or actual offenders, it may be that difference in police attitudes and activity also account for some of the differences.

The latter suggestion is reinforced by a small study based on a South London Court in 1978 and 1979. They found that 47 per cent of 58 West Indian defendants had been charged as a result of police initiatives as compared to 19 per cent of 276 white defendants[80] so that more than one-third (27 out of 79) of those charged with public order offences were black. Walker criticizes the study for not relating these numbers to the population at risk[81] but, if she had not done that she would have found that, according to the Census SAS, less that 13 per cent of the area's population was black.

The decision whether or not to arrest very much depends on the individual police officer and the interaction between him/her and the potential arrestee. The PSI survey asked police officers to describe the last person they arrested.[82] Seventeen per cent were classified as ID3 (black-skinned, West Indian/African), three times the proportion of blacks in the London population. The police thought that the subject was unco-operative on 50 per cent of incidents involving blacks as compared to 37 per cent of incidents involving whites;[83] reciprocally, blacks were more dissatisfied with their treatment by the police than the whites.

Table 3.6
Race of arrested persons for selected offences in MPD (1975 and 1982) (row percentages)

	1975				1982			
	White	Black	Asian	n=100%	White	Black	Asian	n=100%
Assault	75	21	4	7,167	72	20	4	8,845
Robbery	68	31	2	2,294	50	45	3	2,466
Auto crime	88	10	2	20,414	80	15	2	17,030
Criminal damage and misuse	88	9	3	7,755	81	13	2	13,032‡
All offences	85	12	3	103,252	75	17	3	100,800
Population distribution	93	4	3		91	5	4	

‡ Criminal damage of value less than £20 was not recorded in 1975, which accounts for the increase.

Source: For 1975, Stevens and Willis, 1979, Appendix D (white here includes all those not black or Asian).
For 1982, Home Office, 1983, *Statistical Bulletin*, 22/83 (white here refers to white Europeans).

EVEN HANDED JUSTICE

Whilst the previous section implicated only the police, the process from arrest to prison also involves other agencies.

After arrest: juveniles

After arrest, a juvenile can be charged immediately or referred to the juvenile bureau which can then take no further action, caution the juvenile, or charge her or him. Clearly the incident/person is being treated more seriously if an immediate change is made.

There have been two studies: Landau who, in 1981, investigated the procedure for 1,448 children arrested in five different police divisions[84] found black children had a higher probability of being charged immediately and concluded that the most important explanation of this differential treatment was police perception of black youths as being more aggressive and antagonistic than white youths. A subsequent study by Landau and Nathan in 1983 reported on decisions as to whether to caution or to prosecute[85] and found that

54 per cent of white children were cautioned (n=753) but only 40 per cent of black children (n=393). Black juveniles continue to have a lower probability of being cautioned even after controlling for age group, whether or not the child is left alone at home, and previous record of criminal involvment. In contrast, Mawby and Batta, in their study of juveniles cautioned or convicted in Bradford[86] found that of all juveniles 68 per cent were cautioned and 32 per cent were convicted, whilst of non-Asians 'only' 50 per cent were cautioned and 50 per cent were convicted. Of course, there are a whole variety of factors which affect the chances of a child being cautioned, including the victim's agreement, but the data support the hypothesis that black children are treated more harshly than white children.

After arrest: adults

The statistics of the race of people arrested in the MPD showed considerable overrepresentation of black people in each offence group (see Table 3.6 above). This pattern is repeated amongst those found guilty,[87] although the percentage of black people among those found guilty is slightly smaller than among those arrested. This could be interpreted to mean that the evidence to sustain a charge against black defendants is less strong than against white defendants. This suggestion is reinforced by the findings of Baldwin and McConville[88] that a relatively high proportion of black defendants have 'confessed' to the police (the weakness of unsupported confessions have been acknowledged in the new Criminal Evidence Act).

Cain and Sadigh's study in a South London court[89] also showed that whilst more than two-thirds of the cases involving black defendants were allocated to a magistrate who had the reputation among court adminsitrators of being 'tough' less than half the white defendants were.

In contrast, the studies by Mawby and Batta show that Asians in Bradford are much less likely to be found guilty.[90] On the basis of magistrates courts records for 1975–6, they found a rate of 12 per 1,000 adult male population for Asians as compared to 44 per 1,000 for non-Asians.

Sentencing

There have been no comprehensive studies of sentencing of people of different ethnic origin in the UK. The main study is by McConville and Baldwin[91] who examined 1,000 cases in Birmingham Crown Court in 1975–76 and 475 cases in a London Crown Court in 1978–79. In order to counter criticisms that the ethnic groups were involved in different types of offence, they matched black and white defendants on eight factors including sex, age, offence type and previous record. However, this procedure reduced their samples to 411 in Birmingham and 108 in London, and the final comparisons between ethnic groups show very little difference (see their Tables 1 and 2).

Possibly the largest data set relates to the sentences imposed on all persons arrested 'during the serious incidents of public disorder in July and August 1981'. A detailed analysis is given in a recent Home Office Bulletin.[92] They found some differences between the ethnic groups – the black were younger, more often unemployed, more often charged for theft and less for public order – but the proportions found guilty and imprisoned in the ethnic groups were similar.

More recently, Coates studied the sentences imposed on 65 white and 48 black defendants who appeared at Sheffield Magistrates and Crown Courts in February-May 1983, and for whom Social Inquiry Reports were available.[93] Data collected included age, sex, employment status, number of previous convictions, plea, recommendation and offence types. Several logistic models were used to investigate the probability of the defendant receiving a custodial sentence. Ethnic origin was not a statistically significant variable, but this could have been due to the small size of the data set. Another study by Mair[94] in West Yorkshire, which involved 1,173 cases, found a smaller proportion of black defendants (5:2) and some differences in sentencing. In particular, black defendants who were younger were more likely to receive a community service order but less likely to receive a probation order than whites.

Overall, as McConville and Baldwin[95] concluded from their study, 'defendants are treated equally once they attain the status of convicted person; not necessarily fairly or appropiately, but equally'. Crow and Cove[96] reached a similar conclusion on the basis

49

of 688 cases of which 124 involved non-whites, in 9 courts in different parts of the country. Once you are caught in the criminal justice net, discrimination in processing is probably unlikely; that happens before and after.

In prison

The proportion of ethnic minorities in custody is growing, particularly among the young[97] and some Young Offenders Institutions in the South of England had about 30 per cent of black youths in 1981. A special study by Fludger[98] of 13,498 trainees who entered Borstal between mid-1974 and the end of 1976 showed how the number of West Indian-born trainees is over five time greater than expected and, in detention centres, is more than three times greater. Borstal later gave way to Youth Custody Centres, but they also are hosts to a 'disproportionately large population of black Afro-Caribbean youths'.[99]

Walker[100] suggests, rather astonishingly, that this happens because the West Indians are committing more serious offences. The data presented earlier in this section have shown how West Indians are also about five time more likely to be arrested and found guilty than whites for the same offences, so their overrepresentation in prison is perhaps not very surprising. But as Guest goes on to remark 'many good offenders ultimately serve adult persons sentences, the social composition of young offender centres will become a feature of future adult prison populations'.[101]

Over the years, the Home Office has dealt with black prisoners only in a piecemeal way. Religious and dietary needs are now beginning to be recognized, following early clumsy moves by the Home Office in a circular on Rastafarianism in 1976.[102] The circular claimed that Rastafarianism was not a religion and denied facilities for visiting ministers, and so forth, as well as requiring hair to be cut. This circular caused bitter resentment and it is now recognized that this was a disastrous policy. Dreadlocks are not supposed to be cut off (although there have been recent incidents) and a new overall prison policy on Rastafarians has been formulated.[103]

Details of black offenders in prison were published in 1986.[104] The proportion of black men in prison was eight times higher than in the general population. About 8 per cent of male inmates and 12 per cent of female prisoners were of West Indian origin, whilst the same groups comprised less than 2 per cent of the total population of England and Wales. People of West Indian and African origin were less likely to have been released on bail and more likely to have been remanded in custody before trial than whites.

BLACK PEOPLE AS VICTIMS

Perhaps more important from the point of view of the black population is their likelihood of being a victim.

Assaulted or robbed

Two local population surveys of victims in Manchester and London[105] both showed apparently higher rates of victimization for all types of offence among whites than among West Indians, with Asians the lowest. Granted that there are evident biases and distortions in the official criminal statistics, the researcher's surveys cannot simply assume objectivity.[106] It is therefore interesting to see that, according to the MPD reports of the ethnic appearance of victims of assault and robbery, the rates for robbery were 23 for white people, 22 for black skinned and 73 for Asians. Table 3.7 gives the percentage distribution of the victim compared with the resident population as a whole. In fact, as the distribution of ethnic minority groups is concentrated in particular areas, these

Table 3.7
Rates of assault and robbery per 10,000 population as coded by the MPD (row percentages)

	White	Blackskinned	Asians
Assault	79	8	7
Robbery	77	4	11
Resident Population	86	5	4

Source: Home Office, 1983a.

figures do not reflect the rates of victimization. The same data, when broken down to each of the 21 police districts, give a much clearer picture, as demonstrated in Table 3.8. For assault, the recorded victim rates for black and Asians are higher in every kind of area, and the recorded rates of robbery are very high for Asians.

Table 3.8
Victim rates (per 1,000 pop.) in four MPD areas, 1982

| | Assault | | | Robbery | | |
	White	Black	Asian	White	Black	Asian
Westminster	67	86	158	66	57	290
Lambeth	44	59	75	125	53	338
Barnet	17	33	27	8	12	20
Richmond & Hounslow	16	27	92	8	19	24
All MPD (as above)	23	38	41	25	22	73

Source: Home Office, 1983a, Table 8.

Racial attacks

The final issue is the extent of specifically racist attacks. The problem of racist violence had been highlighted in a report prepared by the Bethnal Green and Stepney Trades Council in 1978[107] and again in the Institute of Race Relations 1979 evidence to the Royal Commission on Criminal Procedure,[108] as well as in regular reports in journals such as *Searchlight*. In the light of an increasing volume of evidence that racist attacks were increasing in number and that black people were the most likely victims, a survey was commissioned in 1981 by the Home Secretary, William Whitelaw.

The Home Office study[109] was based on 2,630 reported incidents that took place in 13 selected police areas between May and July 1981. The working definition used was 'an incident, or alleged offence by a person or persons of one racial group against a person or persons of another racial group, where there are indications of a racial motive'.[110] Incidents were coded according to the strength of evidence for a racial motive and compared the number of attacks

with the population size in the area. The victim rates are shown in
Table 3.9.

Table 3.9
Victims of racially motivated interracial incidents (racial attacks)

Ethnic origin of victim	Estimated Population ('000s)	No. of Incidents	No/100,000 pop.	No. of serious offences	No/100,000 pop.
White	16,047	217	1.4	154	0.9
Black	242	124	51.2	47	24.0
Asian	482	336	69.7	205	42.7
Others	240	27	11.3	23	8.8
All	17,011	704	4.2	429	2.6

Source: Home Office, 1981, Table 3.4

The number of victims of racial incidents per thousand of the
population is 50 times higher for Asians and 37 times higher for
black people than for white people. There has been an attempt
by the MPD Statistical Department[111] to claim that these figures
are a statistical artefact because the white population is so much
larger than the black population so that, if the percentage of
attackers were the same for both groups, this would still lead
to many more victims in the minority group. This argument
simply misses the point, which is the exceptionally high rates
of racially motivated victimization experienced by the black
population. Moreover, recent evidence suggests that these
attacks are becoming not only more numerous but also more
violent.

Of course, many attacks, whoever the perpetrator, are never
reported to the police; in the Bethnal Green study victims
were even unwilling to talk to the researchers.[112] But the reported incidents paint a nasty picture of racial violence in Britain
today.

Incitement to racial hatred

The offence of incitement to racial hatred was introduced in Section 6 of the Race Relations Act 1965.[113] It said:

> A person shall be guilty of an offence under this section if, with intent to stir up hatred against any section of the public in Great Britain distinguished by colour, race or ethnic or national origins –
>
> a. he publishes or distributes written matter which is threatening, abusive or insulting;
>
> or
>
> b. he uses in any public place or at any public meeting words which are threatening, abusive or insulting being matter or words likely to stir up hatred against that section on grounds of colour, race or ethnic or national origins.

In the 1976 Race Relations Act the requirement of *intention* to stir up hatred was replaced by the phrase 'hatred is *likely* to be stirred up'. This led to a very few prosections: three cases in 1978 but only Weston was convicted – with a £150 fine; six cases in 1979 with five convictions but only McLaughlin and Relf were imprisoned; there were no cases in 1980.[114] Not only have there been so very few prosecutions, those convicted, often of very nasty attacks, were given relatively light sentences.

At a time of increased racist and fascist activity in the United Kingdom, the law has been heavily criticized, by those who support its intentions, for being ineffective. In 1978–79 the Commission for Racial Equality submitted 74 items – and these were only some of the total number of referrals made to the Attorney General – yet there were only nine prosecutions.[115] Sir Michael Havers QC MP, the Attorney General in 1981, claimed that the offence was extremely difficult to prove; that there had to be an identifiable person to prosecute which was not easy when publications were the sources of evidence; and that, where material was distributed only to community leaders or the offices of Jewish organizations, 'it is impossible to say that racial hatred would be stirred up'.[116]

British law on incitement to racial hatred has been far from successful. But that is not surprising, as the success of any law against incitement to racial hatred will, of course, depend on the extent to which racism and discrimination are officially practised or tolerated.

CONCLUSION

This chapter has described the position of black people vis-à-vis the institution of law and order, ranging from their relations with the police to their considerable overrepresentation in prison. It is clear that, whether as victims of racial attacks or in terms of their representation at each stage of the criminal justice system, blacks are heavily disadvantaged. Four points need to be emphasized.

First, the general problems of interpreting criminal statistics make it impossible to make any comparisons between the involvement of black groups and white groups other than at the stage of entry into the judicial system itself (for example, on arrest). Moreover, we have to be cautious about interpreting comparisons even at that stage or subsequently because the data available is limited to London and only a few other areas. This chapter has therefore focused on the way in which black people are caught up in the criminal justice system rather than on a direct comparison.

Second, the statistics of racial attacks and cases of incitement to racial hatred reflect a hostility to black people which encourages a climate of fear and confrontation. The portayal of black people in the press encourages the reader to make a crude equation between race and crime as indicated by the *Daily Mail* headline at the beginning of the chapter. There is also considerable evidence of hostile police attitudes and racism within the police force.

Third, whilst we believe that the role of the police is crucial in determining the position of black people, it is important to emphasize the interdependence of the criminal justice system and how this affects the way black people (will) experience and respond to that system. For discrimination at any one point is likely to feed through to other parts of the system and reinforce the view that the whole system is racist.

Finally, it needs to be emphasized that no-one experiences the criminal justice system as isolated from other social institutions. As Stafford Scott said:

> Unless you understand what being black in Britain really means, you will never understand why people are prepared to stand up and fight the officers of the Law.[117]

Notes

1. New Scotland Yard Press Release, 'Recorded Crime in London rises by 8%', 10 March 1982.
2. Ibid.
3. Lord Justice Scarman, *The Scarman Report*, Harmondsworth: Penguin, 1982.
4. Quoted in P. Scraton, *The State of the Police*, London: Pluto Press, 1985, p. 95; G. Murdock, 'Reporting the riots: images and impact', Chapter 7 in J. Benyon (ed.), *Scarman and After*, Oxford: Pergamon, 1984, also gives an account of 'The Yard fought back' 1984, (pp. 90–2).
5. P.Sim, 'Scarman: The Police Backlash' in M. Eve and D. Musson, *Socialist Register*, London: Merlon, 1980, pp.57–77.
6. See also P. Gilroy, 'Police and Thieves', Chapter 4 in Centre for Contemporary Cultural Studies. *The Empire Strikes Back*, Hutchinson University Library,1982. An even more detailed history stretching over 70 years is given in H. Joshua, T. Watson and H. Booth, *To Ride The Storm*, London: Heinemann, 1983, Parts I and II.
7. See, for example, A. T. Turk, *Criminality and the Legal Order*, Chicago: Rand McNally, 1969.
8. S. W. Coleman, *The Criminal Elite*, New York: St Martin's Press, 1985.
9. S. Box, *Power, Crime and Mystification*, London: Tavistock, 1983; F. Pearse, *Crimes of the Powerful: Marxism, crime and deviance*, London: Pluto Press, 1976.
10. A. Stinchcombe, 'Institutions of privacy in the determination of police administrative practice', *Amer J. Sociology,* no. 69, 1963, pp.150–60.
11. One self-report study found that a sample of 180 adolescent males aged 15 to 17 admitted to 122,471 offences over one year, of which 2,596 were detected by the police; see M. L. Erikson and L. T. Empey, 'Court records, undetected delinquency and decision-making', *J. Crim. Law, Criminal and Police Sci.*, no.54, 1963, pp. 456–89.
12. M. Hough and P. Mayhew, *Taking Account of Crime: Key Findings from the British Crime Survey*, HO Research Study no.85, London: HMSO, 1985.
13. Ibid., Appendix A, Table A.
14. Home Office, *Criminal Statistics 1980*, London: HMSO.
15. Home Office, *Unrecorded Offences of Burglary and Theft in a Dwelling in England and Wales: Estimates from the General Household Survey*, HO Statistical Bulletin 11/82, London: HMSO, 1980.
16. Hough and Mayhew, op. cit.
17. For example, A. E Bottoms, 'Delinquency among immigrants: a further note', *Race*, vol. 9, no. 2, October 1962, suggests that white victims would be more likely to report a presumed black offender; and D. Jones, *Blood on the Streets: a report on racial attacks in East London* for Bethnal Green and Stepney Trades Council, 1978, suggests that Asian victims of white attacks rarely report them.

18. K. Pease, 'Crime, Race and Reporting to the Police', unpublished MS, University of Manchester, 1984.
19. D. Steer, *Uncovering Crime: The Police Role*, Royal Commission on Criminal Procedure, Research Study no. 7, London: HMSO, 1980.
20. West Midlands County Council, *A Different Reality*, Report of the Review Panel into the Handsworth rebellions of September 1985, 1986 pp. 71, 73.
21. R. Moore, *Racism and Black Resistance*, London: Pluto Press, 1975.
22. The process is described and modelled in both D. Chapman, *Society and the Stereotype of a Criminal*, London: Tavistock, 1968; and L. T. Wilkins, *Social Deviance, Social Policy, Action and Research*, London: Tavistock, 1964.
23. P. Stevens and C. F. Willis, *Race, Crime and Arrests*, Home Office Research Study no. 58, London: HMSO, 1979.
24. For a fully worked-out example of such a model, see R. A. Carr-Hill and N. H. Stern, *Crime, Police and Criminal Statistics*, London: Academic Press, 1979.
25. The tradition probably started with Sir William Petty (1623–87), who called for information on 'the number of . . . persons committed for crimes, to know the measure of vice and sin in the nation', see Marquis of Landsdowne (ed.), *The Petty Papers*, vol. 1, Boston: Houghton, Mifflin, G., 1927, p. 197.
26. M. A. P. Willmer, 'Is the Battle Being Won?', *Police Research Bulletin*, no. 7, 1968.
27. P. H. McClintock, *Crimes of Violence*, Cambridge Studies on Criminology no. 24, London: Heinemann, 1965.
28. M. Winters and J. Hatch, 'Colour Persecution on Tyneside', *Pan Africa*, February 1947, reprinted in *Race and Class*, Autumn 1982, pp. 184–8.
29. J. Hunte, *Nigger Hunting in England*, West Indian Standing Conference, London Region, 1966.
30. G. John, *Race in the Inner City*, London; Runnymede Trust, 1970.
31. Parliamentary Papers, 1976–77, *Select Committee on Race Relations and Immigration*, The West Indian Community, London: HMSO (HC 180).
32. National Council of Civil Liberties, *Minutes of Evidence to the Royal Commission on Criminal Procedure*, London: HMSO, 1978.
33. Institute of Race Relations, *'Police against Black People'*, Minutes of Evidence to Royal Commission on Criminal Procedure, op. cit.
34. D. Humphrey and G. John, *Police, Power and Black People*, London: Panther, 1972.
35. All Faiths for One Race, *Talking Blues*, AFFOR. 1978.
36. NCCL, Minutes of Evidence, op. cit.
37. Ibid.
38. National Council for Civil Liberties, *Southall, 23 April 1979*, London: NCCL, 1980.
39. Southall Rights, *A Report on the events of 23 April 1979*, 1980; see also NCCL, op. cit., Southall Rights Action Group.
40. Lambeth Borough Council.
41. B. M. Blob, *Like a Summer with a Thousand Julys*, London: Rising Free, 1982.
42. Scarman, op. cit., paras. 4.1–4.46.
43. Runnymede Trust Bulletin, 'Police and unlawful killing verdict', *Race and Immigration*, no.191, May 1986, p.l.

44. see Runnymede Trust Bulletins no 184–6, October, November and December 1986.
45. West Midlands County Council, *A Different Reality*, op. cit., p. 69.
46. A. M. Colman and C. P. Gorman, 'Conservation, dogmatism and authoritarianism in British Police Officers', *Sociology*, no. 16, 1982, pp. 1–4.
47. Ibid.
48. D. Smith with the assistance of J. Gray and S. Small, *Police and People in London*, vols. I-IV, Policy Studies Institute, 1983.
49. Ibid., vol. I, p. 113.
50. G. Gaskell, 'Black Youth and the Police', *Policing*, vol. 2, no.1, 1986, pp. 26–34.
51. See, for example, the results reported in the basis of a study by M. Tuck and P. Southgate, *Ethnic Minorities, Crime and Policing: A Survey of the Experience of West Indians and Whites*, Home Office Research Study no. 70, London: HMSO, 1981, based on a study in Manchester.
52. This sometimes seems to be taken as the problem to be explained even by those who should know better. See, for example, J. Lea and J. Young, *What is to be done about Law and Order*, Harmondsworth: Penguin, 1984.
53. S. Hall, C. Chritcher, T. Jefferson, J. Clarke and B. Roberts, *Policing the Crisis*, London: Macmillan, 1978, p. 378.
54. Ibid., p. 359.
55. Tuck and Southgate, op. cit.
56. Smith *et al.*, op. cit.
57. See Table 3 in M. A. Walker, 'Interpreting Race and Crime Statistics', *J. Royal Statistical Society*, Series A, January 1987.
58. Home Office, 'Crime Statistics for the Metropolitan Police Districts analysed by ethnic groups', Statistical Bulletin 22/83 unpublished, 1983.
59. Tuck and Southgate, op cit.
60. H. Garfinkel, 'Research Notes in Inter and Intra Racial Homocides', *Social Forces*, no. 27, May 1949, p. 370.
61. Home Office, op. cit., 1983.
62. Stevens and Willis, op. cit.
63. See, for example, M. Phillips, 'Brixton and Crime', *New Society*, 8 July, 1976; and C. Demuth, *'Sus': a report on the operation of Section 4 of the Vagrancy Act, 1824*, London: Runnymede Trust, 1978.
64. Thus, Stevens and Willis, op. cit., analysing the 1975 MPD data show 57.9% of suspected person arrests were of whites, and 40.4% were of blacks, as compared to the population proportions of 92.9% and 4.2% respectively.
65. Demuth, op. cit.
66. Royal Commission on Criminal Procedure, op. cit.
67. See Lea and Young, op. cit., p. 177.
68. Evidence to the Scarman Inquiry, Chief Constable of Merseyside, Kenneth Oxford, 1981, p. 6.
69. Merseyside Police Authority, *Report of the Working Party on Police Public Relationships*, para. 3.1(2), October 1981.
70. Smith, op. cit., vol. I.
71. Ibid., vol. III, Table V.10, p. 96.
72. Ibid., vol. III, Table V.13, p. 102.
73. C. F. Willis, *The Use, Effectiveness and Impact of Police Stop and Search*

Powers, HO Research and Planning Unit Paper no. 15, London: HMSO, 1983.

74. M. McConville, 'Search of persons and premises, new data for London', *Crim. Law Review*, 1983, pp. 605–14.
75. C. F. Willis and P. Stevens, *Ethnic Minorities and Complaints against the Police*, Home Office Research and Planning Unit Paper no. 5, London: HMSO, 1982.
76. Smith *et al.*, op. cit., vol. I, pp. 269–73.
77. Stevens and Willis, op. cit., pp. 18–19 and Table 2.
78. Smith *et al.*, op. cit., vol. III, p. 89.
79. Stevens and Willis, op. cit., Chapter 4.
80. M. Cain and S. Sadigh 'Racism, the Police and Community Policy: A comment on the Scarman Report', *Journal of Law and Society*, vol. 9, no. 1, 1982.
81. Walker, op. cit.
82. Smith *et al;* op. cit., vol. III, pp. 79–85.
83. Smith *et al;* op. cit., vol. III, Table V.17, p. 108.
84. Landau, op. cit.
85. S. F. Landau and G. Nathan, 'Selecting delinquents for cautioning in the London Metropolitan area', *Brit. J. Crim.* no. 23, 1983, pp. 128–49.
86. R. I. Mawby and I. D. Batta, *Asians and Crime, the Bradford Experience*, Southall, Middlesex: National Association for Asian Youth, 1980.
87. Home Office, Statistical Bulletin 22/83, 1983.
88. McConville and Baldwin, op. cit.
89. Cain and Sadigh, op. cit.
90. Mawby and Batta, op cit.
91. McConville and Baldwin, op cit.
92. Home Office, 'The Outcome of Arrests During the Serious Incidents of Public Disorder in July and August 1981', Home Office Bulletin, October, 1982, unpublished.
93. E. Coates, 'An Investigation into the Effect of the Race of a Defendant on the Court's Decision', unpublished MSc. thesis, Sheffield City Polytechnic Department of Applied Statistics and OR, 1983.
94. G. Mair, 'Ethnic Minorities' probation and the magistrates' courts: a pilot study', *Brit. J. Crim.*, vol. 26, no. 2, 1986, pp. 147–55.
95. McConville and Baldwin, op. cit.
96. I. Crow and J. Cove, 'Ethnic minorities and the courts', *Crim. Law Review*, 1984, pp. 413–17.
97. Home Office, *Annual Report of the Prison Department, 1981*, London: HMSO, 1982.
98. N. Fludger, *Ethnic Minorities and Borstal*, Home Office, London: HMSO, 1981.
99. C. Guest, 'A Comparative Analysis of the Career Patterns of Black People and White Young Offenders', MSc thesis, Cranfield Instituteof Technology, 1984.
100. M. Walker, 'Interpreting race and crime statistics', *Journal of the Royal Statistical Society*, Series A, January 1987.
101. Guest, op. cit.
102. Home Office, 'Interpretation of prison rules for dealing with ethnic minorities', Home Office Prison Department, 3/76.

103. Ibid.
104. Home Office, *The Ethnic Origin of Prisoners: the prison population on June 30th 1985 and persons received July 1984–March 1985*, Home Office Statistical Bulletin, London: HMSO, 1986.
105. For Manchester, see Tuck and Southgate, op. cit., Table 4.3; for London, Smith *et al.*, op. cit., vol. I, Tables A.8 and III.6.
106. N. Christie, 'Hidden Delinquency: Some Scandinavian Experience', 3rd National Conference on Research and Teaching on Criminology, University of Cambridge, Institute of Criminology, 1968.
107. Bethnal Green and Stepney Trades Council, *Blood on the Streets, A Report of Racial Attacks in East London*, 1978.
108. Institute of Race Relations, *Police against Black People*, IRR, 1979.
109. Home Office, *Racial Attacks*, London: HMSO, 1981.
110. Ibid., p. 3.
111. A study by J. Custance, quoted in Walker, op. cit.
112. Bethnal Green and Stepney Trades Council, op. cit.
113. See P. Gordon, *Incitement to Racial Hatred*, London: Runnymede Trust, 1982.
114. Ibid.
115. Ibid.
116. Ibid.
117. Stafford Scott, speaking for Broadwater Farm Youth Association and Defence Campaign, 16 January 1986.

4

Racism, Employment and Unemployment*

Sushel Ohri and Shaista Faruqi

INTRODUCTION

As a result of the demand for labour in a number of industries in the immediate post–1945 period, workers from the Caribbean and the Asian sub-continent began to arrive in substantial numbers during the 1940s and 1950s. Initially, most were single men who readily found employment in the manufacturing industries, particularly the foundries and textile mills, and in the transport and health services. The negative political and social response to the presence of these workers and how they coped with the harsh realities of living in this country have been well documented.[1] Despite the wider economic context of full employment, the level of discrimination and racism they encountered was fairly evident from the moment they landed on these shores. Many trade unionists blocked the employment of black employees or insisted upon 'quotas', fearing that black workers would take their jobs or push wages down. The 1950s witnessed routine protests by white workers against the employment of black workers. It was not uncommon to find the notice 'no coloureds' at factory gates, and it was an even more common occurrence for blacks to make enquiries regarding

* We sincerely wish to thank David Hickmanm, Jacqui Cooper, Amen Ali, John Wrench and particularly John Solomos for their advice and support in completing this chapter.

61

vacant positions only to be told they had been taken and then find that a white worker would be interviewed later.[2] Employment exchanges coped with repeated instructions to discriminate by noting NBI on the records ('No Blacks or Irish').

Disappointment and disillusionment of many kinds was the everyday experience of the 1950s settlers.[3] This is still the reality today for many black workers and their children. Although legislation was enacted to eliminate racial discrimination from 1965 onwards, the level of discrimination according to a recent PSI study[4] remains the same as it was in the 1960s. It is useful to recall how this situation came about and how racial inequality in employment has been reproduced.

This chapter substantially updates material used in Chapter 3 of the first edition and moves away from the theories and explanations put forward at that time for patterns of unemployment amongst the black population. The assumption underlying that chapter was that racial discrimination was one amongst a range of factors explaining higher than average unemployment rates of the black population.[5] It is the argument of this chapter that some earlier explanations (discussed later) are not adequate, and that the importance attached to others has been greatly exaggerated. It is rather our contention that systematic, rather than incidental, discrimination is taking place and that, notwithstanding the importance of other disadvantaging factors, structured racism operating in the organization of the economy continues to have a deliberate and powerful impact on the lives of black people.

This chapter has six main objectives. First, it examines the experience of blacks in employment. Second, it analyses the impact of the recession upon the black communities and examines some of the explanations for the over-representation of blacks on the unemployed register. Third, it examines the employment position of young blacks. Fourth, it looks at the response to racial discrimination by the state, local authorities and trade unions. Fifth, it draws attention to the black communities' own response to the employment crisis, including their own attempts to create jobs and the promotion of a political lobby to promote equal opportunity policies. Finally, it shows how more positive strategies of change in the field of employment might be attempted by the government and other bodies.

BLACK WORKERS IN THE LABOUR MARKET

Black people on the whole have very different employment characteristics from white people. They are concentrated in semi-skilled and unskilled jobs, and earn less than white people in the same job levels despite more shift-work and greater unionization. Colin Brown in the third PSI report, *Black and White* (1984) argues that '. . . the position of the black citizens of Britain largely remains, geographically and economically, that allocated to them as immigrant workers in the 1950s and 1960s'.[6] The occupational distribution of black workers is summarized in Table 4.1.

Table 4.1
Job level: all employees by ethnic group and sex

	MALE					
	White	West Indian	Indian	Pakistani	Bangladeshi	African Asian
Professional, employee management	19	5	11	10	10	22
Other non-manual	23	10	13	8	7	21
Skilled manual and foreman	42	48	34	39	13	31
Semi-skilled manual	13	26	36	35	57	22
Unskilled manual	3	9	5	8	12	3

	FEMALE			
	Column Percentages			
	White	West Indian	Indian	African Asian
Professional, employee management	7	1	5	7
Other non-manual	55	52	35	52
Skilled manual and foreman	5	4	8	3
Semi-skilled manual	21	36	50	36
Unskilled manual	11	7	1	3

Source: Colin Brown, *Black and White*, Policy Studies Institute report, 1984.

While 19 per cent of white men occupy professional or managerial positions, only 5 per cent of West Indians, 11 per cent of Indians and 10 per cent of Pakistanis and Bangladeshis hold comparable positions. As shown in Table 4.1, West Indian women are the least likely to occupy the top jobs – a minuscule 1 per cent hold professional or managerial positions, compared with 7 per cent among white and 6 per cent among Asian women. At the other end of the scale, more than two-thirds of Bangladeshi men have semi-skilled or unskilled jobs, compared with only 16 per cent of whites. For Pakistanis the figure is 43 per cent, for Indians 42 per cent and West Indians 35 per cent. Differences between whites and blacks, therefore, seem well entrenched with regard to jobs and there is little evidence of change. As Brown argues: 'The difference in occupational level between the ethnic minorities and whites were fairly wide when measured in 1974, and there is little indication of any changes since then.'[7]

Blacks and whites in the labour force not only differ in the kind of jobs they do, but also in their distribution among different industries. According to the 1985 Labour Force Survey (LFS),[8] 25 per cent of employed men from ethnic minorities are in 'distribution, hotels, catering, repairs' – industries well known for low pay rates and poor working conditions. On the other hand, the largest concentration of white employed men – 18.2 per cent is to be found in 'other services'. A greater proportion of black men than white tend to work in the transport and communications industries – 12.4 per cent as against 8 per cent among whites. Among women, the industry distribution between the two groups is roughly the same, except in banking, finance and education where there is a larger concentration of white women than black. On the other hand in 'other manufacturing' industries and the health services, there are more black women employed than whites (see Table 4.2).

Research suggests that where people live has a significant bearing on inequalities in incomes. Comparing gross earnings of white men on the one hand and Asian and West Indian men on the other, the inequalities are greatest outside London and the South East. The PSI (1984) study found that, in the North West, blacks earned nearly £43 per week less than whites and in the East Midlands, over £39 less. The overall picture is represented in Table 4.3.

Table 4.2
Persons aged 16+, in paid employment or on government scheme, by ethnic origin, industry division and sex, UK spring 1985

| | (Percentage) | | | |
| | Males | | Females | |
Industry Division	White	Ethnic Minority	White	Ethnic Minority
Agriculture, forestry and fishing	3.1	0.2	1.3	0.1
Energy & water supply	4.4	0.9	1.0	0.8
Other mineral & ore extraction etc.	4.4	2.5	1.8	1.4
Metal goods, engineering and vehicles	14.7	15.7	5.0	6.5
Other manufacturing industries	10.6	14.7	9.9	15.4
Construction	11.7	5.2	1.6	1.0
Distribution, hotels, catering, repairs	15.8	25.1	25.5	23.0
Transportation and communication	8.0	12.4	2.9	4.5
Banking, finance insurance etc.	8.6	6.3	10.3	6.3
Other services of which:	18.2	15.1	40.2	39.5
education	4.2	3.0	11.4	6.0
health services	2.1	5.3	10.5	16.8

Source: *Employment Gazette*, January 1987.

Table 4.3
Gross earnings of full-time employees, by regions (£ median weekly earning)

Regions	Whites	Blacks
England and Wales	128.90	110.20
North West	141.50	98.60
Yorkshire/Humberside	116.20	103.70
West Midlands	130.20	105.90
East Midlands	135.40	96.00
South West	129.20	107.50
South East (excl. London)	126.90	115.20
London	129.90	118.70

Source: Colin Brown, *Black and White*, 1984.

Differences of this magnitude cannot simply be attributed to the different sorts of work done by whites and ethnic minorities.

Comparing whites and blacks of similar job levels, the PSI study still found significant disparities. As shown in Table 4.4, male professionals and managerial workers, for example, were found to be £33 per week worse off if they were Asian or West Indian than if they were white, while among women, the greatest difference in income between whites and blacks is at the professional employee and manager level.

Table 4.4
Gross earnings of full-time employees, by job level (£ median weekly earnings)

Job Level	Male		Female	
	White	Asian/West Indian	White	Asian/West Indian
Professional Employer Manager	184.70	151.80	106.80	122.10
Other non-manual	135.80	130.40	81.70	86.00
Skilled manual	121.70	112.20	(66.90)	(74.40)
Semi-skilled manual	111.20	101.00	66.50*	72.40*
Unskilled manual	(99.90)	97.80		
All	129.00	110.20	77.50	78.50

*' This figure is semi-skilled and unskilled manual.

Source: Colin Brown, *Black an White*, 1984.

Between 1978 and 1983 the number of black women registered as unemployed increased from 14,900 to 74,000, an increase of 397 per cent. This compares with an increase of 137 per cent in the total number of women, both black and white, registered as unemployed in the same period. Black women now make up 6.7 per cent of all unemployed women, while they constitute only 3.7 per cent of the female labour force. By 1985, 19 per cent of the black female labour force was unemployed, compared with 10 per cent of the white female labour force. Within the black female population, Pakistanis and Bangladeshis have the highest unemployment rates (44 per cent) followed by West Indian women with 19 per cent and Indian women with 15 per cent.

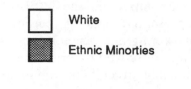

White

Ethnic Minorties

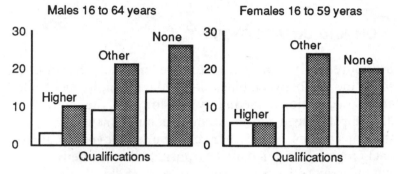

Source: *Employment Gazette*, January 1987.

*Fig. 4.1   Unemployment rates by qualification, ethnic origins and sex,
UK Spring 1985*

Figures from the LFS, 1985, show that qualifications significantly reduce the chances of being unemployed if you are a white man, but they have much less impact if you are an Asian or an Afro-Caribbean man. This is shown in figure 4.1. The figures for white, Asian and Afro-Caribbean women reveal that only when they become *highly* qualified do they decrease their chances of becoming unemployed.

Where ethnic minorities have been successful in breaking into the upper reaches of the job market, it has generally been achieved outside the normal avenues of advancement. The persistence with which African Asians are found at or near the top of jobs indicators has a great deal to do with the fact that they tend to run their own businesses. The experience of blacks competing for executive posts in Britain's companies illustrates how necessary that is. In a survey of 'New Commonwealth' executives in the Midlands, Mark Shaw found that 'individuals of New Commonwealth extraction have very little chance of attaining executive or managerial positions in British industry unless they set up in businesses of their own'.[9] Black executives, when compared with all executives in the Midlands, were found to be well underrepresented among corporate managers, and specialist jobs like marketing and accountancy are proportionately overrepresented among those who described themselves as partners, owners or joint managing directors of companies.

RECESSION AND UNEMPLOYMENT

Blacks are more likely than whites to lose their jobs because, as Brown says, 'the gap between black and white unemployment rates is related to occupational inequality'.[10] However, he notes that the relationship between job level and unemployment is actually strongest among whites, with 52 per cent of unemployed white men having backgrounds in semi-skilled or unskilled work. Only 14 per cent of whites in work have jobs that are semi-skilled or unskilled. Among West Indians in Brown's survey, 50 per cent of the registered unemployed had jobs in those categories, compared with 61 per cent among Asians. Yet 33 per cent of all West Indians and Asians currently hold semi- or unskilled jobs. Brown also reports that the industrial distribution of blacks has little influence – but with some exceptions. Asians, for example, have been particularly hit by the decline of Britain's textile and clothing industries.

This is supported by a Commission of Racial Equality (CRE) survey published in 1983 on Asian workers in the Lancashire textile companies:

> The Asian community in Lancashire has traditionally been self-supporting. A man made redundant or even one seeking a change of employment could usually find employment through a relative or friend without recourse to the Job Centre. In the economic climate which prevailed last year, with night shifts closing and short-time working, the old methods had started to break down and most of our sample were registering at the Job Centre and claiming benefit for the first time in their lives.[11]

Among women, the relationship between joblessness and former job levels is not so strong, largely because women in all ethnic groups are more likely than men to be found in non-manual jobs (see, again, Table 4.1). But again, the exceptions are Asian women, who are particularly vulnerable to unemployment – more so than Asian men – due to the comparatively large numbers of women formerly employed in the recession-hit textile and clothing industries. Overall, however, differences in occupational structure between black and white women contributes little to differences in unemployment levels.

The true figures of black unemployment are unknown due to the fact that the Department of Employment no longer maintains ethnic records, and so the figures that are usually quoted are based upon Labour force sample surveys or the Census. However, the unemployment figures for blacks from the 1960s have always been high as compared to whites, with the minor exception of 1970 (when it was in line with its total population) and between 1973 and 1975. Over the past decade, unemployment has continued to affect blacks disproportionately.[12]

There is little doubt that downturns in the economy hit blacks first. Over the last two decades, differences in unemployment rates between blacks and the general population are usually narrowest at times of low unemployment, and at their widest when unemployment rises. As Thomas points out, some companies actually structure their recruitment policies in such a way as to create two tiers of employment – one for an inner core of secure highly paid professionals, usually white men; and the other, an outer core of clerical and blue-collar jobs, for which women and blacks are more readily taken on.[13] The latter category consists of jobs that can be shed in a fall of business.

Figures from the LFS have consistently shown that unemployment rates for white men and women are lower than the corresponding unemployment rates for men and women of all other ethnic origins. According to the LFS 1985, the unemployment rate for West Indian men is twice that of white men. Pakistani and Bangladeshi men are over two-and-a-half times more likely to be unemployed than white men; and only Indian men, with an unemployment rate of 18 per cent, come at all close to the 11 per cent rate for whites (this pattern is summarized in Figure 4.2).

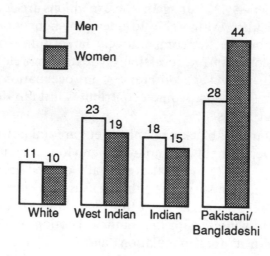

Source: *Labour Force Survey*, 1985.

Fig. 4.2   Unemployment rates by ethnic origin, UK 1985

The rates for Pakistani and Bangladeshi women (44 per cent) and for Indian women (15 per cent) reveal a similar pattern, although West Indian women fare better, with 19 per cent compared with 10 per cent for white women. But these unemployment rates are based only on those who are *registered* unemployed.[14] Taking this into account and the fact that some blacks do not register as unemployed, due to stigma and the appalling service they receive from DHSS officials, the unemployment figures for blacks do not reflect the true picture.

The wealth of evidence shows that, when those seeking work and those not seeking work are taken together, West Indian women are more likely to be unregistered unemployed. A fifth of unregistered West Indian women reported that they did not sign on for reasons to do with children and looking after the house, compared with only a tiny proportion among white women who had not registered.[15]

Different age groups within a population show different levels of unemployment, with young people more likely to be unemployed than older people. The black population as a whole is younger than the white population, with very few over retirement age. According to *Employment Gazette* figures published in 1980, 80 per cent of

West Indians born in Britain were under 30, compared with about 30 per cent among whites.[16] More recently, the 1985 LFS places the under–30s among Bangladeshis (69 per cent) and Pakistanis (68 per cent) ahead of West Indians (59 per cent) with British-born whites under 30 amounting to 42 per cent.[17]

Such wide age differences between black and white populations results in a far greater proportion of the black population being adversely affected by unemployment and leaves blacks particularly vulnerable to the threat of unemployment, even when the consequences of discrimination are discounted. A Department of Employment study in 1981 found that 1 per cent rise in the general level of unemployment led to a 1.7 per cent rise among males under 20 years old, excluding school leavers.[18]

YOUTH UNEMPLOYMENT

Since the rebellions of 1981–85 in Handsworth, Tottenham and Brixton, the question of black youth employment has become a recurrent, if transient, concern amongst policy-makers.

Employment opportunities are unequally distributed between white and black young people on leaving school, on entering YTS and on leaving YTS. Birmingham's annual *Career Service Report* for 1985 indicated, for example, that 13 per cent of white school-leavers found employment but only 4 per cent of Asians and 5 per cent of Afro-Caribbeans. Fewer than 5 per of black youths from Handsworth schools had found jobs four months after leaving school.[19] Not only was this striking difference evident over a long period in Birmingham, it was, and is, applicable to many other towns and cities throughout the country.

The young account for an increasing proportion of those out of work. *Employment Gazette* figures (November 1985) give school-leavers as 0.9 per cent of the unemployed in 1973, rising to 3.6 per cent by 1983 and 6.4 per cent by November 1985. It should be noted that, in November 1985, 36 per cent of all unemployed were aged under 25. As Newham points out, while employment prospects are discouraging for all young people, black youth unemployment has reached astronomical proportions in some areas. The differential unemployment rates between blacks and whites are generally

71

far greater for this age group than any other. When we take account of the fact that black people are far more likely to go into further education than their white counterparts, often to avoid unemployment, we can see 'that young black people in the 1980s are facing a desperate situation'.[20]

The 1985 LFS showed that over 30 per cent of West Indian, 28 per cent of Indian men and 37 per cent of Pakistani and Bangladeshi men in the 16–24 age group were unemployed, compared with less than 20 per cent among white men. As for women in the same age group, 33 per cent of West Indian and 20 per cent of Asian women were unemployed, compared with roughly 15 per cent among white women. The overall picture is summarized in Figure 4.3.

A survey by the CRE found in 1982 that six out of ten West Indian teenagers were unemployed.[21] The direct cause of such a high rate was identified as racial discrimination. West Indians were experiencing no more difficulties than whites in getting interviews, but were then less likely to emerge with a job. The Commission's chairman, Peter Newsam, commented at the time: 'The combination of high level of unemployment and discrimination is potentially explosive.'[22]

Young Asians in Bradford, although on the whole better qualified than their parents, were regarded as

. . . unsuitable for the jobs their parents had done. They nonetheless found it more difficult to move into other areas of employment because semi-skilled jobs in textiles became defined as 'Asian' work. They therefore had difficulty in getting themselves considered for other types of work.[23]

Black school-leavers seeking work through apprenticeships are likely to find that the search for a skill is going to be several times harder than it is for their white former classmates. Lee and Wrench in 1981 followed the careers of youths leaving school in 1979 and seeking craft apprenticeships. Among white youths, 50 per cent were successful in getting the apprenticeship they wanted but, among equally well qualified blacks, only 14 per cent succeeded at this first hurdle.[24]

For many young blacks, the practical choice for those who want some income falls between two options: join the dole queue or

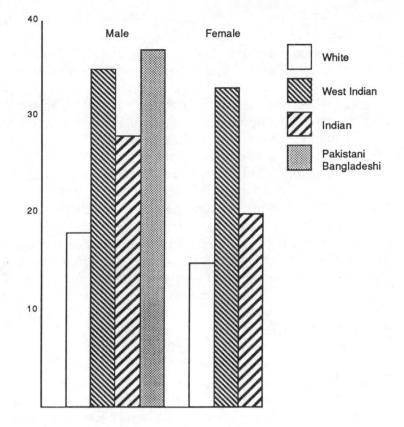

Note: Unemployment rates for women of Pakistani/Bangladeshi orgins in this age group are not available.

Source: *Employment Gazette,* January 1987.

Figure 4.3   Unemployment rates for 16–24-year-olds by sex, UK spring 1985

the Youth Training Scheme (YTS). It seems that, with YTS, the experience of young blacks reflects, rather than compensates for, discrimination in the wider jobs market. YTS was introduced in 1983, and divided into two types of schemes, depending on who organized them on behalf of the Manpower Services Commission (MSC).

Those on 'Mode A'; schemes have tended to work with employers who have a commitment to training and, to that extent, have an even chance of getting work with the same employer after the year's (from now on, two years') training. 'Mode B' schemes have, in many cases, been operated in training centres, where there are few, if any, placements, and therefore less chance of a job leading directly on from the training. There is evidence that young blacks have been channelled into Mode B schemes, and those Mode A schemes which are less likely to lead to work afterwards, while whites take a disproportionate share of employer-based Mode A scheme places. [25] Anna Pollert, in a study of YTS, found that some of the largest West Midlands employers of YTS trainees had poor records in taking on black trainees. Of 27 employers in the Birmingham area who operated Mode A schemes, only 10 employed blacks in June 1985.[26] A study of Mode A schemes in Coventry found only 25 per cent of private employers had a black trainee, most of the blacks being concentrated with four companies.[27] Birmingham City Council's own YTS scheme was found to be discriminatory. Due to an active black community lobby, the Council decided to carry out an elected-member-led investigation into its own scheme and came forward with a 12-point plan to rectify 'inequality' practices.[28]

So far as the recently introduced two-year YTS is concerned, a Coventry survey found that only five of 26 retail schemes had any black trainees, there were only two black trainees on the Construction Industry Training Board out of 263, only one of 82 hairdressing placements had a black trainee, and Jaguar Cars had none at all.[29] The latest figures for the destination of young people on leaving YTS show the same differences in outcome by racial origin. According to the MSC, 56 per cent of white trainees obtained employment on leaving YTS in 1985 in contrast to only 33 per cent of Afro-Caribbean youngsters and 31 per cent of Asian youngsters. One of the paradoxes of the situation concerns those YTS schemes which have a high proportion of black trainees. This is precisely where differences between black and white youngsters are most apparent in relation to success in finding employment – schemes which may be popular with black youngsters and sympathetic to their situations may be less likely to provide a link to work afterwards.

In summary, therefore, it is obvious that at every stage from leaving school, into YTS and beyond, black young people are now finding equal opportunities in the labour market.

EXPLANATIONS OF BLACK UNEMPLOYMENT

There have been a number of explanations as to why blacks are overrepresented in the unemployment statistics. The more common amongst them are:

1. The black population is younger;
2. The black population lacks appropriate skills and qualifications;
3. Discrimination increases when there is a surplus of labour;
4. Black workers are concentrated in particular areas and in particular industries like manufacturing which have been more adversely affected by the recession';
5. The 'last in, first out' rule during redundancies.

Similar explanations to the above were endorsed by the earlier edition of this book and an additional factor of 'last in, first out' rule, applied at times of redundancy, was added.[30] It is worth briefly examining all of the above arguments prior to advocating our own explanation towards the end of the chapter.

Argument 1: The black population is younger

Brown's 1984 PSI survey of unemployment rates by age, sex and ethnic group confirms that the level of white unemployment is consistently below that of the West Indian and Asian populations for all age groups. The age effect can also be allowed for by calculating what the overall unemployment rate would have been for each ethnic group, if they all had the same age distribution.

Figures published by the Department of Employment in 1984 show that the age effect accounts for no more than one-tenth of the difference in unemployment rates; and, in the case of Asian men, allowing for the effects of age actually increases the unemployment rate.[31] Differences in unemployment rates among black and white women is influenced by the proportion of married women in the labour force, as the registered unemployed rate is higher for unmarried than for married women. However, with the exception of married West Indian women, for whom the rate was slightly lower, the unemployment rates were higher for all black women than for white women, irrespective of marital status or age group, (as shown in Table 4.5). Therefore, age structure does not explain more than a fraction of the differences in levels of unemployment among blacks and whites.

Table 4.5
Female unemployment rates by ethnic origin, age and marital status, spring 1981

	White	West Indian Guyanese	Percentage Indian Pakistani Bangladeshi	All Ethnic Groups
Married				
16–24	16	18	34	17
25–44	7	7	14	7
45–59	4	3	8	4
Unmarried				
16–24	16	30	27	17
25–44	9	19	15	10
45–59	9	14	27	9

Source: *Employment Gazette*, June 1984.

Argument 2 : The black population's lack of skills and qualifications

This argument does not hold water because first-generation blacks were often overqualified for the jobs they carried out, and recent evidence confirms that qualified second-generation blacks do not gain the more desirable jobs anyway. Two recent reports on doctors and black graduates made it blatantly obvious that qualified blacks are being discriminated against not only when seeking appropriate employment, but also in terms of salary and status.[32]

Although some of the first-generation settlers did have language difficulties, this no longer applies to the majority of those on the dole. Further, it needs to be emphasized that, in many cases, blacks had more skills and qualifications than were required for the tasks they performed and the level of verbal communication that was necessary was minimal given the tasks to which they were confined. The key point, however, is that, over the past decade or so, the issue of communication has little relevance as more and more blacks speak with ordinary local accents.

Differences in educational qualifications have less effect on black unemployment than at first might appear. As the *Employment Gazette* notes:

> The fact that non-white men were on average less well qualified than their white counterparts tended to increase the difference between the unemployment rates of whites and non-whites, but by no more than one per cent.[33]

An analysis of unemployment rates among those with similar qualifications reveals some striking disparities. The 1981 Labour Force Survey found, for example, that 25 per cent of unemployed West Indian men had 'O' levels; the corresponding figure for whites was 9 per cent. By far the most highly qualified unemployed among all ethnic groups however, were Asians. Among men and women, unemployed Asians with degrees or with membership of professional institutes proportionately outnumbered similarly qualified unemployed whites two to one.[34] David Smith, in a study published in 1981 by the PSI, found that gaining qualifications was a protection against unemployment only for whites.[35] Drawing from results of the 1976–7 General Household Survey, Smith found 'that West Indian and Asian men have much the same risk of being unemployed regardless of their qualifications, whereas among whites it is particularly the unqualified who are at risk'. These sorts of findings are confirmed by local studies, which also show how difficult it is for unemployed blacks to get back to work. In Liverpool, for example, a report published in December 1985 by the local Area Manpower Board found that 'black Job Centre users tended to have more academic qualifications', but they generally have to make twice as many applications as whites before finding a job.[36] In 1980, a CRE survey in Nottingham tested employers' reactions to well qualified black applicants in competition with similarly qualified whites and found that systematic discrimination was prevalent for black applicants.[37]

More recently, a Sheffield City Council report found that discrimination against young blacks was greater if they were highly qualified than if they were less qualified. The unemployment rate among young whites with only up to three 'O' Levels was 48 per cent; for similarly qualified young blacks, 79 per cent. But for young whites with four or more 'O' Levels, the unemployment rate fell to 13 per cent, and for young blacks with similar qualifications, to 38 per cent. Thus, blacks with low qualifications were one and a half times more likely than whites to be out of work; but blacks with high qualifications were nearly three times more likely than similarly qualified whites to be unemployed.[38]

Argument 3 : Discrimination increases when there is a surplus of labour

A surplus of labour may give more rein to the practice of discrimination as employers have more freedom to pick and choose without threatening their profits. This is supported by comparative figures for unemployment rates according to ethnic groups. Except on rare occasions – for example, 1970–74 – unemployment among black people has always been higher than among whites – that is, black people have greater difficulty in finding new employment. It is, however, relevant to mention here the fact that in 1966 at a time when unemployment was very low (approximately 1 per cent) PEP (Political and Economic Planning) found that black minority applicants for employment were treated worse than whites on 90 per cent of occasions. The level of unemployment in 1974, at a time when PEP found a 30 per cent level of primary discrimination, was approximately 2.5 per cent, whereas the 1985 level was 11 per cent the level of discrimination was still 30 per cent. This may suggest that the level of discrimination remains the same regardless of the state of unemployment. Alternatively, it is still possible that the discrimination rate might have declined from 30 per cent to much less if unemployment had not drastically increased. One has to wait for a period of lower employment in order to find out whether the level of discrimination has dropped.

Argument 4 : Black workers are concentrated in areas and industries which have been adversely affected by recession

Black communities are grouped in certain regions in Britain and, given the unevenness of the effects of the recession, this might be expected to have had some impact on higher levels of unemployment among blacks. But, according to the 1984 LFS, the great majority of blacks live in London and the South East – that is, in areas *less* affected by economic downturns. For example, 68 per cent of West Indians in Britain live in the South East, all but 10 per cent of whom live in Greater London. Only Pakistanis and Bangladeshis live in significantly fewer numbers in the South East, with only 23 per cent living in Greater London. Blacks tend *not* to live in proportionately the same numbers as whites in areas which have been worst hit by recession. The exception is the West Midlands, where 9 per cent of whites, but 13 per cent of West Indians, 17 per cent of Indians and 22 per cent of Pakistanis and Bangladeshis live. According to Colin Brown:

Overall, the regional distribution of black people tends to deflate their national unemployment rate rather than inflate it: if Asians and West Indians had the same regional distribution as whites then their unemployment rates would be even higher than they are already.[39]

In March 1986, the MSC carried out a survey of usage of 150 Jobcentres and found that the submission to placement ratio varied considerably according to ethnic groups as shown in Table 4.6.

Table 4.6
Submission to placement ratio, by ethnic group, March 1986

	White	Afro-Caribbean	Asian
South East	12:1	19:1	25:1
London	8:1	13:1	16:1
West Midlands	13:1	34:1	32:1
East Midlands	14:1	31:1	24:1
Yorks/Humberside	19:1	21:1	24:1
North West	15:1	20:1	29:1
All	13:1	16:1	21:1

Source: MSC, *Ethnic Minorities and Jobcentres*, February 1987, Table 4.9.

The 1971 Census showed black workers were concentrated largely

79

in manual occupations, namely textiles, clothing, foundries, engineering and manufacturing. However the argument that the concentration of black people in declining industries makes them especially vulnerable to unemployment may be convincingly attacked as an oversimplification. First, the concentration of black people in certain occupations is itself a result of racist attitudes towards the employment of black people, which prevented them from taking other work. Second, the industrial distribution of the black workforce does in itself account for disproportionately high unemployment; as Smith (1981) points out, most industries give rise to a rate of unemployment roughly proportionate to their share of the workforce, except construction, miscellaneous services and textiles.[40] Third, even in the textile industry it is argued, jobs have been decreased by technology while at the same time black workers are seen as unsuitable for new work requiring mental rather than physical attributes. Ralph Fevre concludes that the main cause of permanent job losses has been the efforts of employers to increase productivity. This, combined with discrimination, has meant that those jobs lost are primarily those of black workers.[41]

Similarly, Colin Brown, in the PSI survey, concluded that the industrial distribution of black workers had been only a limited factor in the disproportionate growth in their unemployment rate. Brown calculated what the white unemployment rate would have been had whites been concentrated in the lower job levels in which blacks are concentrated. He found the white unemployment rate would have been higher than it is at present, but still not as high as present black workers in low job levels, and further discrimination results in blacks being more likely to lose their jobs in these low levels than their white counterparts.

Argument 5 : 'Last in, first out'

'Last in, first out' was a policy advocated by the trade unions as a 'fairer' process of deciding who should be made redundant and therefore safeguarding their longer-serving members. It should, however, be noted that by 1980–85 many black workers had put in 20–30 years service, similar to their white workmates. Therefore, the effect of the 'last in, first out' rule should, theoretically, have the same impact upon all ethnic groups. However, there have been cases where this 'rule' has only been enforced by trade unions when it has been in the interest of their fellow white workers. For example, in 1967–68, at the Coneygre Foundry in the West Midlands the golden rule of 'last in, first out' was not applied despite the long service of black workers. Twenty-one Indian members of the TGWU (and no whites) were made redundant; they reacted by going on strike but the union argued that racial discrimination had not occurred.[42] This limited evidence suggests that there is a need for a more detailed enquiry into the process used when a multi-racial workforce is threatened with redundancy, so that the whole issue can be fully examined.

RESPONSES TO RACIAL DISCRIMINATION

In this section, we shall look at responses to racial discrimination, by (a) the state; (b) local authorities; (c) the trade unions; (d) employers; and (e) black communities.

The state's response

Legal response. From the expulsion of Jews in 1290, to Queen Elizabeth I's Privy Council decision to remove 'blackamores' in the sixteenth century, to action against Welsh, gypsy and Irish minorities, to the hypocrisy over the abolition of slavery in the eighteenth and nineteenth centuries, immigration restrictions and repatriation have been persistent themes of government's approach to legislation on ethnic and racial minorities. In this century the 1905 Aliens Act, the 1914 Status of Aliens Act and the 1919 Aliens Restriction (Amendment) Act were the precursors of the Common-wealth Immigration Acts of 1962, 1968 and 1971 and the 1982 British Nationality Act.

Unsuccessful attempts were made in the 1950s by individual Labour MPs to introduce Private Member's Bills to outlaw racial discrimination in various areas of life. In 1965 and 1968 the Labour Government was under political pressure to adopt further restrictions on immigration but as a token to left-wing and liberal opinion passed two Race Relations Acts. The 1965 Act established a Race Relations Board (RRB) and made discrimination in hotels, pubs and public places unlawful. It was still common, however, for advertisements for flats to state 'no coloureds' and for employers openly to reject black job applicants purely because of their colour.[43]

As a result of the manifest indadequacies of the 1965 Act, illustrated by PEP research and through the RRB's own work, it was clear that further legislation was required. The 1968 Act, passed in the shadow of the Commonwealth Immigration Act, resulted in the disappearance of racist advertisements, and the incidents of overt discrimination by employers subsequently dropped. However, the limitations of the new legislation were soon exposed. The 1968 Act depended for its effectiveness on black people being willing to take their complaints to the Race Relations Board. However, the number of complaints averaged less than 1,000 per year. Furthermore, most cases were conciliated, little financial compensation was negotiated in the small number which reached a hearing and courts showed little sympathy or appreciation of the spirit of the legislation. House of Lords' decisions on the cases of the refusal of admission to working men's clubs and refusal on grounds of nationality of registration on a council house waiting list provided examples of this.[44] Further research indicated a continuing level of direct discrimination in operation.[45]

Pressure for further legislation was resisted until 1975 when the Labour Government announced a new Race Relations Bill. Eventually, in June 1977 the 1976 Race Relations Act came into operation. In addition to plugging the loopholes in respect of clubs and nationality, the Act introduced the concepts of indirect discrimination and positive action. The former was intended to deal with rules which applied to everyone but had a disproportionate and unjustifiable impact on racial minorities, while positive action envisaged redress for past discrimination. Complainants themselves were now able to take their cases to court or tribunal, and the successor body to the RRB, the Commission for Racial Equality (CRE), was given powers to issue Codes of Practice and to carry out investigations on a strategic basis into employers and organizations providing housing, social welfare, education and legal services, and so on. The inadequacies of the latest Race Relations Act have been described elsewhere, notably in the CRE's proposals for amendments to the Act.[46] The courts have once more placed restrictions on the interpretation of the law, few individuals have been able to prove their cases successfully, and patterns of discrimination in 1985 were similar to those of 1974. Four aspects of the legal approach may be identified: the effect of the law in itself; tribunal proceedings for individual complaints; pressure to discriminate; and formal investigations. First, so far as the declaratory impact of the 1976 Race Relations Act is concerned, there is no evidence that it has led to the volume of changes in overt discrimination achieved by earlier legislation. Comparatively few employers understand indirect discrimination, let alone take action to eliminate it. The law also introduced the notion that local authorities had a special responsibility (under Section 71 of the Act) to promote equality of opportunity. This was worded in such a convoluted manner that it has no legal force whatsoever, although Leicester City Council did make an attempt to enforce it in 1986. There is no evidence that any local authority has been moved solely, or mainly, by Section 71 to embrace equal opportunity policies.

Second, according to the annual CRE reports, the level of individual complaints remains constant at approximately 1,000 per year, the same as under the RRB. One should compare this figure with the 'tens of thousands' of cases which the PSI survey estimated were taking place each year. The success rate furthermore is still low. By the end of 1980, according to the CRE's own research, 936 complaints of racial discrimination had been registered at industrial tribunals.[47] Only 45 per cent of complaints proceeded to a hearing; 9 per cent were upheld and 36 per cent dismissed. Awards were made in 25 of 33 upheld cases. Nearly 80 per cent of tribunal financial awards were below £300. The present position is that between 300 and 400 applications are made each year to industrial tribunals (more, as it happens, than under the Sex Discrimination Act), mostly by the CRE. Approximately 10 per cent are settled out of court and about one-half proceed to a hearing where the success rate is between 10 and 21 per cent. Compensation averages a few hundred pounds and it is rare for an award to exceed £1,000. Most recently (1986), a case against a health authority has received the highest financial award so far of £5,000 but that has been turned down on appeal. Black people would argue that the above figures speak for themselves and confirm why they have little faith in the legal system. For a start, it is difficult to obtain evidence to show discrimination and further, even where proven, the compensation for hurt feelings is pitiful, quite apart from the trauma of appearing in court and facing hostile or bigoted cross-examination. What this experience confirms to the black community is that, although racial discrimination and harassment are issues of paramount concern to them, the institutions are unable or unwilling to take them seriously. It should also be pointed out that a substantial number of tribunal cases are handled by the CRE. Clearly, if black organizations, Councils for Community Relations, law centres, and, above all, trade unions were themselves registering and pursuing allegations of discrimination, whether in terms of recruitment, working conditions, promotion, dismissal or redundancy, then the total number of complaints of discrimination recorded would be well above the present figure of 1,000. In this respect, one should ask why the CRE appears to insist on occupying centre stage in terms of complaints and does not do more to develop self-help amongst community organizations and to press trade unions to act on behalf of black members. The CRE has arranged training sessions for outside organizations, published an information pack and offered to provide grant aid for an additional member of staff at law centres, but that is not enough. If the potential number of complaints is legion, perhaps the CRE should review its own procedures for handling cases. Theoretically, it only pursues cases which raises a special principle or are particularly complex (Section 66 of the Act). However, when one considers that some of the successful cases supported by the CRE fit none of the criteria laid down, it seems possible that it simply keeps likely numbers for itself. If other organizations are to play a part, the CRE must be prepared to let them sometimes have winners as well.

Third, the CRE has had a unique power to prosecute in cases where instructions or pressure to discriminate racially have occurred. However, this power is rarely used – in 1985, 43 pressure cases were received (15 in 1984) and less than 20 were taken to tribunal. Successful hearings are of limited value in any case as they only result in a declaration and are not accompanied by any fine or compensation to injured parties. None the less, they may have value in educating referral agencies such as Careers Services, Job Centres and YTS Schemes in how to respond to discriminatory pressure.

Fourth, the CRE also has the special power to carry out formal investigations. To date (end of March 1987), the Commission has carried out 42 investigations, 22 of them into employment or training matters. Most recently these have concerned access to nursing and medical schools, accountancy, retail and hotel industries. While many of the investigations have involved household names such as British Leyland, Prestige, Abbey National and major local authorities (for example, Birmingham, Kirklees and Westminster), their effectiveness has been limited both by repeated legal challenges and by feeble requirements in non-discrimination notices. There has also been a trend away from the 'belief' type of investigation which starts with allegations of discrimination towards a more general kind of enquiry which relies upon the co-operation of respondents and which in any case works at the level of questionnaires and selected follow-up interviews.

One of the other contributions made by the CRE has been the drafting of the Code of Practice for the elimination of discrimination and the promotion of equality of opportunity in employment. Although drafted in 1978, it was only passed by Parliament in 1983, coming into effect in April 1984. The Code gives guidance to employers on how racial discrimination in employment can be eliminated, by advocating the implementation of an equal opportunities policy, which, when applied to recruitment and treatment of employees, theoretically reduces racial discrimination. A key aspect of the Code is the emphasis on monitoring, not only in relation to the appointment of staff but also to promotion, transfer and so on. In evidence to the Select Committee on Employment in 1986 the CRE was obliged to accept that the impact of the Code of Practice was relatively marginal.

Legal measures have therefore a very limited role to play in challenging and changing patterns of discrimination and disadvantage. The government's response generally to discrimination and prejudice in terms of its employment policies has been varied. In some cases, such as the decision to introduce ethnic records into the civil service (1981) and the armed forces (1987), the change came about as a result of social and community pressure. There had been internal discussions within the civil service about 'equal opportunity' for years , culminating in 1975 with the commissioning of the Tavistock Report. However, no real progress was made until sufficient long-term political pressure had been exerted to bring about the recent changes.

Central government and contract compliance. Since 1969 the government has had simple non-discrimination clauses in its contracts with suppliers. These have never been monitored and no action has been taken to exclude or even warn employers about their position in relation to equal opportunities or the Race Relations Code of Practice. No government has been particularly enthusiastic about such clauses and the present government even less so as indicated by its anxieties about local authority action in this area.

The advocacy of contract compliance policies has generally been based upon the relative success of such a policy in the United States in tackling racial and sexual discrimination. In Britain, this idea was first mooted by the 'Street Report' way back in 1966 as a positive suggestion in overcoming discrimination.[48] Contract compliance *per se* has been in operation for some time. Local authorities, prior to agreeing to a contract, always seek information regarding a company's financial viability in relation to particularly large contracts.

According to Mr Peter Bottomley, former Under-Secretary of State at the Department of Employment (1985–86) (and soon moved to a less crucial area), high levels of unemployment among black youth were a major factor in the government's surprise announcement in November 1985 that some version of contract compliance could be introduced for companies tendering for government-financed work.[49]

Central government's response to contract compliance policy has been contradictory to say the least. Patrick Jenkin, whilst Minister for the Environment, stated that contract clauses will have to be limited to 'technical, managerial and financial capacity' thus ruling out any possibility of an equal opportunity clause. David Waddington, as Home Office Minister, stated in 1986 that contract compliance was 'under serious consideration' and believed that an equal opportunity clause would force contractors to adopt fair employment practices for government contracts. Douglas Hurd, the Home Secretary, whilst Secretary of State for Northern Ireland, ensured that contractors complied with policies geared towards the prevention of discrimination against Catholics on grounds of their religion. More recently, after the civil disturbances in Birmingham and London (1985), and after a great deal of criticism by black people[50] that funding 'bypassed' local people, the government has now supported the conditions upon contractors seeking contracts under the urban programme to employ a percentage of local employees. At the time of writing the government is proposing new legislation to ensure further tendering of local authorities services; it is an ideal opportunity to ensure that an equal opportunity clause becomes a norm and that the clause is monitored vigorously.

Furthermore, the government itself, as an employer, has a fairly dismal record for employing and promoting blacks, and so could not, with much moral force, point an accusing finger at private sector employers. But the fact remains that, for all the Codes of Practices and Equal Opportunity Policies, the one method that might alleviate the enormous problem of racial disadvantage and discrimination is the more direct one of *forcing* the better representation of ethnic minorities in companies and in the state. One reason it has failed, of course, is that it has not yet seriously been tried on much of a scale. Yet it is clear that attempting to catch individual acts of racial discrimination with the existing legal apparatus is, with very few exceptions, hopelessly elusive and piecemeal.

Therefore the introduction of an effective monitoring policy and contract compliance, rigorously enforced by government, may prove an important first step in breaking down the well entrenched and deep-rooted problem of jobs discrimination.

Local authorities' response

The limited progress made by local authorities in introducing equal opportunity policies, and thus fairer recruitment procedures, and the positive impact it has had upon black people has been briefly documented in Chapter 1. The reasons for the launch of such policies stem from the political pressure over a period of time from the black community and the few black elected members of local councils. The initiative has primarily centred around inner city authorities.

The concept of equal opportunities was brought to the forefront by the Greater London Council's (GLC) Contract Compliance Unit, established in 1983. The GLC devised a questionnaire covering issues related to areas of equal opportunities policies. At the beginning of 1986, 134 firms had satisfied the GLC that they were operating adequate equal opportunities policies. Twenty-five companies – including Rowntree McIntosh and Hoover – failed the test. However, as John Clare points out: 'disqualification is not the object of the exercise. The point is to educate employers by offering them hope and advice. Most accept it, so the GLC has been performing a notable public service.'[51] The fact that the Labour-led GLC adopted such a policy may have been a sufficient reason for the government to back away from it.

For the purpose of this chapter it is worth emphasizing the impact on racial discrimination achieved by the launch of contract compliance policies. By far the largest success has been by the now defunct GLC and, to a lesser extent, the West Midlands County Council. Other local authorities, for instance Sheffield, have also had success with contract compliance policies, particularly in relation to the construction industry.

Trade unions' response

According to the 1984 PSI Survey, 56 per cent of black employees are union members compared to 47 per cent of white employees, but nevertheless the trade union movement has a history imbued with racism.[52] Trade unions operated the notorious 'colour bar' policies between the two world wars.[53] The trade union movement did not learn its lesson, for history was to repeat itself in the 1950s and 1960s. Even on the fundamental trade union issue of the right of workers to join a trade union, the wider union movement was unwilling to take the action that was necessary to pursue the Grunwick dispute successfully in the 1970s.[54]

The Special Restrictions (Coloured Alien Seaman) Order 1925 laid conditions on the employment of black seamen. Other legislation includes restrictions on the appointment of aliens to occupations such as those of pilot, civil servant and soldier. The 1701 Act of Settlement barred aliens from public office in general. Collective agreements between unions and employees in the 1950s and 1960s discriminated against foreign nationals – for example, the Amalgamated Union of Building Trade Workers, National Union of Hosiery and Knitwear Workers, NUR and ASLEF. A survey in 1966 indicated that 22 unions still had some agreements or rules relating to 'foreign', 'immigrant' or 'coloured' workers and, even after the 1968 Race Relations Act, the Power Loom Carpet Weavers and Textile Workers Association, the National Union of Dyers, Bleachers and Textile Workers, the Brith Airline Pilots' Association, ACTT and Musicians Union still applied restrictions in respect of particular groups or those who were not British subjects. Even today, civil service nationality rules only allow British subjects and even these have to provide full details of their parents' place of birth and nationality at birth and death.

In 1955, although the Trades Union Congress (TUC) passed a resolution condemning racial discrimination, the mover expressed his worry that 'immigrants' would form a pool of cheap labour, thus undermining unions' bargaining power. No doubt the set of attitudes that this reflected contributed to the fact that there was no trade union opposition to the 1962, 1968 nor the 1971 Immigration Bills.

The trade union movement was in broad agreement with the view that what was required was the integration of black workers into the host white culture, thus ignoring the day-to-day issues that were encountered by the blacks, including the issue of racial discrimination at the workplace from white union members. A recent review of the British trade union movement record on racial issues summarized the main failings of the movement with regard to its black membership.

1. The failure of the trade union leadership to entertain the idea that black members were faced with any different problems from those of the ordinary white membership, or that this necessitated any special policies.
2. Cases of direct and active collusion of local shop stewards and officials in arrangements of discrimination. (In addition to this, in some notorious cases, the union withheld support from striking black workers who were protesting about this adverse treatment in relation to white workers.)
3. Cases of more passive collusion of union officers and shop stewards in practices which were demonstrated to have been discriminatory in outcome, along with a resistance to change these practices.
4. Individual cases of racism by unsympathetic, unenlightened or even racially bigoted shop stewards and local officials, and

89

a reluctance on the part of unions to take disciplinary action against racist offenders.

5. A general lack of awareness of the issues of race and equal opportunity and the particular circumstances of ethnic minority members, which may not manifest itself as racism but in effect lessens the participation of black members in the union.[55]

Examples of such racism were Mansfield Hosiery, where 500 Asians were denied access to better-paid jobs on knitting machines for years and when they went on strike in 1972, employers, with the support of the local union, recruited 36 new white trainees for the knitting jobs. At Imperial Typewriters the employers underpaid the bonus to its black employees for over a year, and when they went on strike the union refused to support them. Further, in 1981, when two black electricians with the GLC won their case over receiving lower wages and bonuses, their own union, the EETPU, refused to defend their black members.

According to Sivanandan, it was the fact that blacks were not able to gain the support of trade unions in the workplace that led to the development of black community projects. This argument has been supported further by Lee's study which highlighted the fact that black union members felt that unions do not look after their interests or take up issues pertinent to them, such as racial harassment.[56]

More recently a number of trade unions have been approving anti-racist resolutions at their annual conferences, but these again have generally been paper exercises. In 1985, the National Union of Public Employees (NUPE) Race Equality Working Party reported that 'the trade union movement had voiced its opposition to racial discrimination and all forms of division amongst working people, but it is a fact that there has been very little concerted action to put the policies into action'.

There is no doubt that, after years of pressure by black activists, a few trade unions are now trying to make visible progress. For example the National Association of Local Government Officers (NALGO) was the first union that sponsored a conference for its black members to meet and draw up their own agenda of issues. This is very much to be welcomed but, at the same time, the same union has also been criticized by its black members for lack of consultation. If trade unions are unable to examine their own internal structures and practices critically they will be unable to recognize the fact that it is institutionalized racism that restricts progress.

The lack of a speedy and adequate response to black members' concerns has contributed to blacks organizing themselves to take up directly issues of racism and discrimination. There is a precedent for this in associations representing Jewish workers in the early years of this century. The Camden Black Workers Group is a modern example, where the Group exercises a right to represent black workers in grievance and discipline cases.[57] If trade unions as a whole do not respond to the needs of black workers, such groups are likely to grow in number and might lead to the alienation of black workers from the trade union movement.

Other employers' response

Employers generally (perhaps taking their lead from the Confederation of British Industry (CBI) made little response to the Race Relations legislation in terms of effective action to identify and eliminate direct and indirect discrimination. As indicated earlier, the Race Relations Code of Practice by itself has had very little effect. It is true that a number of major employers in public and private sectors have taken a first step by adopting equal opportunity policies of one kind or another and these include major financial institutions, retail and manufacturing companies and public corporations such as British Rail and the Post Office. It is possible to conclude that these developments were motivated by selfless concern for the principle of racial equality, but it is more likely that the street rebellions of 1981 and 1985 were a key factor. In any event, it is rare for employers, having once adopted an 'equal opportunity policy' to monitor it thoroughly and then to take positive steps to redress past injustices.

The black community's response

The blatant racial discrimination against black people politically, socially and economically by the state, institutions and individuals has compelled the black community, over the years, to organize itself against the unjust treatment it receives daily. The black community has been active for decades in challenging racism at every level from their community-based organizations. These independent groups, centred around the theme of religious beliefs and industrial issues, took on the responsibility of offering not only welfare services but also political campaigns to ensure that they and their members received equal treatment from the state and its institutions. There is a whole history of campaign work against racist and unfair employment restrictions.

In 1943, Learie Constantine, a cricketer from Trinidad who encountered discrimination when trying to stay at a hotel, won his case in court prior to any race relation legislation. Organizations like the Indian Workers Association and the Standing Conference of West Indian Organizations have a long history of defending individuals over cases of discrimination in the labour market. More recently, welfare advice centres have emerged as leading activists in demanding equality of opportunity in employment policies and practices of employees. In so far as black workers in positions of some responsibility – for example, as councillors, race relations advisers, or shop stewards – retain their links with the black community, it is possible to place their activities in the context of the community's response. The issue of youth unemployment and the continual inequality that is embedded in the YTS schemes prompted a small number of black organizations to become managing agencies themselves in order to ensure more black people received appropriate training and support in applying for work.

It could be argued that the government is keen to promote 'black entrepreneurs' and black business through financial assistance so that it can create a 'manageable black middle-class' which could then act as a buffer by creating divisions amongst the black community. Similarly, in pursuance of division amongst the black community in Birmingham during the urban rebellions of 1985, the media attempted but failed to hype-up the so-called tensions between the Asians and Afro-Caribbean communities.[58]

Having lived with racism and discrimination in the labour market it perhaps should not be too surprising to note that the black community was forced into self-employment as another solution to overcoming the frustrations of being made redundant, of not being

92

promoted for jobs for which they were well qualified and of not gaining the support of trade unions on issues that mattered to them. Within the black community the direction taken in self-employment has been influenced by certain stereotypes of the Asian and Afro-Caribbean community. In the case of the latter, the 'alternative market' has come to the fore – that is, the establishment of co-operatives promoting Agro-Caribbean culture, diet food and music. For decades, blacks in the United States have had a proud record in relation to their contribuiton to the music industry. More recently, we have seen the emergence of black sportspersons gracing Britain at the Olympics and on the sport fields, and black talent has been recognized in the competitive world of fashion and design. On the other hand, Asians have been placed in situations of having to take advantage of the extended family in purchasing retail shops and sweatshop industries. The extended family has pulled together to raise the initial capital outlay (often because loans were less likely to be forthcoming from banks) and the use of relatives has kept the wage bill to a minimum. There is a great deal of evidence which reinforces the view that Britain's black entrepreneurs are at a disadvantage, particularly in relation to raising finance and their overdependence upon the local (inner city) market.[59]

For the purposes of this chapter, the key point is that black people's experience in the area of self-employment is one of the continuation of racial discrimination. However, the particular exploitation of labour (in the sweatshop industry) with poor wages, bad health and safety conditions and even the illegal employment of children, coupled with no trade union recognition and a lack of government determination to stamp these practices out, is very much the reflection of the present government's political ideology. This avenue has helped to keep many off the unemployment register even though, in real terms, many are not receiving any wages. Evidence is accumulating on the exploitation of black workers by black employers, particularly in the textile industry. In these circumstances, *capital* becomes the key factor and not the colour of employees.

As highlighted earlier, black business has enabled a few black people to reach executive-level positions but there is no evidence that this has played any part in reducing or even challenging racial discrimination. The emergence of black business is also seen by some as a way towards solving the problem of black unemployment. This however can be overstated. On the face of it, these sorts of findings appear to lend weight to some of the policy conclusions drawn by the Home Affairs Committee which says:

> It cannot be through equal access to employment opportunities alone that racial disadvantage in employment is overcome. It is equally important that ethnic minority businessmen should be enabled to play a full part in the nation's economy as employers and as self-employed.[60]

There seems little reason to suppose, however, that blacks can substantially overcome inequalities at work simply by setting up their own businesses.[61] The possibility of overestimating the opportunities for black businesses is recognized in Shaw's survey;[62] he found that not only are black executives as a proportion of the black population fewer than average but that, when compared with the population as a whole, blacks were underrepresented, even in 'owner', 'partner' and 'joint' managing director positions.

AN ALTERNATIVE EXPLANATION: A NEED FOR POSITIVE ACTION

What this chapter clearly highlights is that, regardless of whether one examines the situation of those blacks in employment, those skilled, unskilled or professional, those unemployed or indeed those on government-sponsored YTS, it must be concluded that blacks have been, and are, discriminated against at every level and in every sphere. Earlier, we highlighted the common explanations given for the disproportionate representation of blacks who are out of work. But we feel to analyse the excessive unemployment figures amongst the black population, there have to be other explanations and indeed other questions which need to be asked. For example, once unemployed, why do blacks stay unemployed for much longer periods than whites? Why is it that blacks are much more likely to experience recurrent unemployment and could it be, as Dex argues, that West Indians constitute 'a reserve or secondary labour force'?[63]

Although we accept that discrimination in the labour market is more prevalent during recessions for obvious reasons, it should not be overlooked that there was discrimination prior to the recession. A recent study confirms that the level of discrimination has remained the same, if not worse, in some areas since the passing of the 1976 Race Relations Act which made racial discrimination unlawful. Therefore, the real explanation for the overrepresentation of blacks in unemployment statistics is due to *racism* both at an *individual level* and *institutional level*. It is this racism which enables white people in power to abuse their position and ensure 'unequal' processes apply in practice when it comes to employment, promotion, redundancy or treatment of black employees. This is the single most important explanation why blacks have continuously suffered adversely in the labour market, irrespective of the market situation.

Given that racism is still endemic in our society, it would seem little has happened over the past three decades to give any clear grounds for optimism for the future. Nevertheless, the following factors have emerged in this chapter. First, racism and racial discrimination accounts for most of the discrepancies in the employment statistics for black people. Generally, the overrepresentation of blacks on the unemployed register and in low-paid jobs still prevails, and now there is consistent research data to verify this in the private as well as public sectors. The progressive policies adopted recently by some of the London Boroughs like Lambeth, Hackney, the former GLC and West Midlands County Council have shown a way forward. They have demonstrated that, through political intitiatives, a great deal can be achieved by adopting effective equal opportunities policies to combat discrimination at the point of entry and in other internal policies like access to training. The emergence of contract compliance in this country has become a much more real option in tackling discrimination, thanks to the GLC and now the Inner London Education Authority (ILEA). Although the Labour Party and the Alliance are now committed to some form of national policy on this, the Conservatives are 'floundering' on this crucial issue.

For decades, the issue of racism in the context of employment and unemployment has been forefront in the minds of black people. Blacks have been persistently informing the politicians that they

95

are receiving a raw deal and that the race relations legislation has been too weak to enable them to receive justice at tribunals. For decades, statistics have been available to verify the inequality in the job market. Attempts that have been made to explain this have, in our view, generally concentrated upon 'cultural factors' and blaming the victim. Hopefully, this chapter has helped to destroy that theory, for what really lies behind the statistics are the many forms of racism which prevent blacks from obtaining fair and equal treatment. Tackling racism is the only way to achieve the necessary changes. Some local authorities have already demonstrated that positive changes can be brought about, and now it is the turn of the government and other authorities and employers to follow their example and demonstrate their concern for all members of our society and eliminate discrimination on grounds of race, gender and other attributes. An implementation of a national contract compliance policy could and should be seen as a major priority in systematically tackling racial and sexual discrimination. There are many weaknesses in the 1976 Race Relations Act and these could be overcome if only the government would strengthen the legislation.

It is the whole issue of racism in our society that needs to be addressed. The institutions that assist in the reproduction of this social injustice need to re-examine their structures, policies and practices and introduce fair and equal opportunities for all. Such a course of action will be one of the most positive ways forward.

Blacks in the late 1980s feel despair at their phenomenal overrepresentation on the unemployment register, attributable to both employers and the state. Not being content with that, the state, through its elected members of parliament and the media, is determined to exploit the black community by using it as a scapegoat for its own crisis. It now seems that by playing the 'black card' and by continuously making insulting, patronising comments, each major political party is determined to outdo the other. The regular hounding by the police of black youths and the constant negative images portrayed by the daily tabloids may well result in the fact that so many blacks are not being given a fair opportunity to contribute to the wealth of their country. Overall the black community's experience in this country is one of exploitation both in economic terms and in the political context. Economically there will no doubt be a steady growth in black businesses, but this is not going to resolve the economic crisis faced by the black community. Politically the black community is now undergoing similar experiences to the ones that Jewish people encountered in the early part of this century. The key difference is that the black community is permanently visible and therefore it is likely to go on being exploited by politicians to further their goals.

The experience of the 1981–85 street rebellions allowed the police to improve co-ordination and training and obtain an increase in their personnel and equipment. Later they were able fully to utilize the extra staff and machinery to handle industrial disputes like the 1984–85 miners' strike and the 1986 News International demonstrations at Wapping. The black community has become a key political football which is regularly kicked by major political parties particularly in the run-up to general elections. The Labour Party, by appearing hell-bent on smashing its black sections, is effectively giving a coded message to white voters 'We'll keep blacks in their place'; while the Conservatives are happy to divert attention from all their shortcomings by linking law and order issues to black people. The Liberals in Tower Hamlets are getting into the headlines for their racist housing policies by evicting black families. Given this scenario it would seem blacks are very much the politicians' pawns.

In terms of the employment situation and black people, it seems unlikely that any government will implement the radical measures needed in order to change the deep-seated patterns of racism and discrimination. Although there is little prospect of them being implemented, a list of basic measures is given below as an agenda for action:

1. New legislation should be introduced to compel employers to provide information about the ethnic composition of their workforces and to take effective action to combat discriminatory practices.
2. Government and all public sector bodies should adopt stringent contract compliance requirements for those providing goods and services.
3. Government and all public sector employers should adopt effective equal opportunities policies, including positive action.

4. Legal aid should be provided for individual complainants to take action at tribunals.
5. The CRE should be given greater powers to investigate employment practices.
6. The MSC should withdraw funding from YTS, new YTS and CP schemes where equal opportunity targets are not being met.
7. Trade unions shoud ensure they do not discriminate in their policies and practices and take a greater stand upon issues confronting the black community.
8. All employers should introduce effective monitoring policies and establish targets for their organization.

This is not an exhaustive list but brings together some well known proposals that, if implemented, will bring about positive changes and contribute towards a more 'equal' society.

Notes

1. R. Ramdin, *The Making of the Black Working Class in Britain*, Aldershot: Gower, 1987.
2. B. Hepple, *Race Jobs and the Law in Britain*, Harmondsworth: Penguin, 1970.
3. P. Fryer, *Staying Power: The History of Black People in Britain*, London; Pluto Press, 1984.
4. C. Brown and P. Gay, *Racial Discrimination: 17 Years After The Act*, Policy Studies Institue, 1985.
5. The Runnymede Trust and the Radical Statistics Race Group, *Britain's Black Population*, London: Heinemann, 1980.
6. C. Brown, *Black and White*, Policy Studies Institute, Heinemann Educational Books, 1984.
7. Brown, op.cit.
8. *Labour Force Survey 1985*, London: HMSO, 1986. The latest in a series of sample surveys of private households carried out every two years until 1983, and annually thereafter by the Office of Population Censuses and Surveys.
9. M. Shaw, *New Commonwealth Executives in British Industry: An Explanatory Study*, Market Location Ltd, 1983. p. 23.
10. Brown, op.cit.
11. Commission of Racial Equality, *In Search of Employment and Training: Experience and Perceptions of Redundant Asian Textile Workers in Lancashire*, Lancashire Industrial Training Unit 1983, p. 27.
12. S. Field, *Ethnic Minorities in Britain: A Study of Trends in their Position Since 1961*, London: HMSO, 1981.
13. D. Thomas, 'The Jobs Bias Against Blacks', *New Society*, 1 November 1984, p. 169.

14. *Labour Force Survey 1985*, op.cit.; also 'Ethnic Origin and Economic Status', *Employment Gazette*, January 1987.
15. Brown, op.cit.
16. A. Barber, 'Ethnic Origin and The Labour Force', *Employment Gazette*, August 1980.
17. *Labour Force Survey 1985*, op.cit.
18. J. Rex and M. Cross, *Unemployment and Racial Conflict in the Inner City*, Working Paper on Ethnic Relations, no.16, SSRC, 1982, p. 16.
19. *The Times*, 11 September 1985.
20. A. Newnham, *Employment, Unemployment and Black People*, Runnymede Research Report, 1986.
21. M. Anwar, *Young People and the Job Market*, CRE, 1982.
22. CRE, *Employment Report*, March 1983.
23. E. Clough and D. Drew, *Futures in Black and White: Two Studies of the Experiences of Young People in Sheffield and Bradford*, Pavic Publications, City of Sheffield Ethnic Minorities Unit, 1985.
24. G. Lee, and J. Wrench, *In Search of a Skill*, London: CRE, 1981.
25. CRE, *Racial Equality and the Youth Training Scheme*, 1984.
26. A. Pollert, *Unequal Opportunities: Racial Discrimination and the Youth Training Scheme*, Birmingham: Trade Union Resource Centre, 1985.
27. Coventry REITS, *YTS or White TS? Racial Discrimination and Coventry's Youth Training Schemes*, Coventry, 1985.
28. Birmingham City Council, *Report of Inquiry into Alleged Racial Discrimination on Birmingham College Group YTS*, 1986.
29. Coventry REITS, *Two-year YTS. Another Whitewash?* 1986.
30. The Runnymede Trust, op.cit. 1980.
31. *Employment Gazette*, June 1984.
32. CRE, *Employment of Graduates from Ethnic Minorities 1987*, and *Overseas Doctors*, 1987.
33. *Employment Gazette*, June 1984.
34. Ibid.
35. D. Smith, *Unemployment and Racial Minorities*, London: Policy Studies Institute, 1981.
36. *The Guardian*, 27 December 1985.
37. J. Hubbuck and S. Carter, *Half a Chance? A Report of Job Discrimination Among Young Blacks in Nottingham*, Nottingham: CRC, 1980.
38. E. Clough and D. Drew, *Futures in Black and White*, Pavic Publications, 1985.
39. Brown, op.cit.
40. Smith, op.cit.
41. R. Fevre, *Cheap Labour and Racial Discrimination*, Aldershot: Gower, 1984.
42. J. Wrench, *Unequal Comrades: Trade Unions, Equal Opportunity and Racism*, Policy Papers in Ethnic Relations no. 5, Centre for Research in Ethnic Relations, 1986.
43. E. J. B. Rose, *Colour and Citizenship*, Oxford University Press, 1969.
44. RRB v. East Ham Conservative Club.45; RRB v. Ealing, London Borough Council.
45. N. McIntintosh and D. J. Smith, *The Extent of Racial Discrimination*, PEP 1974.

46. CRE, *Review of the Race Relations Act, 1976: Proposals for Change*, December 1986.
47. Vinod Kumar, *Industrial Tribunal Applicants under the Race Relations Act 1976*, London: CRE, 1986.
48. H. Street, G. Howe and G. Bindman, *Report on Anti-Discrimination Legislation*, Political and Economic Planning, 1967.
49. *News of the World*, 5 January 1986.
50. H. Ouseley *et al.*, *A Different Reality*, WMCC, 1986.
51. J. Clare, 'Job discrimination and the remedies we ignore', *The Listener* 2 January 1987.
52. Brown, op.cit.
53. Wrench, op.cit.
54. Fryer, op.cit.
55. See Wrench op.cit.
56. G. Lee, *Trade Unionism and Race*, a report to the West Midlands Regional Council of the Trades Union Congress, December 1984.
57. Camden Black Workers Group *Report*, 1982–86.
58. Ouseley *et al.*, op.cit.
59. P. Wilson and J. Stanworth, *Black Business in Brent*, Small Business Research Trust, July 1985; London Borough of Lambeth, *Black Businesses in Lambeth*, March 1982; F. Leo, *Ethnic Minorities and Small Firms, Problems Faced by Black Firms – Lambeth*, a case study, 1982;
60. *Racial Disadvantage*, Fifth Report of the Home Affairs Committee, London: HMSO, 1980–81.
61. Thomas, op.cit.
62. Shaw, op.cit.
63. S. Dex, 'The current unemployment in young black and white males', *Industrial Relations Journal*, vol. 14, no. 1, 1983.

PART II
RACISM AND WELFARE

5

Race, Community, Housing and the State – A Historical Overview

M. S. Luthera

Although it has been argued that housing, along with employment, has been a key factor in shaping race relations,[1] little community action emerged in the context of housing from *within* the black communities until the 1980s, and even then this has been very sporadic. This is not to suggest that there has been no debate on the subject, but that such a debate has arguably not led to political community action in the UK mainly because the level of segregation here is much lower than in certain other countries, for example the USA.[2] While this may have been a contributory element, the main reasons lie in two other factors. First, the nature of the race relations debate over the last two decades has been devoid of any civil rights concept, a void which has been filled substantially by the 'moral panics' related to immigration and, second, as British blacks were originally settlers or refugees, their energies were channelled into organizing in relation to employment, immigration and to some extent education – all areas in which they have been dependent upon the state or private sector. In housing, however, they could create their own sub-markets and survive in them or, to some extent develop their own self-help initiatives.

To understand this process it is important to grasp the history of race and housing in terms of the role of the state, the changing housing market and the changing housing ethos in a social policy context over the last 30 years. These changes then have to be related to different phases in the development of black communities, followed by an analysis of their interaction in the economic and social markets with the private sector and two layers of state – local and central.

Two other factors have to be kept in mind when discussing race and housing. First, although by the early 1950s housing had been established as a social service, it nevertheless has retained substantial features which can be included on the list of commodities: that is, it is a good way of developing equity; it is inheritable; it has been a means of safeguarding against inflation; and, in recent years, it has increasingly become an investment or collateral. In other words, owner-occupied housing, like education, can be a significant variable influencing economic mobility as it becomes a major source of gross personal wealth – for example 40 per cent in land and dwellings in 1975 in contrast to 21 per cent in 1960.[3] Second, if one considers the strong notion of privacy in Britain[4] and the laws relating to trespassing, the British tend to be obsessively territorial in a housing context. Consequently the combined effect of property/equity/territorial rights encapsulated in racist feelings often leads to local political action with a view to protecting what Karn has described as the 'white interest', similar to the notion of class interest.[5]

The other players, or rather 'aiders and abettors', in this process are the 'urban gatekeepers'[6] (council housing visitors, building society managers etc.) and 'exchange professionals' (solicitors, estate agents etc.) in the public and private sectors respectively. They operate to protect this 'white interest'[7] supported by a climate of moral panic and nativism generated and nurtured by the central and local state. This interest could include housing as a combination of equity, property and territory, or protection of an ethnocentric view of the quality of life. The politics, or rather the political economy, of these interests holds the key to understanding race and housing, with sociological or geographical/ecological analysis playing a secondary role – although hitherto the emphasis has been placed on the latter.

For the purpose of our analysis we have divided the history of race and housing into the following phases:

1. Economic migrants[8] and settlement in slum housing – the *'laissez-faire'* period (1950–67).
2. Arrival and relocation of families, token state intervention and development of equity in the inner cities (1968–75).
3. Access and entry into public sector housing, state intervention and emergence of qualitative debate (1975–80).
4. Entrapment in new slums, racial harassment, both leading to community action and development, maturation of the qualitative debate on housing.

It would seem obvious that all of these stages include significant elements of the previous stage which continue to be operative parallel to the dominant trends. In each of these stages the intrusion of politics can come from either or both of two directions, either as a state (mostly local) initiative, or emanating at grassroots level from the black or indigenous population. In each case, the interest of the groups involved surfaces through a focus on either access to or quality and/or location of housing. Throughout this chapter we have used the term 'black' for the group comprising those who were born in the New Commonwealth of Pakistan, and their descendants.

ECONOMIC MIGRANTS AND THE EARLY SETTLEMENT PROCESS

References to racial discrimination in housing prior to the arrival of economic migrants in the 1950s have been recorded by Fryer in relation to black seamen in Cardiff in 1937 'paying higher rents than white families of similar social status', and he also refers to six families sharing a six-roomed house with a common staircase. In the early and mid–1950s many prominent Asians and Carribeans were refused entry into hotels. The difficulties and racism experienced by black apprentices seeking accommodation in the 1950s in Liverpool is well documented.[9] Constantine noted that 'most British people would be quite unwilling for a black person to enter their homes'. The colour-bar period had continued into the 1950s with many 'no blacks or coloured' signs, supplemented by the general concensus of the British public that black people should not be offered jobs or public housing on an equal footing.[10]

Part of this attitude could be attributed to the fact that British people in the early 1950s were still 'bearing the stubborn imprints of nineteenth century culture'.[11] Despite the decrease in sense of deprivation,[12] the important amenities of life – housing in particular – were still in short supply.[13] The 1950s were characterized by a rapidly declining private rented sector and a very sensitive credit market still tightly controlled by government rules and notions of creditworthiness.

Immigration to Britian was employment-directed and, since most vacancies in the 1950s were concentrated in the conurbations, particularly London and the West Midlands, it was in these areas that the immigrants settled.[14] Settlement was concentrated in areas that have been variously labelled 'decayed inner city areas', 'twilight zones' or 'zones of transition'.[15] Originally suburban areas of middle-class residencies in the last century, they had been vacated as the middle-classes spread ever outward. Many of the larger houses had been subdivided for renting. Landlords, such as Rachman in Notting Hill, maximized their profits by subdividing properties to the maximum and maintaining them to a minimum.[16] A study group report compiled by Patterson in 1963[17] also noted how settlers were sometimes used by landlords to make life difficult for already existing protected tenants – subsequently and eventually evicting these statutorily unprotected settlers and enabling the landlords to divide the flats and houses and put them on sale. These housing tensions were to contribute substantially to the Notting Hill disorders in 1958.

Patterson[18] has specifically linked West Indian settlement in Brixton to the availability of cheap accomodation in the old air-raid shelters at Clapham, the London County Council single men's reception centre at Peckham and the large number of theatrical and other boarding houses. Alavi[19] mentioned a similar concentration of Pakistani single men in cheap run-down hotels. Generally, the areas of settlement were all within easy (and therefore cheap) travelling distance of the central city and the peri-urban industrial areas (for example, Lambeth, Hackney and Hammersmith in London and Sparkbrook and Handsworth in Birmingham). Therefore, immigrants settled in areas that were already declining and were not themselves the cause of the decline.[20]

The Caribbeans, because they were relatively early arrivals and in particular because Afro-Caribbean women arrived early,[21] moved rapidly from being short-term economic migrants to putting down roots and establishing households by the end of the 1960s.[22] The Asian immigrants, however, were still mainly single and mobile – a situation dictated by the nature of the labour market.[23]

The census data for 1951 and 1961 is rather unreliable; nevertheless it characterizes two trends. One is the overrepresentation of migrant families in the highly overcrowded privately rented furnished sector; another is the acquistion of tenancy from a landlord of the same ethnic background[24] – overwhelmingly so in the case of Asians – in most cases the landlord being the established mediator between the white world and new arrivals.[25] The spatial distribution of Asians, coupled with the necessity to form transient landlord/tenant relationships in an environment insulated by language, religion and kinship ties, contributed to a higher tendency towards owner-occupation. Caribbean immigration compacted in the space of less than a decade was characterized by a two-way flow and concentration in the South East, and orientated more towards the movement of the individuals rather than dependants seeking to join households. This pushed Afro-Caribbeans into the private rented sector, although owner-occupation did develop significantly among the West Indians.[26] Davison recorded figures between 27 and 40 per cent of households in owner-occupation in the seven London boroughs he studied, a significant proportion of which were to be affected by demolition in the 1960s. Another factor which may have prevented the moving-out rate of Caribbeans from the private rented furnished sector was that Afro-Caribbeans nurtured a strong myth of return up until the early 1960s.[27] The uptake of owner-occupation was also slowed down by the fact that at the time of the Afro-Caribbeans' arrival, the private rented sector was quite large (58 per cent in 1947), whilst it was half this figure (28 per cent in 1961) by the time Asians started arriving.[28]

In political and economic terms this was a *'laissez-faire'* period in the history of race and housing with little central government intervention, a policy which allowed the indigenous population to do its utmost to exclude black people from acquiring decent accommodation, developing good equity in property and consequently inhibiting mobility in terms of employment, and economic mobility in general.

By the early 1960s, the Afro-Caribbean population had already established a balanced sex ratio among their population[29] although the myth of return still prevailed strongly, mainly due to the treatment meted out to them.[30] On the other hand, the dependants and families of the Asians were in the process of joining them.However, the 1962 Immigration Act was to end the *'laissez-faire'* period in the labour market, as immigration was used to control the entry of black workers into Britain according to the needs of the labour market.[31] The British colour bar, however, had become an embarrassment to the state, and the governments had taken note of the 1958 Notting Hill riots and similar developments in black politics in the USA. Nevertheless, for a while, the 'black problem' became more manageable,[32] and to counteract the adverse impact in public relations terms of the Immigration Act the government launched a policy of 'integration' – its first steps being the 1965 Race Relations Act which did not cover discrimination in housing and employment, thus almost sanctioning racism in areas other than those which were 'public resorts'. Notably the 1965 Act remained totally uninfluenced by the 1964 Civil Rights Act in the USA which, amongst other things, did attempt to tackle racism in housing, albeit only in federally-assisted housing. One could attribute this to either British obsession with privacy and/or simply the fact that central state still hoped that blacks would go back, and therefore should not be encouraged to feel too comfortable in the housing market. The British progressives have generally relied on political pressure and public opinion to seek change and have been suspicious of the use of law for such purposes.

ARRIVAL AND RELOCATION OF FAMILIES

By 1965 a large proportion of dependants had joined their heads of household, with the earlier settlers' households acting as reception centres. The constraints in the social and commodity market continued as the dependency ratio of an average settler's family increased, aggravating housing stress, particularly overcrowding – an issue highlighted a great deal in the media, to such an extent that Birmingham Corporation passed a bylaw under which it could compel evictions from existing and proposed lodging houses containing more than one family. Permission to take in lodgers could be denied if the house or its owner was found to be unsuitable or if it was in 'a locality the amenity or character of which would be injured'.[33]

The White Paper on immigration, while promising to extend the above practice to other areas, also declared: 'Local authorities already have a wide range of powers, which if judiciously used, can make a major contribution to this end' (i.e. of relieving the settlers' housing problems).[34] History was to prove otherwise.

Despite the re-establishment of rent control, the decline of the private sector continued as landlording became less profitable in comparison with other activities. Housing was at the centre of the British political scene with the Conservatives having lost the election partly on the basis of low output of public-sector housing in their period in power. The 1964 Housing Act set up the Housing Corporation and promoted Housing Associations to complement the role of the local authority. For at least a decade the Corporation and the Associations were to remain almost irrelevant to the black communities.

It was slum clearance which was now seen as a major objective, and this was seriously and disproportionately to affect many black communities by virtue of their overrepresentation in run-down stock. As stated earlier, most New Commonwealth settlers found that the only housing available to them was in shrinking privately rented accommodation in the cheaper deteriorating inner city area. According to Milner Holland's report, only 11 per cent of privately-let accommodation was being advertised, and at a later stage Hiro calculated that only 3 per cent of all private sector landlords acted in a non-discriminatory fashion.[35] When this sector was tested in PEP,[36] almost all landlords admitted to discrimination. A similar observation was made in relation to accommodation agencies and estate agents who offered fewer addresses to blacks and withheld information about building societies or other sources of lending. This was mainly for two reasons: first, vendors were not prepared to sell these properties to blacks and, secondly, building societies were loath to give them mortgages. Their general justification was that they would go out of business as the white customers would withdraw business from their establishments. Another way of discriminating was to ask for higher or advanced deposits from immigrants, and they were rarely given unfurnished accommodation.[37] The immigrants, particularly Asians, insulated themselves from the private-rented sector discrimination (with the exception of middle-class Asians) as they mainly approached accommodation sources where they were likely to be refused.[38] This insulation was further amplified by language problems and unfamiliarity with the English way of life. Generally, most immigrants avoided discrimination by not approaching the open market.[39] Most of the properties, particularly those which were owned, were exposed to the redevelopment schemes of local authorities. This probably had the effect of moving people time and again, weakening community development and lowering the proportion of the Caribbean population in owner-occupation as many of them, having received little compensation, moved into council accommodation.

The irrelevance of class as a factor in such dynamics was well illustrated by the fact that half the participants in the PEP test who claimed to be professionals were discriminated against just as much as when they claimed to be bus conductors.[40] Follow-up interviews with the discriminating landlords and estate agents showed that two stereotypes existed.[41] The first was that blacks were, amongst other things, unclean and noisy and would upset the existing (white) tenants and, secondly, they would be bad payers, break the conditions of their tenancy or contract of repayment and reduce the area to a slum (with a consequent fall in property/rental values).

In fact, Patterson[42] found just the opposite in Brixton. There, not only did managing estate agents report settlers to be prompt payers, but they also paid above the average rental. In the early years this was regarded as a 'colour tax' necessary to induce landlords to rent to them, but after a period of familiarization with Britain many settlers, particularly Caribbeans, started appealing to Rent Tribunals.[43]

Age, income, reliability of payments, mobility and subletting were indirectly discriminatory criteria applied by many of the building society managers. Estate agents charged higher deposits, higher interest rates on short-payment periods, and offered premises on hire purchase. Many local authorities also applied residential qualifications of five years in assessing suitability for mortgages. Indeed, many estate agents justified their discrimination on the grounds that they were acting on behalf of vendors and were also responsible, in a way, for putting forward the viewpoint of building societies or the local council.[44]

It is not as if blacks were receiving any better facilities in return. Davison,[45] in an analysis of the 1966 Census, found that, of all immigrant households, New Commonwealth settlers enjoyed the least in terms of access to facilities such as a cold-water tap, hot water, fixed bath and a water closet (shared versus exclusive use), and suffered from a high degree of persons-per-room density compared to the English mean.[46] Most literature attributes this to three factors: the higher rentals (both absolute and relative to wage levels) paid by non-whites; larger-than-average family size; and the use of the 'partner' or 'pool' system of house purchase. Generally, the housing situation had greatly worsened in the five years since 1961.[47]

Discrimination in the mid–1960s continued to play a key role in pushing settlers into multi-occupation. The settlers, particularly Asians, created their own small private-rented sector with resident landlords and with restricted entry to all tenure types including that of council accommodation – the houses with multi-occupation of 'individuals' became houses with multi-occupation of 'families' as the wives and children arrived. In our view, the sustained and prolonged period of such arrivals played a key role in developing Asian owner-occupation as it allowed the receiving household to clear their 'informal' debts with the assistance of the new arrivals who, in turn, could accumulate a deposit on low rent to move into their own property.

Municipal onslaught

The press had a field day portraying blacks as 'living and breeding like rabbits' thus creating frequent moral panics, particularly focusing on local authorities' action as regards overcrowding, as many followed Birmingham's practice on multi-occupation, supported by the White Paper. Davison failed in political analysis when he stated 'periodical raids by public health inspectors are undertaken from *wholly admirable* motives, but it may be doubted whether any useful purpose is served by simply turning people out of one house to overcrowd another'.[48] He further appealed to the local authorities actively to pursue a more positive policy, but moral panics had gripped municipal minds with the Ealing Labour Council setting up a sub-committee to deal with 'multi-occupation', yet never discussing the use of public-sector housing for such purposes, and the Conservatives in Ealing asking for a 15-year residence rule for inclusion on the housing list.[49] Whilst councillors justified their action on the basis of crude majoritarianism, the urban gatekeepers such as housing visitors and letting officers were busy applying crude subjective standards or keeping secret records[50] to allocate slum housing, often restricted to certain areas, for blacks. At some places, for instance in Sparbrook, clearance was delayed on the grounds that it would mean rehousing a substantive number of black families.[51] This is not to imply that clearance was welcomed by black families, as they were usually left to their own devices after such action in the 1960s.

The municipal onslaught on the black minorities through the erection of barriers spread like fire. Patterson[52] reported that the qualification for inclusion on the Lambeth housing list was three years' residence in the borough, and that no one was offered accommodation until they had been on the waiting list for at least one year. In fact, most London boroughs had a five-year residence rule and would not allow people living in furnished accommodation on the list.[53] Many other authorities, such as Slough and Wolverhampton,[54] were able to indulge in nativism and erect all sorts of barriers against the guidelines offered by central government in the 1965 White Paper[55] which stated that 'the sole test for action in the housing field is the quality and nature of housing need without distinction based on the origins of those in need'. Nevertheless, when a council like Slough eliminated the factor of housing need in assessing elegibility for accommodation, central government did nothing.[56]

This was bound to affect the uptake of housing by blacks; for instance a survey by PEP [57] showed that 22 per cent of West Indians questioned thought the waiting period for council accommodation too long and 29 per cent preferred to buy their own house anyway. There were only 10 per cent of West Indians, and even fewer Asians, on the waiting list. The figures generally indicate that, until 1966, the main trend in accommodation was away from private-rented and into owner-occupied housing, particularly in areas of concentration. In 1966 in the inner London boroughs, 22 per cent of 'immigrant' housing was in owner-occupancy and in central Birmingham 56 per cent of immigrant household heads were owner-occupiers – nearly twice the percentage of white ownership in those areas.[58]

Home ownership

The extent to which obstacles to council housing may have encouraged disproportionate entry, particularly of Asians, into owner-occupation is debatable. Considerable speculation has taken place as to why owner-occupation is high among Asians, with Rex relying on economic, political determinism and discrimination,[59] Dahya on the immigrant's cultural background,[60] and Davies arguing that owner-occupation is higher among Asians due to the 'risk-taking element' or the enterprise spirit.[61] In our view, the truth lies in immigrants reacting to a variety of restraints, economic and other (discrimination, language, lack of 'know how') *differently* at various stages of their settlement process and taking control of their lives as the 'ethnic' self-help economy develops (estate agents, ethnic banks, for instance). Within these constraints they make a rational response based on their historical experiences to maximize the use of personal and family resources, limit vulnerability and exposure to uncertainty and racism, as well as to enhance their status.

A number of studies have recorded the ability of Asians to buy, with a limited degree of 'shopping around',[62] cheap-end properties, as well as their over-reliance on banks or council loans or property companies.[63] These buyers hardly merit Davies' classification as 'housing entrepreneurs.'[64] The aspiration to own property was to lead to conflict with local residents' associations on the basis of unsubstantiated fear of decline in the value of properties.

Home ownership was not easy for the first generation to achieve. Lower-than-average wage rates, combined with higher-than-average rents, reduced their disposable income and, as with private tenancies, there was no free market in house purchase for blacks. They had a higher dependency ratio than the average indigenous white family, including those dependants in the country of origin, as well as having to save for travel to their country of origin.

All of the early surveys reported white home owners who refused to sell to blacks and estate agents who either refused to show them

113

any properties or explicitly limted them to the least saleable ones on their books.[65] However, despite these difficulties, black home ownership did develop.

Two types of home ownership were identified by Patterson (1963): West Indian landlords who rented to other blacks, and 'partners'.[66] A similar system of pooling clubs existed among Asians.[67]

Patterson[68] found that, because of ignorance of house ownership laws, protected tenancies and compulsory maintenance orders, many early purchasers were taken advantage of. The nature of property within their economic reach (terraced, pre–1919 and without a garden) was such that building societies would not risk their capital,[69] and vendors often granted short-term, high-interest mortgages. Some estate agents in Brixton reported sales to West Indians at increased prices,[70] or for extra commission or cash under the table.[71] The result was that black landlords, in order to maximize savings, subdivided the property to the maximum and, in the case of owner-occupiers, could afford to purchase only by several families pooling their money in a 'partners' scheme and occupying the house jointly. Therefore, both types of purchaser preferred the larger properties.

The colour bar of the 1950s was turning housing into a business bonanza in the inner-city slums. It allowed many landlords to charge excess rent without spending money on repairs, it indirectly did business a good turn by helping to boost demand for new houses from white people fleeing from the older areas[72] and it kept the housing market buoyant.[73] By the late 1960s the government had realized that the integration drive, aimed earlier mainly at the Asian communities, should include the West Indian communities. The 1965 Watts Riots followed by agitation to push for the Civil Rights Act in the USA influenced the government, in addition to the publication of the PEP (1967) report. The black communities in the UK were evolving organizations,[74] and were shedding the myth of return.[75] Paul Rich has recently argued that, in the case of West Indian organizations, their location in London coupled with the failure to set up a black civil rights organization compounded the problem of confronting 'nativism' in the Midlands.[76] Whilst this may partly explain the situation in the Midlands, it is our contention that emphasis on other issues, and channelling of energy into responding to 'moral panics' based on immigration, have been detrimental to the development of organized response on the part of the black community to nativism and racism in housing.

In addition, the Heath Government was agonizing over the Kenyan Asian arrivals, while Enoch Powell was warning people (April 1968) that their neighbourhoods had 'changed beyond recognition'. Polls carried out in April 1968 indicated that 70 per cent of the British thought that there was some danger of race riots. More British than in 1967 (45 per cent in 1967 and 53 per cent in 1966) thought that there should be no law against refusing to rent or sell someone a house because of their race and colour. There had been, however, some support emerging in relation to admitting blacks on to the housing lists on some conditions[77] although, in areas of ethnic concentration, there was a strong feeling that council accommodation should not be given to immigrants but that discrimination in the private-rented sector should be removed.[78] The working classes were reviving the old notion of 'housing for the working classes'.[79] Nevertheless 42 per cent of the British people supported the 1968 Race Relations Bill,[80] which included some very ineffective changes and equally ineffective machinery of enforcement to deal with discrimination in employment and housing.

Subsequent analysis showed that only 5 per cent of complaints were in housing,[81] that the majority of blacks did not know about the 1968 Race Relations Act, and that those who did thought it to be ineffective. There was, however, one success the Act could claim, and that was the disappearance of 'no blacks/coloureds' advertisements. The British were to improve their techniques of discrimination – in other words, racism in housing was to acquire a sophisticated and subtle form.

In May of the same year, Harold Wilson announced the Urban Programme which could give substantial aid to authorities in special need. The government had also established a source of funding by developing Section 11, a clause in the 1966 Local Government Act, although it was rarely used for housing and substantially abused by local government in education.

The 1968 Act was, however, to establish a Community Relations Commission which was to fund a number of Community Relations Councils (CRCs) (in Ealing and Camden for instance) which were beginning to engage significantly in housing casework in the late

1970s. This was a time of mounting housing pressure and increasing homelessness in London where 30 per cent of homeless families applying for hostel accommodation were from the New Commonwealth, pushed out by landlords seeking vacant possession for their own use or due to a breach of mortgage terms.[82]

The end of the 1960s was marked by the failure of central government to provide a lead on an objective debate on race and housing. The government's meek attempts to do something (the 1965 White Paper and the 1968 Race Relations Act) were found to be ineffective in relation to its 'integration drive'. Black minorities were still highly segregated by socio-economic and political forces and by a constantly reinforced sense of insecurity as elements in both central and local government-initiated and perpetuated moral panics.

Dispersal and the state

The 'busing' issue in Southall, riots in Notting Hill and Nottingham presented blacks as a 'cultural problem' which had to be hidden away. Indeed, many officials wanted to put blacks in slum housing so that they could be kept out of sight to avoid embarrassment.[83] When they were rehoused it was begrudgingly, and often in slum clearance areas, often in short-life property and, even when clearance was planned they were left to 'get themselves sorted out' and make their own arrangements.[84]

Constant reference to riots, ghettos, and so on by certain politicians of both parties meant that government had to be seen to be doing something at both local and central levels, particularly when British citizens of Asian origin from East Africa were knocking at their doors as refugees. Thus, the scene was set for state intervention with what was described later as a 'laudable aim of dispersal'. Within a decade, the state had moved from encouraging migrants to move out of London to using housing policy as a means of dispersal. Like the 'busing' issue in relation to education, it had bowed down to crude nativism and racism.

Meanwhile, racism was taking violent forms with white gangs breaking windows of Asian shops and houses,[85] an issue on which little concern was shown by the state. Insofar as state intervention to tackle discrimination was concerned, it came too late and offered too little. Blacks had got the message that 'white owned houses' were not open to them, so they strengthened their own private-rented sector which, although shrinking rapidly as families joined residential landlords, was nevertheless providing stop-gap accommodation. Alternatively, and particularly in the case of Asians, they were purchasing cheaper run-down properties using their internal financing systems whilst Caribbeans were beginning to seek to enter the public sector having fulfilled the residential qualifications[86] and aided by relatively smaller household size (see Figure 5.1) and acquaintance with the English language.

It is notable that, whilst the proportion of Asians and Afro-Caribbeans in the private and public sector converged in 1966 and 1971, Afro-Caribbeans started mainly in the private-rented sector while Asians did the same but rapidly moved into owner-occupation (see Figure 5.2). Although there were geographical variations,[87] for instance in Birmingham where West Indians were under-represented, on the whole, different needs and nego-tiability/familiarity, coupled with social arrangements and preferences, had created two distinct patterns of response by the Asian and Afro-Caribbean communities. For example, while equally represented in the private-rented sector, the former had moved mainly into owner-occupation while the latter were also utilizing council accommodation to a significant extent – a difference which was to be amplified later on (Figure 5.3). The process was very much aided by the local authorities giving loans in the inner city, basically offering these as a politically acceptable substitute to offering council accommodation.

As Figure 5.3 suggests, the proportion of Asians in council accommodation in 1977 was thought to be 10 per cent. Earlier censuses in 1966 and 1971 indicated a higher proportion of Asians in council accommodation, while PEP in 1974 suggested the figure to be nearly 4 per cent. The previous figures, in our view, were inflated due to the presence of as much as 30–40 per cent of New Commonwealth whites being included in the data. According to the recent Labour Force Survey half of the New Commonwealth white persons born before 1950 were born in the Indian sub-continent.[88]

The 1960s ended with the local state condoning and legitimizing urban fencing and discrimination to protect the interests of, mainly, the local working-middle-class-white people. Racism was

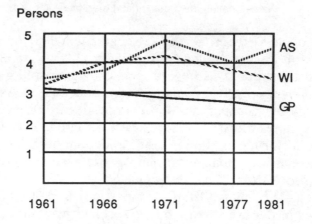

Fig. 5.1   *Average household size*

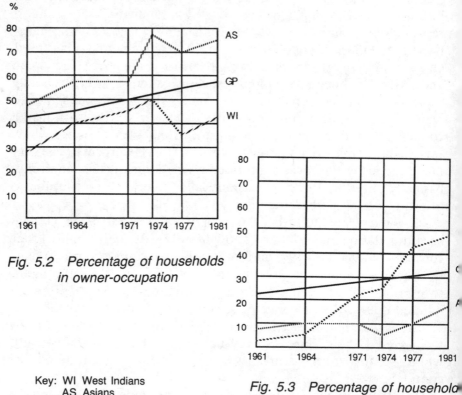

Fig. 5.2   *Percentage of households in owner-occupation*

Fig. 5.3   *Percentage of household in council housing*

Key: WI West Indians
AS Asians
GP General population

Sources: NDHS 78, Census 81, PSI 82, PEP 7A.

institutionalized and discriminatory policies were openly implemented by the local state in the inner city. From now on a large number of blacks were to share the abandoned inner-city pockets with disgruntled and sometimes racist working-class elements unable to move to the outskirts of cities or to the newly-built public sector.[89] The black communities, far too busy fighting battles related to immigration, uniting their families and generally establishing and familiarizing themselves with the system, were unable to fight off the well organized white residents' and tenants' lobby with the local state or to compete with their electoral clout or influence.

The early 1970s were marked by a continued decline in the private-rented sector and an economic downturn leading to the intervention of the International Monetary Fund (IMF) in Britain. This eventually led to a 23 per cent cut in building [90] after 1975–76, the first decline in new building being in 1973 – the last year of the Heath Government. Councils such as Ealing and Nottingham found it convenient to follow the declining commitment of central government to public-sector housing by withdrawal of funding from new building. The government machinery was mobilized to avoid further flack from the working classes – East African Asians were to be dispersed by establishing a settlement board, through public-sector housing, with a view to increasing integration. The board was to aid local authorities for one year with no direct help given to the arrivals once they had left the settlement centres, nor were they allowed to return once they had left. The government saw its responsibility terminating once 'the Asian families had taken their rightful place on the poverty line'.[91] The dispersal through selected centres proved a failure as a survey of four target areas in different authorities showed. The majority of the settlers were unsettled in the absence of any aftercare and in response to the hostility expressed by some sections of the white community.

By 1975 the government had assessed that the 1968 Race Relations Act was not delivering, even as a good public relations exercise. The black communities were not interested in participation in such an ineffective set of arrangements.

The experiment in dispersal at central government level was accompanied by many councils also experimenting at the local level – including Birmingham Council which was to adopt it as a policy.

Later on this policy was supported with some caution by Cullingworth who regarded such policies as laudable, but with due consideration to be given to choice – a position taken by the DoE in 1975 when it devolved the issue to the local authorities and expected them to formulate a balanced view on it.[92] It was, however, Birmingham which was to come under scrutiny in *The 'Practice of Racial Dispersal in Birmingham' 1969–75*.[93] The author found that the effects of dispersal on blacks were most substantial in 1974, with migration to the outer ring originating predominantly in the middle ring; whereas in 1971, 20 per cent of blacks were rehoused in the outer ring, that figure had risen to 44 per cent in 1974. There was a similar trend in suburban migration among whites, though the proportion of whites already in the outer-ring council estates far outweighed that of blacks. This trend, furthermore, represented voluntary white exodus from the more depressed inner-and middle-ring council housing and into the suburban estates where white majorities were higher.

Black and white populations, the authors report, also expressed markedly different area preferences when questioned by housing visitors. Equally contrasting were the outcomes of these expressed preferences. Blacks generally preferred inner-ring housing – whites tended to nominate the suburbs and the outer ring. Flett[94] showed that such preferences were used by the councils to keep their inner-city stock fully tenanted – in some cases, she argued, preferences may have influenced the outcome in terms of property type, as flats are often located in the inner city. Yet, in 1974, when the dispersal policy was well under way, as few as 23 per cent of West Indians were housed in preferred areas, compared with 39 per cent of whites. Asians did best of all, with a 63 per cent success rate, but this was largely due to the fact that most were being rehoused under slum clearance and renewal programmes and so had prior claims to housing in the inner ring. Only in 1976, after the abandonment of the dispersal policy, did West Indians have roughly the same opportunities as whites in preferred areas. Allocation policies were finally coming under fire, although central government was still not providing any lead as the issue focused on quality of housing.

The qualitative and quantitative debate

The major issue at this stage, in the early 1970s, remained the question of access to council housing. Smith examined the access question in his study of Ealing which he disguised by calling it Eastwich.[95] He found that half the deterrents in allocation of housing to blacks were primarily due to lack of residential qualifications and they were having to wait longer; this emphasis on waiting allowed the white applicants to fare better. The applicants from black communities were well represented on the waiting list, but a 'nationality' clause had been included in Ealing to sift out black people[96] – criteria that had to be rendered illegal in the House of Lords. The case also highlighted a grave conceptual flaw in the 1968 Race Relations Act – namely, its inability to deal with 'indirect discrimination'.

Some councils, such as North Bedfordshire, did make limited changes. This council was the subject of a detailed study carried out by Skellington for the Open University's Urban Research Group.[97] The council's housing allocation policy was redrawn in 1975 in response to criticism of discrimination, and a points scheme was introduced designed to take greater account of 'housing need' and time spent on the waiting list. The study highlighted the persistance of disadvantage, despite these changes. Although the scheme had improved the process of housing allocations and extended housing opportunities, there is still evidence of indirect discrimination when the allocation of properties is examined. At the allocation stage itself, ethnic minorities in Bedford were found to be less likely to occupy newer, and presumably better, dwellings than whites. He adds, 'Only if the coloured minorities conform to the typical council house applicant norm – a married couple with one child – do West Indians and Asians achieve outcomes similar to the studied groups.' Skellington also found some 'urban gatekeeping': whites could expect to receive favourable accounts in housing visitors' reports in well over 80 per cent of cases, whilst ethnic minorities received negative comments in 70 per cent of instances. Skellington found these trends in housing visitors' remarks:

Visitors made reference to colour or ethnic origin, recommended applicants for a particular standard of housing and implicitly

121

matched applicants with 'good' house-keeping practices with allocations to new estates.

Skellington further concluded:

> . . . that despite the Borough Council's new points scheme it is evident that the outcome for both West Indians and Asians differs widely from the studied European minorities and the white comparison group. It has been shown that provided West Indian and Asian applicants conform to the typical council house applicant norm – a married couple with one child – equitable outcomes emerge. However, on all other criteria of evaluation West Indians and Asians have been shown to receive inferior treatment.

The black communities were engaged in a battle over, and were suffering from anxieties in relation to, the consequences of the 1973 Immigration Act which presented enormous problems in relation to entry of dependants and turned the prospective black settlers into 'guest workers'.[98] The slowing down of the dependants' arrival meant that many of them came after the introduction of the Homeless Persons Act (1976) thus linking the immigration, race and housing debate, similar to the earlier situation in the 1960s.

Preparation for state intervention

The 1971 Census data was to show some improvement in conditions of black households particularly in relation to overcrowding (Figures 5.4 and 5.5) although 36 per cent of the New Commonwealth households still did not have exclusive use of all amenities. On the whole, education, employment and immigration continued to be the key issues facing black communities – housing came low down on the agenda. The State however noted the US response to the black struggle and realized that steps needed to be taken to emulate the 1964 Civil Rights Act in the USA which had embodied a notion of indirect discrimination. Like the previous legislative measures, it fell victim to British consensus politics, and hence was weakened. Although central government shrewdly put itself above discrimination, or any responsibility to promote good 'community relations' (Section 71, Race Relations Act 1976), it did not,

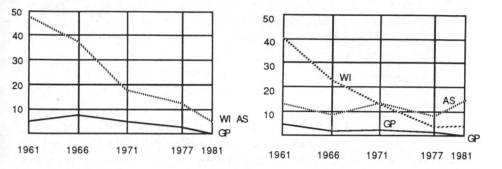

Fig. 5.4   Percentage of households   Fig. 5.5   Percentage of households living
in shared dwellings   at more than 1.5 persons per room

however, allow the local state a similar exemption, perhaps
knowing well that nativism and local racism would be sufficient to
control the pace and degree of implementation, if indeed any came
about, given the inherent weakness of the clause.

Rapid building in the 1960s, often below standard and based on
new techniques, had lead to the development of 'new slums'. This
polarization in the quality of housing was to allow the public-sector
urban gatekeeper to allocate housing on the basis of 'deserving' and
'non-deserving' categories. The non-deserving were often allocated
poor-quality housing – these included the homeless, single parents,
large families, the unemployed and so-called 'problem' families. In
most cases, blacks were over-represented in the first four categories
so that, in addition, as studies showed later on, 'race' was to be a
further key factor in including blacks in the 'non-deserving' categories.[99] In many cases, the urban gatekeepers also facilitated the
flight of 'good' white families (known as the 'tipping the balance'
theory) from these estates: those estates with a significant number
of blacks then became 'problem' estates which everyone wanted to
escape - but only whites managed to do so as they had the heavy
advantage of waiting, residential and 'local connection' points on
transfer lists. It was in these decaying concrete jungles that many
of the young blacks were to be raised amidst race hate, perpetuated
amongst the 'lumpen proletariat' and working classes by organized
National Front activities or by opportunistic politicians. The bound-
aries of the inner-city map of violence were already well marked,

123

although the first-generation blacks had some breathing space since they perceived race relations to be better.[100] Nevertheless, a significant realization of the declining building boom and the housing crisis was indicated by a poll carried out at the time.[101]

The private sector continued with its old problems including 'red lining' (areas regarded unsuitable for lending) observed by Karn in the late 1960s/early 1970s.[102] She also noted in a follow-up study in the Midlands in 1984 the role played by solicitors and estate agents and this, coupled with the lack of minority staff in building societies, contributed to the creation of a non-lending ethos.[103] Insecurity in terms of employment and the possibility of compulsory purchase orders owing to their disproportionate ownership of older properties, helped to push Asians in particular into seeking short-term loans with higher interest rates, often given without too many questions. Many local authorities stepped in to lend in the inner city, which has had the twin effect of coaxing minorities into purchasing inner-city properties. The CRE's later investigation in Rochdale showed the complex nature of 'red lining' and its effect on blacks,[104]but it was the Leeds study which showed that, irrespective of the nature of areas of lending and the status of applicants (savers or non-savers), blacks were less likely to be given a mortgage.[105]

ACCESS TO PUBLIC SECTOR AND STATE INTERVENTION

During the run-up to the formation of the CRE in 1976, the debate on race relations among black groups had shifted from community relations to race equality. The passing of the Race Relations Act in 1976 was to coincide with the government introducing more control on local authority capital expenditure, severely curtailing improvement work using Section 105 resources. The government also introduced the Housing Investment Programme Strategy (HIPS), adding to the bureaucracy and uncertainty to such an extent that it led to a number of authorities such as Ealing underspending the resources.

The advent of the Conservative Government merely accentuated this process by the introduction of a council housing sales policy without a requirement on councils to make good any loss. The mid-

124

and late 1970s saw the production of many studies pointing towards the spectrum of structural barriers leading to black disadvantage in housing.[106] The conventional wisdom at the time was that qualitative imbalances in allocation between different groups existed primarily due to overrepresentation of blacks in the homeless and letting categories, which generally led to them being allocated poor accommodation.

Private-sector racism continued, perhaps taking a more sophisticated form, with estate agents giving limited information and funnelling black purchasers into existing areas of concentration.[107] Fenton (1977) showed that Manchester Asians were paying more, particularly in the unfurnished sector, thus weakening their bargaining position.[108] The ring fencing of good areas continued, with the suburban residents harassing Asians moving into surburbia[109] or even buying the properties which they were intending to buy.

However, the Asians had by now evolved a semi-separate housing market with their own estate agents, ethnic and overseas banks and insurance agents, thus loosening the grip of white operators in the market who were beginning to realize that they were losing business. The gentrification of inner cities and continued expansion of bank-lending in the inner city was finally to initiate a change in policy by the building societies.

The 1977 Homeless Persons Act made the position of the state quite clear – it saw public-sector housing mainly as a means of providing for 'families' with children or the elderly, with considerable discretion given to urban gatekeepers to define 'intentionality' and even what constituted a family. Hillingdon Borough Council led the way in generating moral panics. Ingenious legal arguments were deployed in Islam vs. London Borough of Hillingdon to deter Asian homeless families from applying for accommodation. A highly complex line of cases was to develop involving Asian families, with the press having a field day. Many a time families were split as a punitive measure, people were shunted across to far-flung properties (GLC properties in London), often through the so-called 'one offer' policies, and with total disregard to place of work, networks or support. Both unemployment and 'families only' policies were to lure some white and Afro-Caribbean women into single parenthood as an only means of entry into the public sector

125

and thus as a means of survival, since single people were rarely classified as 'vulnerable' under the Act. Local authorities, although under considerable pressure, were quick – or at least the 'gatekeepers' were more than zealous – to invent passport checks and liaise with the DHSS or Home Office in deciding upon 'intentionality' or the right to housing, often misinterpreting the data due to unfamiliarity with the complexity of immigration and nationality rules. This was to lead later to the 'no pass laws' campaign by the Joint Council for the Welfare of Immigrants. The DoE, however, finally recommended that 'residence points' should be abolished and that allocation schemes should be published.[110] Some local authorities had already acknowledged the problems.

The late 1970s led to initial developments on the part of local government ostensibly to deal with racism within the housing departments. Between 1978 and 1980 about five London boroughs appointed race advisors[111] to monitor allocations and other policies related to housing because the CRCs in areas of high concentration were becoming saturated with casework as the housing crisis mounted, trapping blacks in the worst housing. Such entrapment at times had a benevolent origin. For instance, Tower Hamlets pursued a policy of actively housing the Bangladeshis in the late 1970s – yet a quantitative measure which may have prevented stress in terms of overcrowding and homelessness was to turn into a qualitative nightmare. Bengalis in particular were channelled into 'problem' estates where the East End working-class youth subjected them to constant harassment which was rarely taken seriously by the police and the local authority. Housing was to enter the arena of debate on police and community relations.

Essentially the perpetrators of violence did and continue to do what a large number of racists of every shade of the political spectrum may have secretly thought of doing. Their perception being that since immigration laws failed to break the spirit of black people and repatriation incentives failed to lure them to go back, then racial harassment might remove what Rushdie called the 'empire within' – thus releasing the meagre housing resources they utilize. The phenomenon of racial harassment was no longer confined to the East End – it was beginning to surface in different parts of the UK.

ENTRAPMENT IN NEW SLUMS, COMMUNITY ACTION AND DEVELOPMENT

The uprisings of 1981 were to make housing a major issue[112] as an explanation of urban frustration, yet little had been done in the fields of race and housing by central government six years after Scarman: the government seemed more interested in cosmetic exercises like recruiting more black police officers rather than getting down to eliminating the causes of urban conflict which was to recur time again in the early 1980s.

It was left to local government to take initiatives in housing which were to be emulated in other areas by the authorities as the CRE housing section skilfully marketed the promotion of record-keeping and monitoring. It was ironic that the CRE was still facing resistance from local authorities to record-keeping, as recommended by Rose *et al.* in 1968, and, as a tool of persuasion, it had little more than the polite recommendations of the DoE acquired after a great deal of persuasion from Sir George Young in 1984. The Housing Corporation was finally to focus the attention of the Housing Associations. The National Federation of Housing Associations was to set up a working party at a Sheffield conference in 1981 to produce a series of recommendations.[113] Understandably central government could not push local authorities to keep such records when it had failed to do so itself. The CRE, however, was criticized for inadequate investigative work in the period of quango-bashing, which amongst other things led to an investigation of Hackney's housing policies.

By 1981 the orthodox position that public-sector differential allocation was primarily due to disproportionate representation of minorities in certain 'administrative categories' of allocation was abandoned as research in Lewisham and Hammersmith[114] showed that differential allocation took place within each category on the basis of race. Simpson's work in Nottingham, CRE investigation in Hackney and subsequent analysis in Liverpool[115] were to support earlier findings that differential allocation takes place even when controlled for various variables and *within* each administrative category. Some backlash to these developments was to occur both on the left[116] where it was argued that such differences could be

127

explained by class and on the right where 'choice' was presented as a key explanation,[117] a matter we touched upon earlier.

Since 1961 there had been a substantial decline in overcrowding levels among both Asians and Afro-Caribbeans (Figure 5.5), partly as families nuclearized and household size decreased, particularly among the Afro-Caribbeans. Similar improvement can be observed with regard to Asians if one excludes the Bangladeshi/Bengali communities from the Asian data, although sharing still survives to a significant extent (Figure 5.4). Similarly 'amenities' levels had improved significantly, but remained extremely poor in the private sector and in general in some areas like Bradford and Tower Hamlets.[118] The real nature of housing stress had, however, shifted into the new public-sector slums which were often damp and were statutorily inhabitable as local government failed to modernize partly due to economic constraints imposed by central government and/or ineffective large local bureaucracies. As the Duke of Edinburgh report pointed out, the older stock in the private sector is in serious disrepair, making it considerably dangerous and unhealthy. As stock continued to deteriorate in the private sector, the decline in building further added to the pressure on the public sector, leading to more homelessness.

Homelessness soared, particularly in London, and many authorities sought to house Asian, and in particular Bengali, families temporarily in unsafe houses, which were prone to fire and racial attacks. Increase in such attacks and entrapment of black families in poor public housing with little outlet was to lead to tremendous individual pressures surfacing in the form of increased caseloads in black agencies and housing advice centres. With building programmes at a standstill, not only were blacks disproportionately affected in housing terms, but the increased tightening of the grip of white unions on the local authority direct labour organizations was contributing to the de-skilling of a whole generation of young blacks, particularly Afro-Caribbeans and East African Asians, thus adding to the already high black unemployment.[119]

The tenure profile differences between Asian and Afro-Caribbean communities were to widen further as newly-formed black households, particularly Afro-Caribbeans by virtue of their concentration in central London, were having difficulty entering the owner-occupation sector.[120] On the other hand, the young Asians were having to stay longer with the extended household, boosting the household size.

The Asian population having acquired low-quality properties were trapped as their property values declined, particularly in the north. Additionally high unemployment and dependency ratios were making the maintenance of these properties very difficult. The north-south divide was to offer a choice between a job or a house, the latter usually saleable at poor value. Given the size of Asian households and the age of housing stock owned by them, the owner-ship of such properties is likely to make an extremely poor inheritance.

In London, housing pressures were to crystallize in some community action, for instance in Ealing where, in 1980, the local authority had to face a gathering of about 100 angry people at a conference in Southall, leading to the declaration of a housing action area. This was followed by a similar meeting with black councillors, criticized for their inability to take visible steps in pressurizing the council.[121] By far the most well recorded community action took place in Camden where Bengali families occupied the Town Hall for a number of weeks without the support of Labour councillors and yet achieved major concessions.[122] Housing was also a key factor in the conflict between the black caucus and the 'militant' Labour Council in Liverpool. More recently the Bengali community in Tower Hamlets are having to fight for their homes in the law courts.

With recurring uprisings which followed increasing racial attacks and the hangover of the Rampton and Swann Reports both focusing and raising serious educational issues, housing as an issue still was not grappled with by stretched black activists. Part of the reason lies also in the fact that argument in housing requires much greater technical and economic understanding of the issue – a process from which blacks have been left out by systematic exclusion from local government. Nevertheless, disenchantment with housing was being expressed, particularly about the public sector, as indicated by one quarter of the respondents in a poll who thought that the Tories had the best policies on housing before the 1979 General Election. Generally the optimism of the mid–1970s in relation to race relations had disappeared.[123]

By the early 1980s, the 'new left' had established itself in urban local goverment. Blacks were beginning to flex their political muscles in some urban boroughs through a number of black politicians as well as through their demographic strength. Most major Labour authorities had appointed race advisors in housing, a small number were in the process of instituting more 'objective' allocation systems based on need (Greenwich), and others have a system of creating mixed property pools for lettings, homeless categories, and so on. All in all, these *may* have been successful in stopping further differential allocation, but little light was at the end of the tunnel in terms of building enough houses to get blacks who were 'ghettoized' on the worst estates into better housing. This would have meant earmarking building for residents of such estates – a programme too risky politically and economically impossible under contraints imposed by central government. Already such changes had led to a great deal of pressure being applied on the council (as in the case of Greenwich) by the organized tenants' movements. Overt racism had moved from a local political plane to become part of the tenants' and residents' associations, with nativism as a firm element in such a philosophy.[124] Black people have come to suffer disproportionately from the conflict between central and local governments, with neither taking the issue of 'race' on board for ideological reasons, although a few local authorities have taken some half-hearted steps.

Unemployment, moral panics on immigration, increasing racial attacks, debate on underachievement and police relations, all issues that continue to deplete the black communities' activists' resources, leaving little scope to take on the issue of race and housing. This is not to say that the white communities have been able to take political 'community' action either; they have failed partly due to the devastation of their communities in recent years and partly owing to a general weakening of the workers' organizations. Over the last decade, there has been, however, a significant rise in tenants' and residents' associations which have been particularly well supported by some Labour Councils. Such organizations, often with formal input facilities in local government, have tried to roll back the limited progress made in the area of sale of housing.

It is not that there are no resources for rectifying such historic social imbalances in housing. Most authorities have land as an asset which can be unlocked to create partnership schemes with the private sector to build specifically for residents of high stress estates. But such a possibility runs contrary to the strong left-wing ideology of many councils. A similar problem exists in relation to breaking the stronghold of direct labour organizations vis-à-vis construction – still dominated by powerful white unions who are hostile to equal opportunities at branch level.

Ironically it is in the private sector where a stronghold of discrimination has been broken by the recent boom in loans – that is, the interest of 'large capital' has to be served even if at the cost of local 'petty capital'. Sadly, at the same time, increase in unemployment and underemployment among black communities has reduced their ability to move and operate in this market. Notably it is also the private sector which seems to offer some degree of protection from racial harassment, although this is limited.[125]

The central state has disproportionately affected black communities by pushing for sales of council housing: as houses – particularly large ones – get sold, black entrapment in the worst public-sector housing is increased, usually in densely built, high-rise flats. Yet, at the same time, resources being generated by such sales cannot be utilized to rectify historical imbalances even if the local government wanted to do so.

Relatively poor share of size and quality of equity held by blacks in the housing market is likely to be a major contributing factor in the cycle of deprivation. Even such minuscule shareholding is sometimes resented by the white working classes. Mainly because of ideological reasons, the local governments in some areas of ethnic concentration are not prepared to improve the quality and size of black people's equity. In local government Labour politics, 'class' still predominates even in areas of high ethnic concentration, and despite the race cleavage in society. Generally with the exception of London, properties held by blacks in the UK sustain their value with difficulty due to overrepresentation of blacks in declining areas and because they find it difficult to repair properties due to mounting unemployment. Asians, having purchased their properties often without benefit of tax relief, now find these just sustaining their value in areas of high unemployment. Unlike many other working-class people, able to buy their properties from the council on discount, that option is not open to them on beneficial terms to the same extent, due to shorter periods of residence.

The voluntary sector

Over this period one may have expected the Housing Corporation to evolve a strategy based on local authority lessons from the public sector. As Colin Brown showed in the PSI study, Afro-Caribbeans are pioneering entry into the voluntary sector, where there is extremely poor representation of Asians, probably partly due to larger household size (Figure 5.1) and partly due to their underrepresentation in the public sector which has usually 50 per cent nomination rights. The magnitude of the difference in proportions (0.4 per cent Asians in contrast to 1.3 per cent of whites and 4.4 per cent of Caribbean households)[126] still cannot be explained by such factors, despite the fact that the location of housing associations overlaps with the spatial distribution of the black population and in particular of the Asian population.

It has taken the Housing Corporation a good deal of time to acknowledge that they could end up replicating many imbalances of public-sector underrepresentation in nominations, a longer wait, and disproportionately low access to houses.[127] In a study in Liverpool in 1983 Ferdi Fru found that a major local housing association catering for the elderly had black tenants in single figures despite the fact that blacks had been living in Liverpool for a considerably longer period than recent arrivals in the fifties and sixties, and constitute about a third of the population.[128] Similar observations, including the lack of equal opportunities policies, were to be later noted in the CRE's investigation of Collingwood Housing Association and in the work of Provan and Jesson on Birmingham associations.[129] Generally, the voluntary sector has been substantially controlled by middle-class whites and highly geared towards catering for the subjectively-assessed 'good tenant'. Their stock has also been developed through a system, particularly the notorious TIC (Total Indicative Cost) system which was introduced in 1982 and generally pushes housing associations towards a high level of conversion into smaller units.[130] The race implication of this was explored by the Ealing Family Housing Association which approached the CRE in relation to such a trend being indirectly discriminatory. The Corporation and the Housing Association staff remain mainly white, middle-class and highly networked, sometimes creating little 'white islands' amidst inner-city areas of high concentration. Its greatest failure has been in catering for vulnerable ethnic groups, single parents/persons, ethnic elderly and large families – a sad observation to make, despite the magnitude of evidence of similar problems in the history of allocations in the public sector.

The Housing Corporation's recent response to appoint a Race Advisor with a tiny budget can at best be seen as philanthropic or as a public relations exercise rather than as a genuine desire to take steps to alter the fundamental imbalances within the organization or in the Housing Associations. In this respect it appears to be following central government's line.

As regards the level of disadvantage, one could perhaps cite the PSI conclusion which summarized the overall position thus:

Blacks are more often found in flats, and those in flats are more often at higher floor levels, and those with houses are less likely to have detached or semi-detached property; black families have smaller property on average and, with larger household sizes, their density of occupation is much higher; black households more often share rooms or amenities with other households; the properties black families own or rent are older and they are less likely to have a garden. These differences are not the product of the different ethnic tenure patterns: they remain when the comparison is restricted to council housing or to owner-occupied property.[131]

However, the private-rented furnished sector is quite similar for both white and black households.

As regards change over the last few years, the general conclusion from the PSI studies, the Labour Force Survey and 1981 Census data is a considerable improvement in amenities and overcrowding (Figures 5.2 and 5.3), particularly in the owner-occupation sector – but the gap between black and white households in age, size and type of property persists. This gap is even wider in the public sector where the concentration of blacks appears to be in pre–1919 or post–1960 properties often on higher floors, and on undesirable estates in the case of the latter. According to the PSI, the disparity

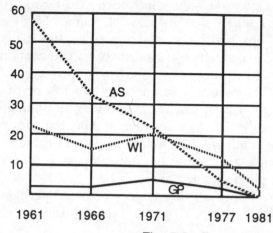

Fig. 5.6 `Percentage of households in private-rented furnished accommodation

Key: WI West Indians
AS Asians
GP General population

Source: NDHS 1978, Census 1981, PSI 1982.

between type of properties allocated since 1972 has grown. It is in this low-quality sub-sector in which one finds the most disadvantaged sections *within* black communities – for example single parents, large families, the newly arrived communities such as Bangladeshis – taking the brunt of racial discrimination and violence ten years after the passing of the Act.[132] The situation is forcing people to make a choice between living near the community or moving to avoid racial harassment. In the 1980s racial harassment in East London was to bring the Asian youth in to confrontation with the police. Racial harassment, although reactively the debate of race and housing, also acted as a sponge to suck in limited resources in the form of 'harassment' monitoring projects and anti-racist campaigns, so much so that many race units in housing departments intended for policy development were being forced to do casework.

One of the most serious observations in the 1980s is the decline in owner-occupation levels of the West Indian communities (Figure 5.2), a trend which, if continued, will have serious long-run implications for urban order.

CONCLUSION, ANALYSIS, AND THE WAY FORWARD

The following issues emerge clearly from the foregoing debate. First, both the central and local state have frequently colluded due to political opportunism or in response to racism and nativism or what can be described as 'Pareto's rationality'. The process continues particularly in the public sector as the debate on race and housing has moved from public health, to access, to quality of access and now to 'entrapment' in high-rise, high-density and poorly-designed housing in which the powerless Afro-Caribbean and poor Asian families are located – prone to racial harassment – their vulnerability perpetuated by sale of council housing. There has been little serious attempt to roll back this process as, with the exception of a few local authorities, the housing establishment, including the voluntary sector, remains mainly white. The situation is no better with regard to the DoE, the Housing Corporation and the Institute of Housing.

Second, the quality and value of equity held by blacks in property is disproportionately low and prone to devaluation, being held mainly in older properties and in poor and declining areas (except London). Occupiers face mounting repair bills and unemployment and have high dependency ratios. Such housing also has poor inheritability, hence offering relatively little in terms of social mobility.

Third, in the world of increasingly centralized building societies and banks, as well as building firms and the concentrated ownership of land,[133] blacks have little or no stake, although they are savers/buyers with many of these institutions. Historically from a Marxist perspective one can argue that these institutions have had a parasitical relationship with the inner city, offering just enough resources to maintain residence of a reasonable pool of human capital. The black communities have increasingly formed a larger proportion of this human capital.

These institutions, including the public sector DLO-controlled (Direct Labour Organization) construction industry, offer little employment to blacks, as was noted in Handsworth.[134] The banks and building societies still have very few black staff, even in areas of high ethnic concentration. Central government still remains non-committed or even hostile to the idea of a centrally co-ordinated contract compliance system.

135

The key people who operate at all levels of state are politicians and gatekeepers. The equivalent for the latter in the private sector would be trustees/shareholders and what would be described as exchange professionals. It is quite clear that, in the public sector, historically through political pressure, in response to direct public pressure, the urban gatekeepers have given differential treatment to blacks. As we indicated, racial discrimination by such urban gatekeepers is intertwined with discrimination on other grounds. Such professionals in our view either discriminate to simplify decision-making[135] or to protect their own territory (hence their own property values) and/or to gain by carrying out what they see at the time as 'good' management rewardable by promotion. The local state controls access of black people to resources through these processes continuously aided by moral panics often generated by the central state.

In the case of exchange professionals, they represent the interest of the majority of clients and are prepared to forgo a small pool of clients, creating a market in which the unscrupulous operators make their money by a 'colour tax' until the market becomes more competitive (for example when banks move in) or the act of discrimination becomes worthless (by, for instance, gentrification) or new competitors emerge (such as the Asian estate agent). The building societies' hierarchies do quite well out of the system in the form of good salaries/perks.

On the whole, one could argue that the local politicians, the urban gatekeepers and exchange professionals all have used racist values to erect barriers and deny equal opportunities to blacks: in so doing they have collectively, politically and economically benefited from racism; and they have been able to do so because the central state has always created other issues (for example, police, immigration) and moral panics to keep the black communities engaged on these other fronts.

There appears to be little by way of a concerted action plan well focused on ethnic minority areas to increase move-out rates from appalling estates or to assist by offering low-interest-rate loans to blacks to acquire some stake in the inner cities or to tackle the amenities problem in areas such as Tower Hamlets, Bradford, and so on. The DoE has failed to provide a lead on tackling racial inequality in housing on a long-term basis, incorporating access, quality, locational, structural and equity issues. A similar failure has taken place in terms of developing measures to increase black employment in the construction industry and housing establishment. The DoE has also failed to develop and subsequently provide any sources to tackle the most pressing issue of racial attacks.

Whilst it is useful to monitor allocations and move towards more objective systems of allocation, in our view the discrimination flowing from misuse of discretion will only abate as and when black people are represented well in organizations involved in housing. Some local authorities are developing 'targeting' systems to offer fair employment opportunities and ensure fair allocation, others are grouping their properties in quality categories and offering choices to queue for any of these categories, with the higher quality property group having the longest wait. Research is necessary in comparative systems of this nature to assess the effectiveness of such systems.

Such measures will not, however, eradicate discrimination altogether as the 'negotiability' and knowledge of 'areas' of blacks will still put them at a disadvantage due to lack of political clout together with limited lobby, poor political representation and multiple disadvantage factors, including the logical preference to stay near their own communities. In particular, the socially vulnerable groups like single parents, large families, recent arrivals, the young and the non-English speakers, all overrepresented among black minorities, will be channelled into the less desirable properties as a 'management achievement' by the urban gatekeepers and exchange professionals.

Thomas Sowell, a black right-wing philosopher in the USA, has argued that exchange professionals and urban gatekeepers have no incentive *not* to discriminate.[136] It would seem that we have to develop a new notion of management performance to create such incentives as an integral feature of race equality strategy, in addition to sanctions.

The way forward

A great deal of ad hoc and limited experimentation in race and housing seems to emanate from the lack of centrally-supported strategy on racial equality. Only such a strategy, hand-in-glove with a well funded partnership with local government, the Housing Corporation, building societies and banks, and well targeted on ethnic minority areas, can improve the quality of housing of blacks, their equity share in the cities, and their representation among urban gatekeepers and exchange professionals in both public and private sectors.

There are various possible key pressure points and channels as candidates: for instance, introducing a factor of racial disadvantage in the HIP's allocation for targeted allocation of monies; use of the recent changes in the Housing and Planning Act, viz. s.16 of the Housing and Planning Act 1986; use of income from Section 11 funding for housing departments and possibly extending to associations soon to create a pool of black housing professionals; and the use of positive actions through relevant sections of the Race Relations Act (ss.35,37,38).

Many local authorities are imaginatively using land on a partnership basis with builders to build homes for local people. The problem is that little finance is available to enable the poorer families to buy equity in such properties. The co-ops still remain on the fringes of housing strategy. Like some Third World countries which have special co-op lending agencies for such purposes there is a desperate need to develop such agencies for housing co-operatives. The Housing Associations with their excellent staff–tenant ratios and building and management experience can assist greatly in giving an impetus to the co-op movement as well as assisting self-build schemes on a large scale, assisting the unwaged. The local authorities are rightly suspicious of the large developers simply coming in and developing housing projects which can only be afforded by middle-income groups or Yuppies.

For a large number of young blacks, even the lower end of the owner-occupation sector is almost unreachable. Lack of equity or no stake in their immediate environment enhances their feeling of disenfranchisement. For such powerless groups as the poor and the unemployed, the electoral carrot of mortgage tax relief is irrelevant and the link between local housing and international money markets (through interest rates) is a sick joke.

Only a variety of options going beyond the crude and polarized owner-occupation and public-sector debate can begin to tackle the problem of race and housing. There is a desperate need to introduce plurality and variation in lending, owner-occupation and other forms of co-ownership housing with increased degrees of participation by black comunities in building, managing and controlling this spectrum of arrangements including the land policy in the inner city. Only such a change, leading to increased equity of the black communities in the inner city, will alleviate the feeling of disenfranchisement on the part of the young blacks.

Much has been said about the poorly conceived election package for the inner city which appears to be poorly costed and over-optimistic about the private-sector input. However, little has been said about land policy or the use of housing policy to create jobs and to facilitate movement of people to enable them to seek jobs.

It is not the government's objective to increase equity or owner-occupation which is objectionable; it is its insistence that no regulation, no control or support is necessary to ensure that the package will work and will not benefit only the developers, speculators and Yuppies, simply displacing young inner-city residents or pushing them further into worse pockets of the inner city. Such an approach has failed miserably in the United States as badly as the large post –1960s public-sector experiment in the UK. A system of controls, a new set of institutions and support mechanisms have to be developed using the technical expertise of housing associations and local authorities to hold a ring around a limited market offering well defined, thought-through support to inner-city residents to acquire equity. This may even necessitate the creation of a separate market for disadvantaged groups to acquire equity in which the local or central state in partnership act as builders, estate agents and lenders offering a variety of flexible arrangements for people who cannot participate in the speculative market. Such a market is separated from speculative markets as all houses in this market have to be exchanged by the aforesaid agencies. The participants have full control of the houses, responsibility for repair and equity but very limited speculative gains mainly to safeguard against inflation. Current lending, building and exchange agencies are too rigid, and their profit orientated policies too heavily linked to the international economy to provide for low income people who want to acquire equity in certain areas. These ideas are being developed in a following paper by the author.

Currently neither the Associations, nor the public sector, or the ownership sector appear to offer adequate competition to the private sector. With liberalization and continued shrinkage of this sector the prices and abuse in this sector will continue to escalate. Co-ownership, and co-operatives and more Housing Associations have to be encouraged through establishing banks, which will support such measures on a bigger scale and offer competition to private sector housing. A different sort of policy has to be developed for local authorities with large run-down public-sector stocks and limited land supply. A policy of 'targeted' building, especially for 'entrapped' tenants, may be necessary using central government funds.

In Britain housing policy has to be linked to creating employment as well as increasing mobility to improve access to employment. Clearly, attempts to move jobs where housing is plentiful have shown little success. If the government is interested in creating a more free market, then a subsidy has to be offered to people funded by industry, to allow unemployed people to accept jobs in booming areas. Such a process will benefit minorities considerably as they are disproportionately located in old industrial heartlands.

Current public interest law and arrangements are not developed in the UK to protect the tenant in the proposed multi-landlord tenure situation. The experience of Glasgow housing, where buildings are often run-down due to the problems of enforcing repair by common users, is instructive in this sense. Predictably, such half-baked arrangements will heighten tension between black and white tenants, increasing racial harassment and undermining racial harassment policies in many areas. The DoE and the Home Office both need to grasp the political, economical and socio legal aspects of racial harassment and segregation, particularly as housing control is expected to drift away into the hands of tenants or social landlords.

There appears to be little reference to the broader 'race' dimension of government policy in the proposed measures. A centre-led strategy is certainly not on the agenda and the government remains hostile to the issue of contract compliance despite previous policy failures in the context of employment generation in Liverpool and Handsworth, in the absence of such compliance. Little appears to exist in government's approach by way of increasing control and participation of blacks in the management and control of this strategy. Despite all the evidence to the contrary, the underlying assumption is that the blacks are equally advantaged, equally networked, equally familiar with the system and have total equal opportunities in access to all the new institutions being planned and have their fair share in housing.

On its current policy course, if the government is not careful it could find itself not only turning all public-sector housing into welfare ghetto housing, it may also find the majority of the inner-city blacks entrapped in such housing and a large number of young blacks, without any equity, concentrated in the inner city. The proposed policies are also likely to undermine some progressive policies adopted by a handful of authorities on equality in housing, and protection of and support for racial harassment victims, as it is unclear whether the new proposed institutions will fall under the Race Relations Act. In particular, section 71 does not apply to these. Instead of taking a lead on race equality, the government appears to be rolling back the small amount of headway made in this direction.

The black communities need to press the government to develop a comprehensive approach to the inner-city partnership in which there would be a centre-led race equality strategy on housing co-ordinated by the DoE. The DoE needs to produce a code of practice for monitoring equal opportunities which should apply to all housing agencies. Adherence to such a code would be conditional for any state funding, essential for registration and planning purposes. Already the government is yet again to link the social policy debate with immigration and nationality in the expected legislation on immigration which will make the entry of New Commonwealth dependants subject to the ability to acquire accommodation, thus returning the local authorities to their role of pay inspectors/immigration officers in order to monitor recourse to public housing. There could not be a better package of moral panics sanctioned by the state to undermine the basic human right to have a complete family irrespective of ability to pay for housing.

A national campaign on housing, aimed at the central government, needs to be launched as part of the inner-city debate. Black and ethnic minority communities need to broaden their campaign from simply lobbying the local authorities. Black professionals and activists have a key role to play in such a development by establishing a non-partisan national housing body to represent the ethnic minority viewpoint. The government in response should create a forum involving the DoE, Home Office, Department of Employment as well as key urban authorities, corporations and Housing Associations together with the CRE and the national black organizations to develop a strategy on race and housing which has an economic basis beyond platitudes offered hitherto by politicians and bureaucrats alike.

Notes

1. J. Rex and R. Moore, *Race, Community and Conflict. A Study of Sparbrook*, London: OUP for IRR, 1967.
2. C. Husbands, 'The Politics of Housing and Race – Perspectives from Great Britain, USA and France', paper presented at Glasgow University, 1986.
3. *Royal commission on distribution of Income and Wealth*, Cmnd. 6999, London: HMSO, 1977.
4. R. Hooper, *Colour in Britain in 1965*, London: BBC Publications, 1965.
5. V. Karn, *Race and Housing in Britain in Ethnic Pluralism and Public Policy*, Aldershot: Gower, 1983.
6. P. Pahl, V. Karn, J. Rex and R. Moore, 'Housing, empiricism and the state, in H. David (ed.), *Social Problems and the City*, OUP, 1978.
7. Karn, op. cit.
8. W. R. Bohning in *Racial Discrimination and Disadvantage in Employment*, Harper & Row in association with the Open University, 1981, chp 1.
9. P. Fryer, *Staying Power*, London:Pluto Press, 1984, p. 58; Richmond, *Colour Prejudice in Britain: A Study of West Indian Workers in Liverpool*, R. K. Paul Ltd, 1954.
10. *Data on 1958, polls in Promotion of Racial Harmony*, IPA, 1958.
11. M. Abrams, in E.J.B. Rose *et al.*, *Colour and Citizenship*, Oxford: IRR, 1969.
12. Runciman, 'Relative Deprivation and Social Justice', in Rose *et al.*, op. cit.
13. Rose *et al*, op. cit.
14. Ibid. pp. 100–3.
15. T. R. Lee, 'Immigrants in London – Trends in Distribution and Concentration', *New Community* vol. 2, no.2, 1973, p. 145.
16. Fryer, op. cit.
17. S. Patterson, *Dark Strangers*, London: Tavistock Publications, 1963.
18. Ibid.
19. H. A. Alavi, 'London Council of Social Services' in Patterson (ed.), op. cit.
20. Lee, op. cit., p. 145.
21. Rose *et al.*, op. cit.
22. Hooper (ed.), op cit., pp. 20–1.
23. Rose *et al.*, op. cit.
24. R. B. Davison, *Black British*, IRR, Oxford Univ. Press, 1966, pp. 39–43, Patterson; op. cit., p. 211.
25. R. Moore, in Hooper (ed.), op. cit., p. 69; also in R. Moore, *Racism and Black Resistance*, London: Pluto Press, 1975.

26. The Economist Intelligence Unit *Social Integration and Housing*, Studies on Immigration, no. 3, 1961.
27. R. B. Davison, *Commonwealth Immigrants*, IRR, Oxford Univ. Press, 1964, p. 107.
28. A. Halsey, *Trends in British Society*, London: Macmillan, 1972.
29. Rose *et al.*, op. cit.
30. Davison, op. cit., 1966.
31. A. Sivanandan, *Race, Class and the State*, RRI (Pamphlet), 1978.
32. Ibid.
33. A. Chater, *Race Relations in Britain*, London: Lawrence & Wishart, 1966, p. 45.
34. Home Office, *White Paper on Immigration*, Cmnd. 2739, London: HMSO, 1965, p. 10.
35. D. Hiro, *Black British, White British*, London: Eyre & Spottiswoode, 1971, p. 73.
36. PEP 1967, *Racial Disadvantage in England*, Harmondsworth: Penguin, 1968.
37. Rose *et al.*, op. cit. Data suggests significant presence in the unfurnished sector. These were probably cheap operators in the inner city, mostly white ethnic minorities of some sort. Quality PRU accommodation has been generally controlled by the 'firms' sector.
38. PEP 1967, op. cit.
39. Ibid.
40. Ibid., p. 194.
41. Ibid., p. 162.
42. Patterson, op. cit.
43. Ibid.; M. A. Malik, *From Michael De Feritas to Michael X*, London: Sphere Books, 1968.
44. PEP 1967, op. cit.
45. Davison, op. cit., 1966, pp. 48–51.
46. Rose *et al*, op. cit., pp. 134–5.
47. PEP 1967, op. cit., p. 232.
48. E. Burny, 'Immigrant Housing in Britain', *New Community*, vol. 1, no. 1. 1971; Davison, op. cit., 1964, p. 30.
49. M. S. Luthera, *Black Minorities and Housing in Ealing – A Comparative Study of Asian, West Indian and Native White Communities*, Shakti Publications, April 1982.
50. PEP 1967, op. cit., p. 86.
51. Rex and Moore, op. cit.
52. Patterson, op. cit., p. 174.
53. Working Party of London Housing Research Group on Race and Local Authority Housing for Ethnic Groups, Community Relations Commission, 1977. In 1967, 26 boroughs in London expected applicants to have lived in the UK for five years and a minimum of one year in the borough.
54. Hiro, op. cit.
55. *White Paper*, Cmnd 2838, London: HMSO, 1965.
56. Hiro, op. cit.
57. PEP 1967, op. cit.
58. Rose *et al.*, op. cit., p. 134.
59. Rex and Moore, op. cit.

60. B. Dahya, 'Pakistani Ethnicity in Industrial Cities' in Cohen (ed.), *Urban Ethnicity*, London: Tavistock Publications, 1974.
61. J. Davies, *Asian Housing in Britain*, Social Affairs Unit, 1984.
62. Karn, op. cit., 1969; Pahl *et al.*, op. cit., 1978.
63. V. Karn, 'Property values amongst Indians and Pakistanis', *Race*, vol. 10, no. 1, 1969; Select Committee, *Report on Race and Immigration 1970–71*, vols. 1–4, London: HMSO; M. Fenton, *Working Paper on Ethnic Relations*, no.2, SSRC Research Unit on Ethnic Relations, 1977.
64. Davies, op. cit.
65. Hill, op. cit., 1965, pp. 86–92., PEP 1967, op. cit., pp. 170–6; PEP 1977, *The Facts of Racial Disadvantage*, Harmondsworth: Penguin, 1977.
66. Patterson, op. cit., pp. 179–81.
67. Hiro, op. cit., p. 131; Rex and Moore, op. cit.
68. Patterson, op. cit., pp. 193–6.
69. Ibid., p. 76; Karn, op. cit., 1969, and *Select Committee Report 1970–71*, op. cit.
70. Patterson op. cit., 1969, p. 194.
71. Hiro, op. cit.
72. Burney, op. cit.
73. Luthera, op. cit.
74. Hiro, op. cit.
75. M. A. Anwar, *The Myth of Return; Pakistanis in Britain*, London: Heinemann, 1969.
76. P. Rich, *The Politics of Race and Segregation in British Cities*, CFHR, Univ. of Glasgow, Dept. of Politics, June 1986.
77. 'The Promotion of Racial Harmony', *IPA*, January 1970.
78. Rose *et al.*, op. cit., p. 580.
79. D. Donnison and C. Ungerson, *Housing Policy*, London: Pelican Books, 1982.
80. 'The Promotion of Racial Harmony' in *IPA*, January 1970; Hiro, op. cit.
81. Hiro, op. cit.
82. Burney, op. cit., 1971.
83. E. Burney, *The Times*, 26 October 1967.
84. Hiro, op. cit., p. 263.
85. Hiro, op. cit.
86. PEP 1967, op. cit.
87. H. Flett, *The Politics of Dispersal in Birmingham*, Working Papers on Ethnic Relations no. 14, ESRC Research Unit on Ethnic Relations, 1981.
88. *Labour Force Survey*, London: HMSO, 1984.
89. P. Harrison, *Inside the Inner City*, London: Pelican Books, 1985.
90. A. Simpson, *Stacking the Decks*, Nottingham CRC, 1981, p. 204.
91. Report by Co-ordinating Committee for the Welfare of Evacuees from Uganda, 26 September 1973; cf. Moore in Hooper (ed.), op. cit.
92. DoE, 1975, p. 9, cited in E. Cashmore and B. Tryona, *Introduction to Race Ralations*, RKP, 1983.
93. R. Skellington, *The Practice of Racial Dispersal in Birmingham, 1969–75*, 1980.
94. Flett, op. cit.
95. Luthera, op. cit., p. 13.

96. D. Smith and A. Whalley, *Racial Minorities and Council Housing*, London: PEP, 1975.
97. Skellington, op. cit.
98. Sivanandan, op. cit.
99. V. Karn and Henderson, *Urban Studies*, May 1984.
100. M. Anwar, *Ethnic Minorities and the Political Systems*, London: Tavistock Publications, 1986, p. 27.
101. Ibid.
102. Karn, op. cit., 1969 and *Select Committee Report 1970–71*, op. cit.
103. V. Karn and J. Kemeny, *CURS – Final Report of the Inner City Home Ownership Project*, Publication Centre for Urban and Regional Studies, 1984; see also Abbey National Building Society, *Report*, CRE, April 1984.
104. CRE, *Race and Mortgage Lending, Report of the Formal Investigation*, CRE, October 1985.
105. L. Steven *et al.*, *Race and Building Society Lending in Leeds*, CRC, 1982.
106. J. Parker and K. Dugmore, *Colour and Allocation of GLC Housing*, GLC Research Report, 1976; H. Flett, 'Bureaucracy and Ethnicity – Notions of Eligibility to Public Housing', in S. Wallman, *Ethnicity at Work*, London: Macmillan, 1979, J. Stunnell, *An examination of Racial Equality in Ponts Scheme Housing Allocations*, Research and Information Report, London Borough of Lewisham, 1975; in 'Is the Borough being fair?' *Power, Racial Minorities and Council Housing in Islington*, North Islington Housing Project, 1977.
107. PEP 1976, *Extent of Discrimination*, Penguin, 1976.
108. M. Fenton, *Asian Households in Owner Occupation*, Working Papers on Ethnic Relations no. 2 SSRC, Research Unit on ethnic Relations, 1977.
109. V. Robinson, *New Community*, vol. VII, Winter 1979.
110. DoE, 1977, op. cit., pp. 79–80, cf P. Pahl *et al.*, op. cit.
111. P. Gallagher, 'Housing and race relations: the role of policy advisers', MA thesis, PSA Dept. of Government, Brunel University, 1980.
112. Lord Scarman, *The Brixton Disorders*, Cmnd 8427, London: HMSO, 1981.
113. *Race & Housing: A Guide for Housing Associations*, NFHA, 1982.
114. T. Reidout and L. Russell in Luthera, op. cit.
115. Simpson, op. cit.; CRE, *Hackney Housing Investigated*, 1984; CRE, Liverpool Housing Investigation, 1985.
116. P. Harrison, *New Society*, 12 January 1984.
117. J. Davies, *Asian Housing in Britain*, Social Affairs Unit, 1984.
118. OPCS, Census 1981.
119. *Labour Force Survey*, London: HMSO, 1984; C. Brown, *Black and White Britain*, PSI, 1982.
120. Brown, op. cit., 1982.
121. Luthera, op. cit.
122. C. Adamson, *CCCR Annual Report*, Camden Committee for Community Relations, 1986.
123. Anwar, op. cit.
124. Tower Hamlets Tenants Federation, *Tenants Fight Racism*, 1984–85.
125. GLC, *Racial Harassment on GLC Estates, 1974;* Home Affairs Committee, *Racial Violence and Harassment*, London: HMSO, 1987.
126. Brown, op. cit., 1982.

127. DoE, *National Dwelling and Housing Survey*, London: HMSO, 1978. F. Fru, *Report to the CRE on EEC Funded Research*, 1983.
128. P. Niner, *Merseyside Improved Housing*, Reports to the Housing Advisory Group, *New Community*, vol. XI, 1984; cf. P. Niner, 'Housing Associations and Ethnic Minorities', *New Community*, vol. XI, no. 3, Spring 1984.
129. *Merseyside Improved Housing*, op. cit.; cf. Niner, op. cit.
130. TIC, *Voluntary Housing*, Special Report, February 1984.
131. Brown, op. cit., 1982.
132. See note 125.
133. M. Ball in *Class and Capital*, no. 24, Winter 1985.
134. West Midlands County Council, *A Different Reality*, 1986.
135. M. Lipskey, *Street Level Bureaucrats*, New York: Sage Publications, 1981.
136. T. Sowell, *Markets and Minorities*, Oxford; Blackwell, 1987.

6

Education*

Roy Carr-Hill and Harbajan Chadha-Boreham

INTRODUCTION

When large numbers of black children first went to school in Britain in the 1950s they entered an educational system organized on the assumption of cultural homogeneity, staffed by people with inappropriate training and a curriculum reflecting the racist ideology of Britain's colonial and imperial past.[1] All the early studies in the 1960s showed the importance of these factors in the educational difficulties encountered by black children[2] whether they were phrased in terms of 'adaptation', 'discipline problems' or 'educational performance', or even 'failure'. The question is: do the curriculum and pedagogy still discriminate against black children? What impact does that have on outcome? How important are those factors compared to the influence of family and social class?[3] And what is to be done?

Black children in British schools used to be defined by many as an 'immigrant' problem.[4] But now that nearly half of the black population in Britain are British-born,[5] the problem cannot be thought of as one of immigrant children. Instead, it is the education

*This chapter is based on an earlier version prepared by Shan Nicholas. The authors would also like to acknowledge the labour of Sally Cuthbert and Jenny Hardy in typing several versions of this chapter, and of Tracy Higgins and Alex Murray in preparing the diagrams.

system, against a background of widespread racial discrimination, which has failed to respond to the new situation of cultural diversity.

Indeed, the main difficulty in writing this chapter – the scarcity of data – stems from this same history. Statistics on the number of immigrant pupils were collected by the Department of Education and Science between 1966 and 1972[7] in order to arrange for the provision of language programmes. In these, an 'immigrant' was defined as someone born outside the UK or born in the UK to parents who had been in this country for less than ten years. But Mrs Thatcher – then Secretary of State for Education and Science – did not see that the data were related to performance or policy, so they were discontinued in 1973.[8] Despite calls for the reintroduction of statistical monitoring by various Select Committee Reports and the National Union of Teachers (NUT)[9] this chapter has had to rely almost entirely on a collection of specific studies.

A whole host of factors affect the educational experience of the black child in the British school: family, class, racism, school organization and language; and their importance will be acknowledged where appropriate. This chapter concentrates on the education system itself, a system which recently prompted an Afro-Caribbean youth worker to say, 'We have been badly educated for years.'[10]

This chapter first considers how racism is expressed in the educational system in terms of power, practices and prejudice; then it reviews research into three key issues – curriculum, teachers and language. We then present the small amount of statistical evidence on achievement and performance and the various 'explanations' of 'underachievement' which have been advanced, and finally discuss very briefly some of the possible – lateral – routes concentrating on the ambiguities of Multicultural Education (MCE).[11]

RACISM IN EDUCATION

Racism is a many-headed Hydra in education as elsewhere: it is a structural characteristic of our society and, like many other deeply embedded institutional inequalities, resists description let alone change. But, at the very least, we have to fight power, practice and prejudice; the inequality of influence as between blacks and whites, the routine expression of racism in day-to-day practice, and individuals' racist beliefs and attitudes.

Structural inequality

Black people have held posts at several different levels in the educational structure both nationally and locally as well as in the schools. Yet their potential power and influence has often been neutralized. Thus, although blacks have been included on many government-initiated advisory bodies and working parties, they have usually been accepted on the basis that they will be easily outnumbered or marginalized at the Committee stage.[12] When they do show independence they tend to be forced to resign: the politics of the Swann Committee with multiple resignations and realignments during its troubled six-year history is a good example.[13]

The story is repeated locally. Some authorities have established consultative structures and machinery but, again, they are advisory rather than decision-making. More poignantly, in using Section 11 funds, which are specifically directed towards the black populations,[14] the local authorities are meant to consult with the 'intended beneficiaries'. But although there has been an improvement since community groups were simply used to 'rubber-stamp' decisions already taken, efforts to consult are still rather restricted.[15]

Within schools, the pattern persists. Whilst school governing bodies include parents as well as teachers and local authority nominees, they tend to be a self-perpetuating oligarchy[16] so that black parents are rarely to be seen. There are, of course, black teachers – although not very many[17] – but it is frequently assumed that, in addition to their usual duties, they can also act as a liaison point with parents, teach the 'mother-tongue', take responsibility for the welfare of black pupils and staff developments[18] – and all this for free. Feeling, not unnaturally, exploited, many become angry, frustrated and alienated from their 'ordinary' duties and seek refuge in the occupational 'ghetto' of Multicultural Education. It, at least, involves some recognition of the extra work they have been doing, provides some kind of career structure for a minority of black (and white) teachers, and it is often more congenial than working in an all-white school.

At all levels, therefore, the unequal distribution of power and influence means that it is the white construction and interpretation of black reality that prevails.

The practice of discrimination

There have now been a large number of studies[19] documenting how the organization of the educational process itself discriminates against minorities. The learning experience itself can be alienating, as the ways school curricula are devised and teachers are trained lead to an educational diet typically based on the preconceptions of established teachers about ethnic minorities.[20] Indeed, often the learning experience is simply alien because the pupil may prefer to use a language other than English, which the school refuses to recognize.[21]

More overtly, the organization of the school itself discriminates. First, the administrative rules and regulations, whilst phrased impartially, ignore the fact of different cultures and, in practice, lead to a disproportionate rate of suspension or exclusion of pupils from ethnic backgrounds from mainstream schools (see below). Second, the assessments or diagnostic tools used for grading, or – more politely – for placing pupils into bands or streams will often favour those of an English cultural heritage and be inappropriate for others. Thus, Wright undertook a comparative study of a sample of Afro-Caribbean, South Asian and white pupils' examination results at the end of their second year, prior to their allocation to ability bands, and also of their performance in certain subjects at the end of their third year.[22] She noted the examination sets to which they were allocated: 'in both instances a number of Afro-Caribbean pupils were placed in groups below their attainment'. When she showed the results to a Deputy Head, he commented:

> Allocations to bands and sets aren't totally done on examination results, that's why it's so fuzzy and inadequate. . . Teachers have notions of children . . . it's often a social business . . . [so that a particular pupil] couldn't do 'O' level because 'O' level is for the good children.

Finally, racism is expressed on a formal and institutional level by the way pupils and staff are chosen. For example, Berkshire Local

Education Authority (LEA) constructed catchment zones for different schools based on characteristics of areas, including the proportion of families whose head was born in New Commonwealth and Pakistan (NCWP);[23] others have *de facto* adopted segregation or dispersal policies,[24] and the admission policies of some denominational schools exclude much of the local (black) population.[25] For staff, whilst the selection, recruitment and promotion policies might espouse explicitly equal opportunity, the practice often leaves much to be desired.[26]

Prejudiced beliefs and attitudes

Racism starts young and spreads. Both pupils and teachers bring with them sets of attitudes towards each other. Whilst racism might be more frequently expressed in school, it must be remembered that these attitudes are not only generated by or within the educational system, but also by the beliefs and attitudes the participants bring with them to school.

Teachers' racism has been an issue for some time.[27] Black parents have attributed their offsprings' 'underachievement' to teachers' preconceptions, stereotyped and negative views and related under-expectation of the average black pupil.[28] But neither teachers nor their unions like it: for example, the final report of the School Council, *Education for a Multi-Racial Society*, was delayed for three years.[29] The NUT blocked the original report which was censored because of its finding that schools were failing black children, failing 'to afford significance to either the everyday reality of the minority group child's existence, or the effects of society on the attitudes of the majority group child'.[30]

The interim Rampton Report pointed to unconscious and unintentional racist attitudes among teachers, but the report of the revamped Swann Committee shifts the emphasis away from racism at school to locate the problem of underachievement elsewhere. First, it argues that

A substantial part of ethnic minority underachievement . . . is thus the result of racial prejudice and discrimination on the part of society at large, bearing on ethnic minority homes and families, and hence, *indirectly*, on children.[31]

Second, it resurrected the 'Race and IQ' debate. The commissioned review[32] reached the obvious conclusion that there was no case to answer, but the whole balance of the report had been shifted. Whilst Swann is clearly correct to point to racism in the wider society, the purpose of the Committee's report was to enquire into the *educational* system; and the research resources available to them would have been more profitably spent on systematic research into the issue of racism in schools, raised by Rampton.

THE CONTEXT IN SCHOOL

Before presenting the data on achievement, this section outlines three aspects of the institutionalized racism to which the Swann Report also drew attention: namely curriculum, teachers and language.[33]

Curriculum

Racism in our school curricula is most obvious when black children are taught about the history and culture of their 'host' society, whilst their own is ignored and implicitly devalued.[34] Racism has been, and is, encouraged among white children; black children were, and are, made to feel inferior.[35] Of course, the racist impact of any material is complex: whites may react by becoming condescendingly guilty and paternalist;[36] blacks may be able to block discordant aspects of the cultural environment;[37] or adopt different criteria of identity.[38] But that does not, of course, excuse any racist material that is used.

Some schools began to include a wider range of multicultural or multi-ethnic materials, including information about other customs, but often without relating this to the peoples now in Britain: some have developed Black Studies with the intention of fostering a positive self-identity amongst black children; but others have done nothing.[39] Little and Willey emphasized the role of examination boards in influencing teachers to press for curriculum changes, concluding that the boards gave little initiative to broaden the syllabus.[40] The Centre for Urban Educational Studies produces and tests materials and the NUT proposed that all children should be taught about different cultures and published guidelines for teachers.[41]

Multicultural education means different things to different people: as a specific approach to curricula development (rather than a general ethos), it is an offshot of one of the many fashions in the sociology of education. When policies aiming to provide for 'equality of opportunity' for (white) working class pupils – such as the Educational Priority Area (EPA) programme – were seen to have failed, many intellectuals pointed to the inappropriateness of the theoretical foundations of those policies. Thus, the macrosociological emphases on education being an avenue – or, conversely, a banner – to mobility were replaced by a narrower microsociological focus on the content of the curriculum, the specific interactions between teacher and pupil and the preconceptions held by the teacher. Manipulation of these aspects of the educational process would, it was claimed, be a more effective measure to promote educational and social change.

Whilst it is important to understand the detail of the educational process, one must also – and, possibly, more importantly – understand the function of education and the influence of power and ideology. Put bluntly in this way, it is obviously idealistic and, indeed, futile, to think that the structural, social and economic inequalities can be ignored.

Nevertheless, some of this microsociological focus has rubbed off into the corpus of ideas labelled 'multicultural education'. For example, Bullivant argues that power and control in the multi-ethnic school *depend* on the way knowledge is selected and transmitted unequally to different ethnic groups by 'knowledge managers';[42] Lawton influenced the emphasis in Brent LEA on the multicultural curriculum,[43] and so on. Not surprisingly, given this origin, multicultural education is not uncontroversial: thus, Dhondy sees it as a means of 'containing the black problem', and argues instead that teachers should represent the present strengths rather than the past history of the black population.[44]

From a totally different point of view, Stone sees multicultural education as compensatory and argues that equal opportunity is best served through traditional formal academic methods.[45] Basically, MCE is not a monolithic and undifferentiated ideological framework: it is a 'catch-all phrase'. At worst, MCE has been a compensatory model based on a pathological conception of the black communities which focuses on culturalism and ethnicism in order to provide 'ethnic life-chances' for black pupils. But it also includes those who argue for a more appropriate education for white pupils and white teachers as well as black pupils. Whatever the right answer (see the section 'The way forward' p. 167), the point is that any educational material is less or more salient to some groups of children. Whilst, of course, a range of material embodying different views should be presented to children, their reactions to a specific mix of material will be reflected in their 'achievement' on that material. Indeed, no one expects a curriculum to be neutral – but it need not be racist.

Teachers

Most teachers are white. Whilst, in the mid–1970s, about 1.5 per cent of pupils in England and Wales were of Caribbean origin; the Caribbean Teachers Association estimated that only 0.15 per cent of teachers were of that origin.[46] At the beginning of the 1980s, about 6 per cent of pupils were of Afro-Caribbean or Asian origin,[47] *yet the estimated number of black teachers was less than 1,000 out of some 500,000.*[48] A study by the Society for Immigrant Teachers in the mid–1970s reported evidence of discrimination against black teachers: they found that the black teachers who were able to find jobs were employed mainly in 'ghetto areas' and were kept on the lowest pay scales.[49] The 1977 Select Committee Report reported that a large proportion of those who had managed to find employment as teachers 'had proved satisfactory, others had not, because of inadequate command over English and inability to adapt to British teaching objectives and disciplinary methods'.[50] Is this, perhaps, a fairly realistic reflection of the institutional racism in the wider society?

More recent studies suggest that the situation has scarcely changed. In 1981, a National Convention of Black Teachers was formed to act as a pressure group on issues facing black teachers. The point is that models of multicultural education presume varying degrees of cultural change by black groups in school and society (and black teachers as privileged mediators of those changes) without any corresponding changes on the part of white groups in school and society.[51]

The attitudes of teachers to different ethnic groups varies sharply so that white teachers tend to see Afro-Caribbean children as a problem[52] and low achievers because they use patois.[53] There is some anecdotal evidence of teachers holding explicitly racial stereotypes[54] and that white teachers do tend to suppose that their white pupils are not racist and so make no effort to educate them about their own racism.[55]

The 'obvious' response to teachers' ignorance was training. In 1973, the Select Committee on Race Relations and Immigration recommended that 'All students at colleges of education should be made aware that, whatever they teach, they will be doing so in a multi-cultural society';[56] this was repeated in a 1974 report by the Community Relations Commission, yet a survey in 1977 confirmed that teacher training had not prepared staff for the needs of black pupils[57] and as recently as 1980 schools still tend to view the special needs of black children as related to the teaching of English as a second language.[58] The interim Rampton Report in 1981 also stressed the need for pre- and in-service training, but the final Swann Committee Report four years later still had to reiterate 'that there is an urgent need for a major expansion in provisions for induction training', and, even 12 years after the Select Committee Report, 'All in-service courses should reflect the multiplicity of cultures, faiths and languages in present-day society'.[59] A report from Her Majesty's Inspectors based on a survey in 1979–80 of 46 out of the (then) 69 public-sector teacher training institutions, concluded that the overall picture 'was not a particularly bright one'.[60]

In contrast, special courses have been established to encourage the recruitment of black teachers.[61] But the expectations of *all* teachers is known to affect the actual performance of their pupils;[62] and, given the sets of attitudes, beliefs and expectations that have been described above, this could obviously have a serious impact upon black children. These beliefs are likely to be deeply ingrained. Whether or not they are correctly described as racist, we know that:

(a) achievement and attainment will be affected – the only question is by how much;

(b) they will be very difficult to change as they are rooted in institutional structures.

The language issue

The 'immigrant problem' was initially defined as the supplementary teaching of English to mainly Asian children who had little or no command over the language. The provisions and facilities varied considerably and ranged from an extra teacher and a few lessons a week to full-time language classes within schools and a language centre. Moreover the scale of provision seemed unrelated to either the size of the black population or any assessment of need.[63]

This situation of dramatically uneven provision despite the availability of funds via Section 11 of the Local Government Act 1966, continued through the 1970s.[64] Moreover, it has taken a long time for the needs of black pupils to be taken seriously and adequate teaching materials to be developed.

The situation is different for Afro-Caribbean children. Many, whether born in Britain or not, speak patois or Creole to some degree, and a whole range of dialects are maintained by black pupils in schools both negatively – in response to rejection and alienation – and positively – as an affirmation of their cultural identity.[65] Because there is a continuum between standard English and patois, there can be 'interference' between the two, and Afro-Caribbean children are disadvantaged when educated through the medium of standard English. There is then a tendency for teachers to presume that the use of patois indicates low academic ability. The interim Rampton Report rejected language as an important explanation of low achievement but recognized the problems of the negative attitudes of teachers towards dialect speech.[66]

When the issue has been recognized the usual response is to attempt to force Afro-Caribbean children to improve their standard English at the expense of patois. This is despite the EEC directive that member governments should 'promote, in coordination with normal education, teaching of the mother tongue of the country of origin'. There have been some recent attempts to encourage the use of patois in drama and poetry by ILEA and in writing by the

Afro-Caribbean Educational Resource Project,[67] but not on a wide scale.

Research projects funded by the Department of Education and Science and the Schools Council to assess linguistic diversity showed, in a sample of 28 schools, that 14 per cent of pupils were bilingual or multilingual.[68] Some local education authorities are now providing mother-tongue teaching in their schools. But parents and pupils are ambiguous as to whether they prefer their children to learn only in 'standard English' – if such a thing exists. Many who want to 'succeed' in the system – that is, reach powerful positions – know that they have to learn the language of the powerful; others wish to retain their own culture possibly at the expense of climbing the ladder of achievement.[69] Whatever the 'correct' view, it is clearly another factor to be taken into account in assessing achievement.

THE 'FACTS' ABOUT ACHIEVEMENT

This background, both of how racism in institutionalized throughout the educational system and of the specific context of curricular facilities and linguistic medium, is essential for understanding debates about achievement. More importantly, the term 'achievement' has been used in a very restricted sense in (nearly) all of these studies to refer to scores on tests designed for, and within, a white British curriculum. This is not to deny the quasi-universal validity of some elements of the curriculum, as some commentators suppose, nor to deny that many black parents are (rightly or wrongly) concerned about achievement in that sense, but to emphasize the importance of considering both the content and the context of any measure of 'achievement'.

The first major impact of the educational system upon black children was their 'selection' out of the normal educational system into schools for the educationally subnormal. Table 6.1 shows how 'immigrant', and especially West Indian, children were dramatically overrepresented in the educationally subnormal (ESN) schools in the late 1960s.[70] No up-to-date statistics are available because their publication was withdrawn after 1972, but a recent estimate suggests the situation has not changed.[71]

Table 6.1
Exclusion and marginalization

(A)   Immigrants as a proportion of children in Inner London

	In all primary schools	In ESN schools
1966 ILEA Inspectorate Report	13.2	23.3
1967 ILEA Inspectorate Report	–	28.4

(B)   West Indians as a proportion of children nationally

1972 DES Statistics	1.1	4.9

(C)   Proportion of different ethnic groups in ESN schools

	Non-immigrants	West Indian	South Asian
1970 DES Statistics	0.68	2.33	0.32–0.44
1981 Tomlinson's Estimate	0.5	2.5	

To the West Indian community the ESN issue symbolized the general underachievement of their children; but during the 1970s it has been progressively overshadowed by the growth in disruptive units, withdrawal classes and guidance units ('sin-bins') which were developed on an ad hoc basis during the 1970s.[72] One unit visited by Tomlinson had 52 per cent black children and 42 per cent of Irish parentage, as against 6 per cent of English.[73] An inquiry into suspensions from schools in Birmingham by the Commission for Racial Equality (CRE) in 1984 confirmed that children of Afro-Caribbean orgin were four times more likely to be suspended from schools[74] for a given level of disruptive behaviour.

It is only too easy to physically segregate minority groups in this way. But these reports also provide a grim context for the discussion of 'underachievement' as defined by the school system. Reports are presented from analyses of school test results and the range of qualifications obtained on leaving school. It is worth emphasizing that these are all *average results and a difference between group averages does not imply that all, or even a majority, of one group score is higher or lower than the mean score of the other.*

School performances

Three major overviews of the literature were published around 1980, and these provide the background to our review. Thus, Bagley presented a comparative picture of black educational performance in the UK and Jamaica and concluded:

The trend in most of these studies is for black children to have significantly poorer scores than their white counterparts.[75]

The following year Tomlinson wrote:

Of the 33 studies of the West Indian educational performance reported here, 26 show the children to score lower than white children on individual or group tests or to be over-represented in ESN schools and under-represented in higher school streams.[76]

Finally, Taylor was given a brief from the Rampton Committee 'to undertake an evaluative survey of the research evidence'.[77] She concluded that 'research evidence shows a strong trend to under-achievement of pupils of West Indian origin on the main indicators of academic performance.'[78]

Once again, it needs to be emphasized that these conclusions all refer to scores on achievement tests designed within the core school curriculum, and can only be interpreted in the context of the curricula, the facilities available and the linguistic medium employed, as well as any racist bias inherent in either the instruction provided or the tests administered. Representative studies from this earlier period are considered below, together with some more recent ones, mostly from the technical point of view, but these factors must not be forgotten.

The first large-scale surveys were conducted by ILEA in 1967 of children born in 1959–60. The survey was concerned principally with reading skills, the main test used was a group test administered by the class teacher. Table 6.2 is taken from the report by Mabey:[79] the scores show that West Indians started, at age 8, 12 points below the national average (notionally 100) compared to 2 points below for the UK. Mabey then breaks down the reading scores according to the amount of education in this country (Table 6.3).

The difference between those who have been 'fully educated' in this country and the other groups is clear. Yet the mean reading score still drops, from age 8 to 10 to 15, as the 'delearning' impact

159

of school increases. Or, as a black woman said, 'We are being made into semi-literates.'[80]

Table 6.2   Mean reading scores at 8, 10 and 15 years by group

Age in Years	UK-born	Eire	WI	IND	PAK
8	98.1	94.8	88.1	89.6	91.1
10	98.3	97.9	87.4	89.6	93.1
15	97.8	96.6	85.9	91.4	94.9
N	12,530	229	1,465	137	74

Source: Mabey, 'Black British Literacy', 1981, p.85.

Table 6.3
Mean reading scores of UK and WI children at 8, 10 and 15 years by amount of education in Britain

Age in Years	Fully Educated		Full Junior Education		Partial Primary Education	
	UK	WI	UK	WI	UK	WI
8	98.2	90.1	95.7	86.6	98.0	82.8
10	98.4	88.7	96.2	86.3	98.3	83.9
15	98.0	87.0	95.3	84.0	97.9	83.6
N	11,075	929	242	113	626	335

Source: Mabey, 'Black British Literacy', 1981, p.165.

The most up-to-date survey is reported in Phillips and Marvelly based on a longitudinal study, between 1976 and 1979, of pupils from a number of infant schools in a West Midlands local education authority.[81] This sample included 246 white and 114 Asian children. Every child completed four tests, English Picture Vocabulary Test (EPVT), mathematics, spelling and reading. Table 6.4 presents the test results, both the raw scores and the 'D-scores' (standardized to a mean of 50 and a standard deviation of 10), the latter representing adjusted estimates after controlling for the effects of age, sex, teacher's grading for language, and 'the level of semantic reference which a child is capable of comprehending as assessed by EPVT'.[82]

On these standardized D-scores 'the mean of the Asian subjects is higher than that of the indigenous, very significantly for reading (p < 0.001), and probably significantly for spelling ability (p < .05) and for number (p < 0.025)'.[83]

Table 6.4
Test results, indigenous and Asian children compared

	Indigenous (N=246) M	Asian (N=114) M	Significance
Age, completed months	86.4	86.3	ns.
Spelling			
Age equivalent	87.0	85.3	ns.
D-score	50.0	52.2	0.05
Reading			
Age equivalent	88.3	86.2	0.025
D-score	50.0	54.5	0.001
Number			
Raw score	15.5	13.5	0.001
D-score	50.1	52.8	0.025
EPVT			
Standardized score	97.2	78.9	0.001

Note: Statistical significance calculated from a comparison of the means, taking into account differences in the standard deviation.

Whilst it is clearly inappropriate to compare the raw scores, the introduction of controls for both teachers' grading for language and for the EPVT may be disputed. But a more simple control for residential areas shows how both groups do equally well in 'low social areas' (mixed working class and disadvantaged, council estates and socially disadvantaged, inner city), but that the indigenous apparently get better scores in 'high social areas' (middle class/owner-occupied, mixed middle class and settled working class). This latter result is probably due to the very different distribution of Asians *within* each of these categories (see Table 6.5), a warning against using such broad categories.

Indeed, one of the main messages of this study is that, whilst it is important to examine the test results of this kind in some detail

Table 6.5
Numbers and percentages by residential area and ethnic group

		White	Col%	Asian	Col%
High	Middle class/owner-occupied	33	22	2	3
	Mixed middle class and settled working class	55	36	4	6
	Settled working class	65	42	58	91
	Sub total	153		64	
Low	Mixed working class and disadvantaged council estates	68	73	2	4
	Socially disadvantaged inner city	25	27	48	96
	Sub total	93		50	
	Total	246		114	

– as Phillips and Marvelly indeed do – broad-brush controls for social background, in terms of high- and low-status areas, are insufficient. The *detail* of discrimination is as important as the detail of the particular tests.

School-leaving qualifications

Several studies of school-leaving qualifications have been undertaken in the context of discovering the employment situation of minority and 'white' young people. Those conducted during the 1970s tended to show Asian pupils performing better or equal to whites, with West Indian pupils trailing behind. These conclusions were relatively 'comfortable' for the white majority - they suggested that the fault lay with the West Indian community rather than with institutional racism. But they were upset by Driver's study, conducted on the basis of school records in 1974–5, 1975–6 and 1976–7 in 12 age-grades in five schools.[84] Using the rather dubious procedure of a ranked overall school achievement, he found West Indian girls coming first six times, West Indian boys first twice, English boys first twice and English girls never first (see Table 6.6).

The pendulum, of course, soon swings. The Swann Report included a table from Craft and Craft, claiming to show, on the basis of a study in 1979 of all fifth-form and second-year sixth-form pupils in each of an Outer London borough's 16 schools, that in public examinations 'the levels achieved by West Indian pupils lagged behind those of all other pupils, even when controlled for social class'.[85]

Table 6.6
Rank order of pupil categories for overall school achievement

School:	A	A	A	B	B	C	C	D	E	E	Aggregate
Age-grade	1	2	3	1	2	1	2	1–3	1	2	
West Indian Boys	1	4	2	3	3	2	4	1½	1	3	24½
West Indian Girls	4	2	4	4	4	4	1	1½	2	4	30½
English Boys	3	3	3	2	2	1	2	4	4	1	25
English Girls	2	1	1	1	1	3	3	3	3	2	20

Source: G. Driver, *Beyond Underachievement*, 1980, Table 16, p. 44.

There is a strong temptation to interpret this as academic jousting whilst children's lives are ruined. Nevertheless, as this was one of the few empirical studies included in the voluminous Swann Report, a sample of its results is shown in Table 6.7. Other possible explanations of the variations might be in terms of the mix of sub-groups of middle class and working class and teachers' expectations and are discussed below; also note the small number of West Indian working class.

Table 6.7
Fifth-form examination performances by ethnicity and social class

Examination Performance	White %		Asian %		WI %		All %	
	MC[a]	WC	MC	WC	MC	WC	MC	WC
High[b]	31	18	32	16	20	9	30	16
Medium	55	62	58	64	49	51	56	61
Low	14	20	10	21	31	41	14	23
Total (N)	445	786	165	359	31	176	761	1,476

Notes: [a]MC = middle class; WC = working class (OPCS classifications)
   [b]High = 5+ passes; Medium = 2–4 passes; Low = 0 or 1 passes

Source: Craft and Craft, 'The Participation of Ethnic Minority Pupils in Further and Higher Education', 1983.

On the other hand, Roberts, Noble and Duggan[86] show that,

within disadvantaged areas, black youth were leaving local schools better qualified than whites (see Table 6.8). Moreover, more received further education.

Table 6.8
Percentages leaving school with qualifications and receiving further training

	White Males	Black Males	White Females	Black Females
At least one 'O' level or CSE equivalent	19	20	24	37
CSEs	20	45	25	38
None	61	35	51	25
N	137	130	134	150
Percentage who had received further education	29	41	26	51

Source: Roberts, Noble and Duggan, 'Racial Disadvantage in Youth Labour Markets', 1983.

However, when Dex[87] compared the first jobs of 285 female black school leavers of West Indian origin with a matched sample of 324 white females (matched for age, educational qualifications, same class or school), she found that blacks remained unemployed longer and were less frequently successful in getting jobs according to their occupational aspirations.

Most of this evidence is of balmier times when white teenagers obtained reasonable jobs and blacks, eventually, obtained some kind of job. Now the issue for many – about one-half of all school-leavers – is which kind of Youth Training Scheme they land in.

Mode A is 'employer-led' and generally leads to more of its trainees being placed in jobs following better training. In Mode B, the MSC acts as managing agent and arranges work experience and training in conjunction with local authorities and local community and voluntary organizations. Despite MSC guidelines, Mode B provision is still seen as a 'sheltered environment' for the socially deprived. All studies[88] show that a greater proportion of young black people are put on Mode B schemes (see Table 6.9) and within Mode A schemes private sector employers take the smallest proportion of black people.

Table 6.9   YTS placements: scheme mode by ethnic group (1983)[89]

	European %	'Ethnic Group' %
Mode A	71	59
Mode B	29	41

Mode A YTS trainees: Employer type by ethnic origin[90]

	Asian/Afro-Caribbean	UK/European	Other
Private Sector (%)	4	91	5
Public Utility (%)	6	94	0
Local Authority (%)	7	93	0

The lack of the necessary trained teachers of Afro-Caribbean origin has been a recurring theme. But the processes we have discussed above as operating in school and YTS also appear to operate even in the courses specifically set up to help solve the problems! Connolly analysed the examination pass rates of teacher trainees in both ACCESS and NON-ACCESS groups.[91] A summary of his results is presented in Table 6.10. They show that the non-access group passes at an equal rate after repetition.

Table 6.10
Results for teacher trainees in a Polytechnic of Further Education

		Non-Access Group	Access-Group
Overall	Passes	2,748	674
Number	Fails	106	80
Unredeemed	Passes	2,716	682
Failures	Fails	37	12

165

Underachievement

There is no easy summary of this material. In general, blacks of West Indian origin do less well out of the educational system than others. The discussion has been confused for several reasons.

1. *The single factor approach.* The effects of racism on the educational system are worked out against the background of a capitalist economy and a paternalist society. This is nicely illustrated by a study of school leavers in six multi-racial neighbourhoods in the UK. The researchers concluded that the national profile of black underachievement 'could be attributable entirely to residing in districts and attending schools where the attainment of all pupils are below average'.[92] But the effects of racism on the educational system work through a capitalist economy and a paternalist society to give such results. As Parekh says, 'a cause is effective only within the context of a specific set of conditions'.[93]

2. *Use of out-of-date research.* This partly occurs, of course, because of the usual delays between research and publication.[94] This is especially important when there is little reason to assume stability, given rapid cultural and social change affecting black groups; unfortunately, as this review demonstrates, we *cannot* avoid using older studies for some arguments – for example, because no statistics are published.

3. *The reality principle.* Much of the debate is conducted at too abstract a level to connect with the reality of the school or of the child.[95] Dharely explains the problem:

    I go on the demonstration and feel all the time that it doesn't take into account my experience of schooling . . . I get the feeling that *my* demonstration has something to do with the building, or something to do with one set of ideas fighting another in this society, *but nothing to do with schooling.*

4. *Special pleading, specious testing.* The different factors involved are deeply committted to particular theories[96] so that any 'debate' is highly political. In consequence, the policies proposed are often simply impracticable because they ignore important effects. For example, the attachment of multicul-

tural, multi-ethnic, multi-racial advisors, and so forth, has some impact, but not much on the atmosphere of schools and does little to affect attainment levels.[97] The basic data on attainment can also be biased by the race-of-tester effect. This may not be inevitable[98] but it should always be taken into account, especially when teacher assessments are used. And, of course, we should repeat that all these 'findings' depend on a very specific notion of 'achievement' and therefore 'underachievement'.

Given these caveats, the evidence presented in this section has illustrated the effects of social class[99] and teacher expectations against a background of institutional and pervasive racism.

THE WAY FORWARD

The recent flurry of committees and their reports has a long history. On the one hand, West Indian parents have been collectively concerned at the difficulties experienced by their children in British schools since the 1960s.[100] On the other hand, there has been a growth of separatist schools started by groups of parents or by community leaders.[101] These have taken various forms, the most common being the 'Saturday morning schools' but recently, under pressure from the community, ILEA agreed to a Muslim primary school.[102] The state, for ever integrative, woke up to the implications of this development. What was the 'expert solution'? The banner of the Swann Committee is 'Education for All':

an educational process which both caters for the educational needs of *all* children with equal seriousness and sensitivity, and which also prepares *all* children, both ethnic minority and majority, through a common educational experience, for life in today's society.[103]

The collective, social and unifying nature of this approach is not always evident in their Report. An Annex to the chapter on 'Achievement and Underachievement' includes the proposal for research on 'Academically Successful Black Pupils' which they had

167

wanted ILEA to carry out but adds that 'it soon became evident that there were serious reservations'[104] from both parents and teachers about the objectives of investigating the factors making for *individual* high achievement.

The point they were making is that attainment levels and the factors which influence them cannot be studied in isolation. Eventually, any research which ignores the selective mechanisms of the school system and indeed the associated parts of the social system as a whole – in short, any study which ignores racism of any kind – serves to perpetuate a specific ideology: an ideology which usually blames – and very occasionally congratulates (as above) – the victim.[105] An individualistic solution of this kind will not work.

What of the possibilities for the 'social' version of 'Education for All'? It is useful to step back a little and re-examine the genesis of current controversies in the light of the material presented in this chapter.

> Multi-racial, multi-ethnic, multicultural education, have grown in response to a number of different but related pressures: first, black parents were concerned at the underachievement of their children and particularly the disporportionate number in ESN schools; second, some white teachers were worried about the classroom control of black pupils; and third, the establishment of supplementary schools by, particularly, the 'West Indian' community was seen as a threat to the state education system.

Mullard claims that there is a more conscious process.[106] He argues that all forms of education policy in this area since the Second World War, from immigrant education to multicultural education (via multi-ethnic and multi-racial education), have been state-constructed and state-sanctioned, and have risen from the way in which the state has intervened and defined structural-cultural relations. This is because they have all been white constructions of black reality and white definitions of the 'black problem'. In particular, multicultural education has perpetuated ethnicism and culturalism by treating black culture as posing a problem for white society. MCE asks how *those* cultures can enrich the overall educational experience of all children rather than asking similar questions about *all* cultures.

The sentiments are right, the emphasis is misplaced. There was nothing *planned* about the introduction of racially explicit educational policies by LEAs. In 1977, only ILEA had any positive statement, and Manchester was the next to adopt a policy in 1980. But twenty LEAs followed suit in 1981–2.[107] Why the rush?

It is difficult to avoid the conclusion that a major contributory factor were the 'riots', starting with St Paul's in Bristol in Easter 1980 and the following year in Brixton with 'disturbances' in over 60 cities later in the year.[108] Extra resources were made available aimed at political and social containment because of the fear and perceived threat of future violence. These reactive policies provided state legitimation for initiatives such as MCE, but to suppose any more conscious process of policy formation is to ignore the overwhelming sense of crisis management in assessing state policies towards the black population: in education, this meant institutionalizing MCE.[109]

Indeed, it is generally true that 'change' has been reactive: for example, the 'ethnic' vote is 'hard currency' which can be exchanged for the introduction of a race-relations policy, aimed at benefiting the black community.[110] This has usually happened with the change from a Conservative-controlled to a Labour-controlled local administration with a new Labour administration's adoption of a 'positive race relations policy' as part and parcel of a package directed at disadvantaged minorities in general. But the reverse has happened, as in Berkshire and Bradford, where Conservative councillors are conscious of the 'ethnic vote'.[111]

The problem is that the rhetoric of MCE as propounded in academic journals is not the same as an analysis of the actual practice. Such an analysis would indeed throw up examples of extremely bad practice, but also examples of those involved in important anti-racist work, that is acceptance of the endemic racism of British society, of racism as a 'white problem' and of the structural inequalities of British society based on race, class and gender.

For the weight of evidence in this chapter is that institutional racism, whether expressed in the classroom, the organization of the school or the social structures in which the school is embedded, prevails. The only answer is an anti-racist education which

. . . rests on and rotates around the question of who should

169

define whose reality or . . . whose definitions and perceptions of history and experience of race, class and gender should prevail and constitute the legitimate values, interests and knowledge to be transmitted within the context and process of schooling.[112]

Such an educational system would not be forever occupied with black children in a white school, but with the development and education of all children.

Notes

1. Examples are given in D. Hicks, 1981 'Bias in School Books: Messages from the Ethnocentre Curriculum' in A. James and R. Jeffcoate (eds.), *The School in the Multicultural Society*, London: Harper and Row, 1981, pp. 163–77.
2. See, for example, the review by R. J. Goldman and F. Taylor, 'Coloured Immigrant Children: A survey of research studies and literature of their educational problems and potential in Britain', *Educational Research*, vol. 8, no. 3, 1966.
3. Cf. the excellent review by B. Parekh, 'Educational Opportunity in Multi-Ethnic Britain' in M. Glazer and K. Young, *Ethnic Pluralism and Public Policy*, Massachusetts: Lexingham and London: Heinemann Educational, 1983.
4. Even in such respected and scholarly books as F. Taylor, *Race, Community and Schooling*, Windsor: National Foundation for Educational Research, 1974.
5. See Chapter 10.
6. The 'situation' of course varies widely from school to school so that, although the overall proportion of black children is 'only' 6% (see Chapter 10), some schools have a majority of black children.
7. Department of Education and Science in *Education, Vol. I: 1967 to 1972*, London: HMSO, 1973.
8. In a classic foretaste of the dictatorial egocentrism which was to come she said: '*My* department makes no use of them whatsoever except to publish them. They do not form the basis of any grant from *my* department' (Mrs Thatcher, June 1973, authors' emphasis).
9. For example, the Select Committee on Race Relations and Immigration, *Report on Education*, London: HMSO, 1977; Department of Education and Science, *West Indian Children in our Schools*, Interim Report of the Committee of Inquiry into the Education of Children from Ethnic Minority Groups (The Rampton Report), Cmnd 8273, London: HMSO, National Union of Teachers, 1981.
10. Report of the Review Panel, *A Different Reality*, Ethnic Relations and Equal Opportunities Section of the West Midlands CC, February 1986, p. 39.
11. Multicultural education can mean all things to all (wo)men: a representative statement is ILEA's wish 'to sustain a policy which will ensure that, within a society that is cohesive though not uniform, cultures are respected, differences recognized and group and individual identities are secure' (ILEA,

Multiethnic Education, Joint Report of the Schools Sub-Committee and the Further and Higher Education Sub-Committee, 1977).

12. The process by which committee pressure can steamroller the effective expression of minority group interest is well described in C. N. Parkinson, *Parkins Law: or the Pursuit of Progress*, London: Moray; and W. F. Whyte, *Organizational Behaviour: theory and application*, Illinois: Homewood.

13. The resignations included both black and white members: see introduction to Swann Report – Lord Swann, *Education for All: The Report of the Committee of Enquiry into the Education of Children from Ethnic Minority Groups*, Cmnd 9453, London: HMSO, March 1985.

14. This section of the 1966 Local Government Act enabled local authorities to claim back 50% (later 75%) of the salaries of people employed to deal with the special needs of immigrants.

15. The take-up of the money has been very uneven and there have been allegations of widespread misuse: see Community Relations Commission, *Funding Multiracial Education: A National Survey*, London: CRC, 1976.

16. See J. Finch, *Education as Social Policy*, Harlow: Longman, 1984, pp. 55–7.

17. See the section 'The language issue' below (p. 156).

18. This comment has been voiced several times in the journal published by the National Association for Multiracial Education since 1972.

19. Multi-racial education: the classic source is. R. Rosenthal and L. Jacobson, *Pygmalion in the Classroom*, New York: Holt, Rinehart and Winston, 1968; and the parallel British study is D. Hargreaves, S. K. Hester and F. J. Mellor, *Deviance in the Classroom*, London: Routledge and Kegan Paul, 1975. Other references are given in Tomlinson.

20. The power of teacher expectations to influence pupils' performance has been demonstrated several times. The classic text is Rosenthal and Jacobson, op. cit.; see also J. D. Finn, 'Expectations and the Educational Environment', *Review of Educational Research*, no. 42, 1972; and M. Stone, *The Education of the Black Child in Britain*, London: Fontana, 1981.

21. Obviously, as half of black British are born in Britain, for many an English dialect – *not* BBC or Oxbridge upper-class English – will be preferred. Indeed, some might prefer their children to learn in 'standard English' even though it is not their vernacular (see the next section). But the issue cannot be prejudged by *taking for granted* that a specific medium is the best.

22. C. Wright, 'School Processes – An Ethnographic Study', in J. Eggleston, D. Durin and A. Mahdie, *Education for Some*, Trentham Books, 1986, Chapter 8, provides a blend of anthropological and statistical evidence to make a very powerful case.

23. In Reading, there was disquiet about changes in the school allocation procedures. After a campaign by black and white activists, the LEA zoning scheme was formally investigated by the CRE and this led, ultimately, to the authority adopting anti-racist policies. For an account see S. del Tufo et al., 'Inequality in a School System', in A. Ohri, B. Manning and P. Curmo (eds.), *Community Work and Racism*, London: Routledge and Kegan Paul, 1982, pp. 75–87.

24. These have a long history. DES Circular 7/65 stated that 'serious strains could arise in schools if the proportion of black children in any one school rose above one third'; see also D. Hiro, *Black British White British*, Harmondsworth: Penguin, 1973, pp. 68–70.

25. Such policies can, of course, avoid any reference to race: for example, by using residence qualifications or by giving preference to those whose parents attended that school.

26. Only a few authorities, such as Berkshire and ILEA, have explicitly attempted to recruit and promote more black teachers, apart from those appointed to specific 'multi-racial' or Section 11 posts, and there is little sign of any change, judging by the newsletters of the Local Authorities Race Relations Exchange set up in March 1984.

27. Several examples can be cited from assimilationist phase of educational policy from the early 1950s to the 1965 White Paper: see C. Mullard, 'Multiracial Education in Britain: from Assimilation to Cultural Pluralism' in J. Tierney, (ed.), *Race Migration and Schooling*, London: Holt, Rinehart and Winston, 1981, pp. 109–19.

28. The first major published statement by a black spokesperson was Bernard Coard, *How the West Indian Child is Made Educationally Sub-Normal in the British School System*, London: New Beacon Books, 1971.

29. Thus parts of the report were published in 1978 – see, for example 'Assumptions and Contradictions'. *New Society*, vol. 43, no. 802, 16 February 1978, pp. 366–6, but the final report was not published until 1981.

30. See *New Society*, ibid.

31. The Swann Report, op. cit., para 8.3, their italics.

32. M. Mackintosh and C. G. N. Mascie-Taylor, 'The IQ Question?', Annex D to the Swann Report, op. cit.

33. The Swann Report, op. cit., section 3.4, pp. 68–70.

34. S. Hatch, 'Coloured People in School Textbooks,' *Race*, vol. 4, no. 1, 1962, pp. 63–72; see also Hicks, op. cit., 1981.

35. D. Milner, *Children and Race*, Harmondsworth: Penguin, 1976.

36. The confusions of policies upon 'benevolent multiculturalism' and 'benign racialization' are examined in detail in B. Troyna and J. Williams, *Racism, Education and the State: The Racialisation of Educational Policy*, London: Croom Helm, 1986, especially Chapter 1.

37. D. London, 'Self Esteem and Locus of Control: Some Findings on Immigrant Adolescents in Britain', *New Community*, vol. 6, no. 3, 1978, pp. 218–34; also 'Self Esteem and Locus of Control in Minority Group Adolescents', *Ethnic and Racial Studies*, vol. 1, 1970, pp. 196–217.

38. L. Young and C. Bagley, 'Identity, Self Esteem and Evaluation of Colour and Identity in Young Children in Jamaica and London', *New Community*, vol. 7, no. 3, 1979, pp. 154–69.

39. R. Giles, *The West Indian Experience in British Schools - The Way Forward*. London: Heinemann, 1977.

40. A. Little and R. Willey, *Multi-Ethnic Education – The Way Forward*, Schools Council Working Paper, no. 18, London, 1981.

41. National Union of Teachers, *In Black and White: Guidelines for Teachers on Racial Stereotyping in Textbooks and Learning Materials*, London, 1979.

42. B. Bullivant, *Pluralism Teacher Education and Ideology*, Melbourne: Faculty of Education and Centre for Migrant Studies, Monash University, Mimeo, 1979.

43. D. Lawton, (1980). *The Politics of the School Curriculum*. London: Routledge and Kegan Paul, 1980; D. Lawton, *Curriculum Studies and Educational Planning*, London: Hodder and Stoughton, 1983.

44. F. Dhondy, 'Teaching Young Blacks' in James and Jeffcoate, op. cit., 1981, Chapter 5.2.
45. M. Stone, *The Education of the Black Child in Britain*, London: Fontana, 1981.
46. Select Committee on Race Relations and Immigration, *Report on Education*, vol. I, London:HMSO, 1977, para 69.
47. See Chapter 10.
48. An article in *New Society*, of 27 November 1980 estimated 800–900 black teachers with some 150,000 pupils of West Indian origin.
49. N. Gibbes, *West Indian Teachers Speak Out: Their Experience in Some of London's Schools*, Lewisham: Caribbean Teachers' Association and Lewisham Council for Community Relations, 1980.
50. Select Committee on Race Relations and Immigration, op. cit., vol. I, para 118.
51. Mullard, op. cit., p. 130.
52. J. Townsend and E. M. Brittan, *Multiracial Education: Need Innovation*, Schools Council Working Paper no. 50, London: Evans and Methuen, 1973; see also Wright, op. cit.
53. For a spirited defence of linguistic diversity and the encouragement of dialectic and patois, see J. Miller, 'How do you spell Gujerati, Sir' in A. James and R. Jeffcoate, *The School in Multicultural Society*, Pitman Press for Open University, 1981.
54. Milner, op. cit.
55. 'Race and Teachers: the Schools and Council Study'. *New Society*, vol. 16, 1980, pp. 366–8; see also W. Yult *et al.*, 'Children of West Indian Immigrants II, Intellectual Performance and Grading attainment', *Journal of Child Psychology and Psychiatry*, no. 16, 1975.
56. House of Commons, Select Committee on Race Relations and Immigration, Session 1972–73, *Education*, vol. 1, p. 56, para 9.
57. Community Relations Commission, *Urban Deprivation, Racial Inequality and Social Policy: A Report*, London, 1977.
58. Little and Willey, op. cit.
59. The Swann Report, op. cit., p. 611.
60. Included as Annex B to Chapter 9 of the Swann Report, op. cit., at p. 549.
61. Department of Education and Science, *Education in Schools*, (Green Paper) Cmnd 6869, London: HMSO, 1977.
62. A rigorous critique of the potential impact of expectations is provided by R. Nash, *Teacher Expectations and Pupil Learning*. London: Routledge and Kegan Paul, 1976. He shows how the possibility is always present.
63. H. E. R. Townsend and E. Brittain, *Organisation in Multi Racial Schools*, London: National Federation for Education and Research, 1972; and H. E. R. Townsend, *Immigrant Pupils in England: The LEA Response*, London: National Federation for Education and Research, 1971.
64. National Union of Teachers, *Section 11: A National Union of Teachers Report*, London: NUT, 1978.
65. V. Edwards, *The West Indian Language Issue in British Schools*, London: Routledge and Kegan Paul, 1979; R. Miles, *Between Two Cultures? The Case of Rastafarianism*. SSRC Research Unit on Ethnic Relations Library Paper no. 10, 1978. Of course, white British also use dialects but they are less easily attached to other personal characteristics.

66. The Rampton Report, op. cit., p. 70.

67. See, for example, L. Garrison, *Black Youth, Rastafarianism, and the Identity Crime in Britain*, London: Afro-Caribbean Educational Resource Project, 1979, judging by the newsletters of the Local Authority Race Relations Information Exchange, which have been appearing since September 1984.

68. J. Rosen and L. Burgess, *Language Dialects of London School Children – An Investigation*, London: Ward Lock Educational, 1980.

69. The whole issue has echoes of a much wider debate in many African nation-states: should the language of the colonial oppressor be adopted as the only nationally available medium? Or should the dominant local language be adopted with many implications for ethnic group rivalry?

70. ILEA Reports nos. 959/1966 and 657/1967; Townsend, op. cit., 1971; Department of Education and Science, *Statistics in Education: Vol. I, Schools, 1967–72*, London, HMSO, 1973.

71. S. Tomlinson, *Educational Subnormality: A Study in Decision Making*, London: Routledge and Kegan Paul, 1981; Black People's Progressive Association and Redbridge Community Relations Council, *Cause for Concern: West Indian Pupils in Redbridge*, Ilford: BPPA and RCRC, 1978.

72. D. P. Tattum, *Disruptive Pupils in Schools and Units*, New York: Wiley, 1982, Chapter 2.

73. Tomlinson, op. cit., 1981.

74. Commission for Racial Equality, *Birmingham Local Authority and Schools – Referral and Suspension of Pupils:* report of a formal investigation, 1984.

75. C. Bagley, 'A Comparative Perspective on the Education of Black Children in Britain', *Comparative Education*, no. 15, pp. 63–81; for an analysis by those most involved see Black People's Progressive Association and Redbridge Community Relations Council, *Cause of Concern: West Indian Pupils in Redbridge*, Ilford: BPPA and RCRC, 1978.

76. S. Tomlinson, 'The Educational Performance of Ethnic Minority Children', *New Community*, vol. 8, no. 3, Winter 1980, pp. 213–34.

77. M. Taylor, *Caught Between: A Review of Research into the Education of Pupils of West Indian Origin*, National Foundation for Educational Research, London: Nelson, 1981, p. 3.

78. Ibid. p. 216.

79. C. Mabey, 'Black British Literacy: A Study of Reading Attainment of London Black Children from 8 to 15 Years', *Educational Research*, vol. 23, 1981, pp. 83–95.

80. Report of the Review Panel, op. cit., p. 41.

81. C. J. Phillips and A. Marvelly, 'Basic Educational Skills of Asian Children at the End of Infant Schooling', *Educational Research*, 1983, vol. 26, pp. 113–29.

82. M. A. Brimer and L. M. Dunn, *English Picture Vocabulary Test, Full Range Edition*, Bristol: Educational Evaluation Enterprises, 1975.

83. Phillips and Marvelly, op. cit., p. 121.

84. G. Driver, *Beyond Underachievement*, London: Commission for Racial Equality, 1980.

85. M. Craft and A. Craft, 'The Participation of Ethnic Minority Pupils in Further and Higher Education', *Education Research*, vol. 25, no. 1, 1983.

86. K. Roberts, J. Duggan and M. Noble, 'Racial Disadvantage in Youth Labour

Markets' in L. Barlow and S. Walker, *Race Clan and Education*, London: Croom Helm, 1983, pp. 191–208.

87. S. Dex 'The Second Generation: West Indian Female School Leavers', pp. 53–71 in A. Phizachlea,(ed.) *One Way Ticket Migration and Female Labour*, London: Routledge and Kegan Paul, 1983, pp. 53–71.
88. J. Wrench, *Ethnic Minorities and the YTS*, Research Unit of Ethnic Relations, University of Aston, 1983; Commission for Racial Equality, 'Racial Equality and the YTS', London, 1984; S. F. Fention *et al.*, 'Ethnic Minorities and the YTS', *MSC Research and Development*, no. 20, MSC, 1984; A. Pollert, 'Racial Discrimination and the YTS', West Midlands YTS Research Project, 1985.
89. Fention, op. cit.
90. Commission for Racial Equality, op. cit., 1984.
91. M. Connolly, 'Achievement of ACCESS Students on a BED Course', *New Community*, vol. 12, no. 2, 1985.
92. F. Reeves and M. Chevannes, 'The Underachievement of Rampton', *Multiracial Education*, vol. 10, 1981, pp. 35–42; quote from p. 39.
93. Parekh, op. cit., p.113.
94. See, for example, the material reviewed in the Swann Report.
95. Dhondy, op. cit., p. 269.
96. There are still enough geneticists around that the Swann Committee felt obliged to commission a research paper – note 9 above.
97. K. Young and N. Connolly, *Policy and Practice in the Multiracial City*, London: Policy Studies Institute, 1981.
98. B. Troyna, 'Fact or Artefact? The Educational Underachievement of Black Pupils'. *British Journal of Sociology of Education*, vol. 5, no. 2, 1984, pp.153–65.
99. See Tables 6.5 and 6.6 on pages 162–3.
100. See introduction to the section 'The "facts" about achievement' (page 157) and note 71 above.
101. See Stone, op. cit., Chapter 4, pp. 171–90.
102. *Runnymede Trust Bulletin*, no. 192, June 1986.
103. The Swann Report, op. cit., p. 317.
104. Ibid., para 429.
105. Victim-blaming as an approach to proposals for policy reform is not specific to education; in the health sector, discussions about prevention are dominated by proposals for health education campaigns aimed at individual change.
106. C. Mullard, 'Anti-Racial Education: The Three O's', National Association for Multicultural Education, 1984.
107. Even his 'numbers game' is a matter of dispute. Thus

Garry German writing in 1983 claimed that 21 Authorities had published documents declaring a committment to anti-racism. But Mullard and his colleagues disagree. In 1982 they wrote to all LEAs and found from the 110 replies received that only about ten per cent had some explicit anti-racist aims.

Taken from B. Troyna and J. Williams, *Racism, Education and the State: The Racialization of Educational Policy*, London: Croom Helm, 1986, p. 74.

108. Anon, *Like a Summer with a Thousand Julys*, B. M. Blob, 1982.
109. This does not imply that any of the parties to the educational process seriously believe it can solve social ills: but it is a useful scapegoat and it is even better if it looks as if something is being done.
110. We can cite the cases of Berkshire, Brent and Haringey.
111. For a boring account of 'ethnic voting' see I. Crewe, 'Representation and the Ethnic Minorities in Britain', in Glazer and Young, op. cit., 1983, pp. 258–84.
112. Mullard, op. cit.

7

Health

Mike Grimsley and Ashok Bhat

In its brief discussion on 'Race, ethnicity and health', the Report
of the Working Party on Inequalities in Health – the Black Report
states that:

> Another important dimension of inequality in contemporary
> Britain is race. Immigrants to this country from the so-called
> New Commonwealth, whose ethnic identity is clearly visible in
> the colour of their skins, are known to experience greater diffi-
> culty in finding work and adequate housing. . . Given these
> disabilities [in finding work and adequate housing] it is to be
> expected that they might also record rather higher than average
> rates of mortality and morbidity. This hypothesis is difficult to
> test from official statistics, since 'race' has rarely been assessed
> in official censuses and surveys.[1]

Later when considering social class inequality in the availability
and use of the Health Service the Report quotes Skrimshire[2] with
approval.

> The data . . . are consistent with a theory of structural determi-
> nation of need and demand for health care from an area, oper-
> ating both through environmental and social conditions on the
> level of health, and through the social pressures and life experi-
> ences that further affect demand. . . .

The Report then comments:

> It is likely that similar conclusions would follow from a consideration of race and ethnicity. However, information on the use of services by ethnic groups is sparse.[3]

Despite this relative paucity of official information concerning the health patterns of ethnic minorities in Britain there is considerable evidence from individual studies, as well as from the available officially collected data, that ethnicity provides a relevant dimension of health inequality. This is so whether one adopts a 'medical model' or a 'social model' of health.

The 'medical model' sees ill health or disease primarily in terms of a mechanistic malfunctioning of the body with a consequent emphasis on drug-bases or surgical treatment, and this appears to be the dominant model in Britain. There are a few conditions and diseases which are specific to, or relatively more common among, black Britons – for example, sickle cell disease and, probably, rickets and osteomalacia. The 'social model' sees ill health as mainly deriving from social factors such as poor living conditions and emphasizes the importance of modifying such conditions and preventive medicine in alleviating ill health.

The following is an attempt to bring together the limited amount of national statistical information on ethnic health and findings from a number of individual studies. The intention is to throw some light on the patterns of ethnic health inequality in Britain.

THE MAJOR INDICATOR OF HEALTH: MORTALITY

The Black Report chose mortality as its surrogate health measure for practical reasons.

> Every death in Britain is a registered and certified event in which both the cause and the occupation of the deceased or his or her next of kin are recorded.

The Office of Population Censuses and Surveys (OPCS) has provided information on mortality rates for different occupational

178

and therefore social class groups, regions, the sexes and so on, for many years. It was only in 1984, however, that the 'first comprehensive study of mortality of immigrants to England and Wales'[4] was published. The opportunity for such an analysis came about when place of birth was included at death registration in 1969. Standardized mortality ratios (SMRs) were calculated by country of birth and sex for all causes and for selected individual causes, which generally followed the numerical ordering of the International Classification of Diseases and Causes of Death (ICD). Analyses excluded deaths of persons less than 20 years of age and referred to the years 1970–78. The SMRs took the England and Wales age/sex/cause specific mortality rates as standard – that is, 100. Figure 7.1 shows the SMRs for those born in the New Commonwealth and Pakistan for all causes and two major cause groups: circulatory diseases, which include heart disease; and neoplasms (cancers). The most strikingly high SMRs for all causes are for males and females born in the African Commonwealth and for females born in the Indian sub-continent and the Caribbean Commonwealth for all causes and circulatory diseases.

Further to this theme of female health inequality and noting that country of birth is used as the indicator of ethnicity, the article by Marmot *et al.* in *Population Trends 33*[5] points out that deaths from true obstetric or associated causes – maternal mortality – are relatively high among those women born in Africa, the Caribbean and the Indian sub-continent. The DHSS enquiries into maternal deaths in England and Wales for 1970–72, 1973–75 and 1976–78[6] show maternal death rates from true obstetric causes to be 0.32 per 1,000 live births for women born in the New Commonwealth and Pakistan (NCWP) compared with 0.11 for all other women. Table 7.1 gives more detailed information. The DHSS reports suggest that a majority of excess deaths are avoidable.

PERINATAL AND INFANT MORTALITY

Although information on adult mortality rates by cause and country of birth has only recently become available, the OPCS has published quite detailed information on deaths at and around the time of birth by maternal country of birth, since the mid–1970s.[7]

179

Country of origin: IND: Indian Subcontinent: CAR: Caribbean Commonwealth; AFR: African Commonwealth

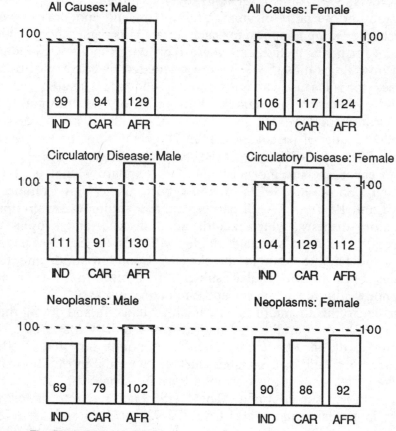

Source: The Black Report, 1982.

Fig. 7.1   SMRs by country of birth and sex for all causes, circulatory diseases and neoplasms at age 20 years and over, 1970–78. England and Wales

Figure 7.2 shows the trends in perinatal and infant mortality rates in England and Wales by mother's birthplace for the years 1975–81 and 1983–84 (1982 figures were unobtainable). There are a number of points to be made. Mortality rates have been consistently higher for mothers born in the NCWP than for those born in the UK. Rates have been coming down faster for mothers born in the UK compared with mothers born in the NCWP. Within the NCWP group, mothers born in India and Bangladesh have shown a

Table 7.1
Maternal mortality rate (deaths per 1,000 live births) by country of origin

Year	Country of origin	True Obstetric Causes		Associated Causes	
		N	Rate	N	Rate
1970–72	NCWP	68	0.50	35	0.26
	Other or not known	287	0.12	216	0.10
1973–75	NCWP	39	0.32	24	0.20
	Other or not known	196	0.11	131	0.07
1976–78	NCWP	44	0.32	28	0.21
	Other or not known	183	0.11	172	0.11

Source: DHSS, *Report on Confidential Enquiries into Maternal Deaths in England and Wales*, 1975.

considerable recent reduction in rates. There was a recent sharp increase, however, in 1980 and in perinatal and infant mortality rates for mothers born in Pakistan and also increases in perinatal and infant mortality rates for mothers born in the West Indies. There appears to be no obvious explanation of why these NCWP groups should have more erratic trends: for example, because of different patterns of parity, maternal age or birthweight. There is, however, accumulating evidence from local investigations of considerable disparities in health experience between white and black populations as a whole at and around childbirth. These differences relate to a number of factors in addition to, or related to, possible causes of infant and perinatal mortality.

OBSTETRIC PROBLEMS AND EARLY CHILD HEALTH

The Second Report from the House of Commons Social Services Committee 1979–80 – the Short Report[8] – examined the problems of perinatal and neonatal mortality in Great Britain. Included was a detailed chapter on causes of mortality and these were divided into four sections. Predisposing factors (before pregnancy) were

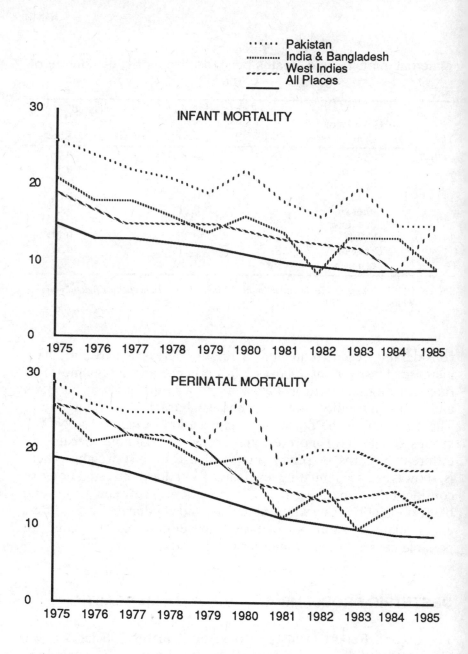

Source: OPCS, *Mortality Statistics*, nos 7, 9, 13.

*Fig. 7.2   Infant and perinatal mortality rates by maternal country of birth
1975–84 in England and Wales*

abnormality of the reproductive system and congenital anomaly, poor education and living conditions and nutrition, attitude to use of health care and chronic ill health. Smoking and physical or mental stress in pregnancy together with environmental toxins, medication and infection were seen as contributory factors. Underlying causes related to particular obstetric experience such as multiple pregnancy, pre-term labour, toxaemia and placental problems were associated with prematurity and low birthweights. The immediate, certified causes of mortality consisted of congenital abnormality, asphyxia, respiratory failure and trauma. Although these conditions were viewed as possible causes of stillbirth they are also 'at risk' factors for live-born children. It is well known, for example, that severely handicapped children are more likely to have suffered difficult births and/or low birthweight than 'normal' children.[9] Most studies into the obstetric problems of ethnic minorities examine one or more of the above factors and often relate these to perinatal mortality or low birthweight. At a national level, the OPCS has analysed the distributions by birthweight of live and stillbirths by mothers' country of birth since the 1983 birthweight statistics.[10] For 1983 and 1984 around 6.7 per cent of all live births were of low birthweight – that is, below two kilograms (approximately 4.4 lbs). There was, however, wide variation in this percentage between different places of maternal origin. Some have said that excess perinatal mortality is due to low birthweights. Indeed, the highest proportions of low-birthweight live births – around 11 per cent – were recorded by mothers from India and Bangladesh. But if one relates perinatal mortality to birthweight, OPCS information also shows that, for low birthweight babies, the overall perinatal mortality rate declined from approximately 96 in 1983 to about 93 in 1984. Rates for mothers born in India and Bangladesh were lower but rose from about 71 to 81. For mothers born in Pakistan, however, rates were higher but fell from around 123 to 106. The comparable rates for West Indian mothers were 83 and 84. Rates have been given as whole numbers as these figures should be treated with caution because of the relatively low number of cases.

In local studies on obstetric problems and child health it is not always clear how 'ethnic' is defined. Research tends to concentrate on 'Asian' mothers and children. In a series of papers Terry,

Condie[11] and Settatree[12] have reported findings on mothers delivered at Dudley Road Hospital, Birmingham in 1979–80. Table 7.2 shows the ethnic distribution and perinatal statistics for the 4,026 babies born in 1979. Since ethnic origin, rather than country of birth, was used to categorize mothers, comparisons with national mortality rates and birthweight data must be tentative. The figures, however, highlight the clear differences in birthweight between ethnic groups. It is perhaps surprising to note the relatively low average birthweight of the West Indian babies. A more detailed study[13] of normal singleton pregnancies delivered in 1979 and 1980 found that 11.3 per cent of normal Indian singleton babies and 10 per cent of Pakistani babies were classified as being of low birthweight compared with 7.3 per cent of European babies.

Table 7.2
Ethnic distribution and perinatal statistics in 4,026 babies

Ethnic Group	No.	Stillbirth Rate/1000	Perinatal Mortality Rate/1000	Congenital Malformation Rate/1000	Mean Birthweights (g)		
					Boys	Girls	Total
Indian	1,126	15.1	27.5	19.5	3,051	2,914	2,986
Pakistani	574	7.0	19.2	29.6	3,091	3,027	3,059
Bangladeshi	92		21.7	32.6	2,991	2,936	2,963
West Indian	422	4.7	16.6	14.2	3,071	3,034	3,051
European	1,698	8.2	13.5	21.2	3,302	3,163	3,231
Other	114	8.8	17.5	26.3	3,105	3,009	3,096
Total	4,026	9.4	18.9	21.6			

‡Patients mainly from Africa, Middle East, and Far East

Source: Terry et al., 'Analysis of Ethnic Differences in Perinatal Statistics', *British Medical Journal*, 1980.

The Dudley Road Hospital serves a community in which Social Class IV and V households predominate across all ethnic groups. Northwick Park Hospital on the other hand is situated in an affluent area of North London. Haines et al.[14] reported on factors, particularly nutritional factors, related to birthweight and complications of pregnancy for 706 singleton deliveries to Asian women defined by country of origin, for the period 1977 to about 1980. Women in the study were interviewed by a dietician at their booking-in visit and later at 28 and 34 weeks' gestation. They were classified as vegetarians if they ate meat on average only every two weeks or less often. Birthweights were adjusted to 'take account of' parity, sex of offspring, gestational age and maternal weight at 20 weeks' gestation. Average birthweight for meat-eaters was 3.020 kg compared with 2.953 kg for the vegetarians, so the difference – 0.67 grams – was small.

Since most of the vegetarians were Hindus, birthweight was compared between vegetarians, Hindu meat-eaters and Muslim meat-eaters. The major difference in average birthweight was between all Hindus – 2.951 kg – and Muslims – 3.133 kg – a difference of about 182 grams. The authors concluded that the heavier Muslim babies could not be explained by differences in gestational age, parity, maternal weight or social class. Also 'vegetarianism does not appear to have a direct effect on birthweight'.[15]

In addition to the higher perinatal mortality rates and lower birthweights there is some evidence that the black (or at least the Asian) population is suffering greater incidence of severe subnormality in children and a higher rate of infant death due to congenital abnormality. Barnes[16] presented time series data on mortality and morbidity rates in the Bradford Health District. The percentage of children of low or very low birthweights has been consistently higher in the Asian population and the incidence of severe mental handicap has shown an Asian rate three to five times as high as the non-Asian rate for the years 1975–79. For the years 1975–79, the infant death rate due to congenital abnormality in the Asian population was between two and five times that for the non-Asian. On the other hand, Dhariwal's[17] more recent figures from Leicestershire show a closing gap in lethal congenital abnormality rates. The Asian rate was approximately five times the non-Asian in 1975 but was down to about two-and-a-half times in 1979.

The above studies have been mainly concerned with the outcome of pregnancy and labour but there has been some information published on the characteristics of labour and ethnic status. In a study of 2,661 pregnancies at Dulwich Hospital[18] labour and delivery characteristics were related to parity and ethnic group.

There were no specific antenatal problems in Asian mothers and all three groups showed similar incidence of anaemia, essential hypertension, pre-eclampsia, placental abruption and prematurity. However 8.6 per cent of Afro-Caribbean mothers showed sickle cell trait compared with 1.7 per cent for Asians and 0 per cent for whites. The 73 Asian primigravidae admitted in spontaneous labour arrived in hospital with a lesser cervical dilation and the foetal head at a higher level than the other groups. Of these mothers, 51 per cent required stimulation of labour and this was evidence of a higher incidence of labour dysfunction. Black women also suffered more labour dysfunction than the white women in the study. Modes of delivery, however, showed a broadly similar pattern for all groups.

There is, then, clear evidence of obstetric health inequality between ethnic groups despite the apparent availability of extensive maternity services. Medical 'explanation' of these phenomena has been limited but there are indications that the quality of service received by black Britons is not at the same level as for whites. Mothers from the Asian community tend to receive shorter periods of antenatal care. Information from Bradford[19] shows that, in the period 1974–78, about 17 per cent of Asian expectant mothers received antenatal care for less than two months before delivery compared with 5–6 per cent for non Asians. For the mothers delivered at Dudley Road Hospital in 1980, the median post-menstrual weeks at booking for stillbirths was 16 weeks for Europeans but 20 weeks for Indian mothers and 23 weeks for Pakistani mothers.

In Leicestershire Clarke[20] and Clarke and Clayton[21] have examined the quality and organization of obstetric care provided for Asian immigrants in some detail. They report that between 1976 and 1981, 939 perinatal deaths occurred to women living in Leicestershire of which 128 were to Asian women. A case control study design was employed whereby cases were defined as perinatal deaths occuring to women resident in Leicestershire regardless of place of delivery. Controls consisted of the next live birth to a Leicestershire woman in the intended place of delivery of the perinatal death to which the case related. Information on GP qualifications, gestation at initial antenatal attendance and category of perinatal death was recorded in addition to other social and medical variables. The percentage of GPs not on the obstetric list was found to be higher for Asian mothers compared with non-Asians, no matter what the outcome of pregnancy. Also initial antenatal care for the Asians tended to start later in pregnancy and this tendency increased if the mother had a GP not on the obstetric list. Even allowing for other relevant variables, mothers of Asian origin had a relative risk of a perinatal death 42 per cent greater than non-Asian mothers. The relative risk to mothers with GPs not on the obstetric list was 81 per cent higher. The relative risk was greatest for Asian mothers. The authors comment that:

In Asian patients, systematic antenatal care, as evidenced by routine recording of antenatal tests and examinations, starts at later stages in pregnancy. This tendency of late enrolment into care increases if the patient's doctor is not on the obstetric list. At first we thought this might indicate only patient behaviour, but it has been suggested that some practitioners might not wish to enrol patients into formal antenatal care until the pregnancy is well established. Consequently the mother herself may not see the value of positive health behaviour. . . . [22]

They conclude that consumer interest and involvement in maternity services should be encouraged in Asian patients by people who can understand and communicate with Asian cultural groups and that postgraduate courses should be arranged especially for doctors not on the obstetric list.

In its deliberations on possible explanations of perinatal and infant mortality and low birthweight the Black Report comments:

Several studies have pointed to the importance of the mother's health, and the quality of obstetric care received, and there can be no doubt, on the basis of the evidence we have presented so far, that these are class-related.

They missed out 'and related to maternal ethnic origin.'[23]

ILL HEALTH SPECIFIC TO BLACK PEOPLE

In 1977 the Community Relations Commission (CRC)[24] in its evidence to the Royal Commission on the National Health Service, presented information which showed that certain sections of the black population have potential or actual special demands on the NHS. The first of these related to low birthweights and the CRC drew attention to the inadequate investigation into the reasons for weight differentials between white and black populations and expressed concern at the low take-up of antenatal and postnatal care services by blacks. That there still must be such concern might be seen as an indication of the veracity of what Torkington[25] refers to as 'institutionalised racism in the NHS'.

Our argument is that, with respect to black people as consumers of the National Health Service, the multi-racial and multi-cultural nature of British Society has not yet been accepted by those who have the power to formulate policies at central and local levels and to decide what health facilities should be available to the community. Consequently diseases specific to black people have received little attention.[26]

These specific diseases or conditions usually refer to anaemias, rickets and osteomalacia and various infectious diseases such as tuberculosis. To this list might be added certain problems of mental health.

The CRC identified certain dietary deficiencies amongst Asians and related these to anaemic conditions. It stated that anaemia caused by deficiencies in iron and Vitamin B12 is probably more common among Asians, particularly among vegetarian Hindus. Roberts et al.[27] measured haemoglobin, serum vitamin B12 and serum red cell follate levels in 322 pregnant immigrant women at their first antenatal booking; 126 women were followed up at 34 weeks' gestation and postnatally. The Indian, East African Indian, Pakistani and Bangladeshi women showed significantly lower serum vitamin B12 levels than the European women. Serum vitamin B12 levels were lower among Hindus and Sikhs than Muslims. The West Indian, Indian and East African Indian women also showed significantly lower initial haemoglobin levels than immigrants from Europe.

Most concern, however, continues to be expressed not so much at the incidence of 'normal' anaemia but at a range of diseases known as haemoglobinopathies. Haemoglobinopathy defines a group of blood-related disorders where anaemia is caused by an inherited difference in the make-up of the haemoglobin in the red blood cells. The most common diseases in this group are sickle cell disease, commonly called sickle-cell anaemia, and thalassaemia (Mediterranean anaemia). The following discussion is based on Clarke and Clare[28] of the Organization for Sickle Cell Anaemia Research and Torkington.[29]

Sickle cell disease describes a group of genetically transmitted disorders of haemoglobin which mainly affects people of Afro-Caribbean origin. Haemoglobin is the chemical in the blood which carries oxygen to body tissues and gives blood its red colour. When the oxygen is used up, red cells circulate back to the lungs to be 'reloaded'. The sickle cell disease sufferer has a less efficient form of haemoglobin and the red cells can take on a 'sickle' or crescent-moon shape as opposed to the normal 'full moon' shape. Because of this lack of efficiency, the body's tissues may be deprived of oxygen, particularly in times of stress, and give pain which may be very severe. There may also be subsequent jaundice and skin ulcers. Children with the condition may be particularly susceptible to infection and, because the disease reduces the life of red blood cells, anaemic fatigue is not uncommon.

The major conditions included in this group are homozygous sickle cell anaemia (HbSS), the most severe type, and the milder forms, sickle cell beta thalassaemia (HbSBThae) and sickle cell haemoglobin C disease (HBSC). The most common state, however, is when about one-third of the haemoglobin is in the S form and the remainder is the normal HbA. This is not a disease as such but sickle cell trait and is believed to affect one in ten black persons in Britain. Its importance lies in the fact that it is a means of passing on the potential for HbS to the next generation. It is estimated that around 1 in 400 black persons in Britain are affected by sickle cell anaemia, but Torkington reports that this could well be a conservative estimate.[30]

In this country, there appear to be relatively few empirical

189

investigations of people suffering from sickle cell disease and information on mortality is sparse and indirect. Anionwu *et al.*[31] reported on 70 cases of the disease which were identified in the London Borough of Brent from records dating back to 1962. Their findings were expressed in terms of the number and duration of sickle cell disease admissions and reasons for admission. They concluded that there are probably many undiagnosed individuals with the disease in the community. The main risk to such individuals would be an unexpected and potentially fatal sickling episode during pregnancy or after surgery.

Tuck[32] discusses sickle cell disease and pregnancy and reports on a survey of 125 pregnancies in women with sickle cell disease. The main findings were a twofold increase in spontaneous abortions compared with racially matched controls not suffering from sickle cell disease and a perinatal mortality rate which was four times greater at 48/1000. Antenatal complications included anaemia, urinary tract and chest infections, sickling crisis and severe pre-eclampsia. The spontaneous premature delivery rate, at 13 per cent, was twice that of the comparative population, and 25 per cent of the babies weighed less than the tenth percentile for their gestational age. Tuck also states that 'the maternal death rate in this country associated with sickle-cell disease remains a matter of educated guesswork'. She estimates that the 18 fatalities associated with the disease reported by the DHSS confidential enquiries into maternal deaths over the period 1964–75 occurred in the context of about 300 pregnancies to affected women. This gives a guess of a mortality rate of about 6 per cent.

Sickle cell disease is a serious condition. It may be even more serious than the above indicates because, as there is no screening to detect the disease at an early stage, 'the pneumococcal infection with which a child presents and for which treatment is given is seen as the cause of death without associating it with sickle cell disease'.[33]

Could there be a connection with the above-mentioned high infant mortality rates in the West Indian community? Anionwu states that early identification of affected infants through umbilical cord blood screening is essential for the prevention of sickle cell disease-related deaths in infancy. We screen for phenylketonuria which has a lower incidence than sickle cell disease. So why not screen? 'Phenylketonuria virtually affects only white children.'[34]

Whereas sickle cell disease affects mainly black Britons of Afro-Caribbean origin, rickets and its adult equivalent, osteomalacia, are conditions which appear to be particularly prevalent in our Asian population. Patterson[35] states that rickets and osteomalacia are conditions caused by defective mineralization of the skeleton. Since rickets affects the growing skeleton and involves both bone and cartilage, it therefore occurs in children and its main features are pain in the bone and bone swelling which may produce obvious skeletal deformities (florid rickets). The main features of osteomalacia are bone pain and tenderness and associated muscle weakness. Both conditions are thought to be caused by a deficiency of vitamin D which is essential for mineralization. According to Sheiham and Quick[36] there is no unanimity about the prevalence of these conditions or whether they are becoming more or less common. In the COMA report[37] rickets is reported to be declining and osteomalacia slightly on the increase. But individual surveys of Asian populations have found alarmingly high proportions of affected individuals. In a 1976 study of florid and subclinical rickets in Glasgow Goel et al.[38] found that about 5 per cent of Asian children had rickets. In Ford et al.'s[39] 1976 investigation in Bradford, around 40 per cent of the Asian study population showed some degree of bone change, and they estimated that one Asian child in forty would have gone into hospital with rickets by the time of adolescence. In addition to the greater prevalence of these conditions in the Asian population, it has been found in a number of studies – for example, Preece et al.[40] and Stamp[41] – that average vitamin D blood levels are lower for Asians than for the rest of the population.

'By far the commonest cause of vitamin D deficiency in Britain is the combination of inadequate exposure to sunlight and low intake of vitamin D in the diet.'[42] There is clear evidence that British Asians do have a relatively low dietary intake of Vitamin D. Singleton and Tucker in a (small) study of infants in Southall found that those aged 6 months had diets with reasonable vitamin D intake, thanks to the consumption of fortified dried milk and cereals and reinforced by health visitors and baby clinics. 'Children aged 18 months however, ate largely Asian diets and had much lower vitamin D intakes . . . with a corresponding increase in symptoms of vitamin D deficiency.'[43] In their summary of other investigations, Sheiham and Quick state: 'All studies have found average

191

intakes in the Asian community to be less than two micrograms per day, which is well below the recommended intakes . . .'[44]

Thus British Asians have a relatively high incidence of two very unpleasant conditions – rickets and osteomalacia. There is strong evidence that these conditions are caused by low vitamin D levels, and British Asians appear to have relatively low levels of this vitamin. Vitamin D levels can be raised by increased exposure to sunlight and by raising dietary input – for example, by vitamin D fortification of foodstuffs. Margarine has been fortified with vitamin D since the war and rickets virtually disappeared from the 'indigenous' population. Some have argued, therefore, that Asian foodstuffs, such as chappati flour, should be so fortified. Indeed Dunnigan et al. report the success of a low-dose vitamin supplement campaign in Glasgow.[45] COMA, however, came out strongly against the idea of fortification. 'Milk, butter and flour, including chappati flour should not be compulsorily fortified by the addition of vitamin D.'[46] Though there are arguments against the fortification of foodstuffs, it does seem strange that it is 'yes' to margarine but 'no' to chappati flour.

It should be noted that there are other conditions which particularly affect other British ethnic groups. Cystic fibrosis, which particularly affects people of northern and central European origin, and Tay-Sachs disease which particularly affects those of European Jewish origin, are well known and well researched examples. From the above discussion we must conclude that much more research needs to be done.

OTHER CONDITIONS

Sickle cell disease and rickets are the two specific conditions differentially affecting the black British population which have received most attention. There now follows a brief discussion of other morbidity issues before a more detailed consideration of mental health. In 1967 the National Institute of Economic and Social Research[47] identified the higher incidence of tuberculosis amongst immigrants as an important factor in assessing demand for health resources. The notification rates of respiratory tuberculosis has declined dramatically since the turn of the century (and before).

Most recently, the number of cases of respiratory tuberculosis noti-
fied in Great Britain has declined from 8.727 in 1973 to 5,318[48] in
1983. However, Darbyshire,[49] in the 1978–79 Medical Research
Council (MRC) notification survey,[50] reports the annual notification
rates for England and Wales estimated for different ethnic groups
as 9.4 per 100,000 population (all ages) for whites and 354 and
353 respectively for the Indian and Pakistani/Bangladeshi groups.
There were also differences in the characteristics of the disease.
Table 7.3 shows that the 'Asian' ethnic group had a greater
percentage of non-respiratory cases than the whites. Darbyshire
concludes that, according to Nunn *et al.*[51] the annual rate of decline
in the incidence of TB is 5.2 per cent per year for white males
and 5.3 per cent for white females born in this country, but the
corresponding reductions for males and females for all ethnic groups
combined are 3.8 per cent and 2 per cent. 'Thus for this disease
active policies of case-finding and chemotherapy, together with
BCG vaccination and chemoprohylaxis, programmes introduced
over the past 20 years will need to continue . . .'[52]

Table 7.3
Ethnic notified cases of TB in 1978–79

Ethnic Groups	All Forms		All Respiratory		All Non-respiratory	
	No.	%	No.	%	No.	%
White	2,121	57	1,785	62	429	9
Indian subcontinent*	1,323	35	890	31	573	52
West Indian	76	2	55	2	24	2
Other	208	6	154	5	76	7
Total patients	3,732	100	2,884	100	1,102	108

* Indian, Pakistani and Bangladeshi.

Source: MRC, 'National Survey of Tuberculosis Notification in England and Wales
1978–79', 1980.

Evidence of ethnic patterns in 'common diseases' is patchy and
local. Reference can be made to the proceedings of a Conference

on Ethnic Differences in Common Disease published in the *Postgraduate Medical Journal* in December 1981. Beevers[53] comments in the Introduction that 'no clinician can fail to notice the high prevalence and severity of essential hypertension in blacks'. Sever's studies of 115 factory workers with the black (West Indian) subjects' age and sex matched with those of whites, showed evidence of higher blood pressure in blacks.[54] Beevers and Cruickshank[55] examined the frequency of admission for heart attack and stroke in Afro-Caribbeans, whites and Asians in 17,739 consecutive admissions to Dudley Road Hospital, Birmingham. These admissions were for 35–64 year old men and women for the years 1975–79. Rates per 1,000 admissions for heart attack by age group were favourable to blacks compared with Europeans and Asians. Admissions for strokes, however, showed consistently higher rates for blacks across all age groups.

In a study of ethnic differences in respiratory disease Jackson *et al.*[56] analysed 40,034 admissions, excluding obstetric admissions for patients aged 30–59 over a six-year period. The distribution of admission by ethnic group for each respiratory diagnosis indicated that Asians were more susceptible to TB and asthma than whites or blacks, whites suffered much more from carcinoma, while blacks had relatively low rates of respiratory disease. The clinical pattern of asthma in 2,331 children of European, Asian and West Indian parentage was reported by Morrison-Smith and Cooper.[57] The children were patients at the Central Birmingham Chest Clinic over a ten-year period. The main findings were that a higher proportion of children born in England of all races developed asthma within the first four years of life than children born abroad.

From the above examples it is impossible to draw any general conclusion about the state of ethnic health with respect to 'common disease'. This problem persists when we turn from 'physical' to 'mental' well-being.

MENTAL HEALTH

When attempting to examine the situation of Britain's black population with regard to their mental health, or more accurately mental ill health, several factors intervene to make such an exercise problematic. First, as in 'physical' health, statistical evidence is ad hoc and hard to come by.[58] NHS and official statistics, such as the Hospital In-Patient Mental Health Enquiry, do not give data by ethnic origin. However, in addition, psychiatry, the medical speciality dealing with this form of ill health, finds itself in the midst of debates about, amongst other issues, the status of the medical model as its paradigm, the validity of its diagnostic categories, and of its phenomenology and its practice.[59] Placed in this context, it is clear that inferences and interpretation of statistical evidence on mental health is limited by the lack of a common framework.

What measures are there to indicate the psychiatric state of Britain's black population? The most accessible is the number and characteristics of psychiatric hospital admissions. There are limitations to this measure however. The likelihood of mental hospital admission is influenced by many factors apart from any psychiatric illness displayed by a patient. Availability of beds, community attitudes, referral practices, other forms of treatment and so on, are all possible alternative determinants of admission to hospital.[60] With these limitations in mind we can look at the evidence available.

There have been two large admissions studies which included some measure of ethnic group in their data. Cochrane[61] analysed hospital admission data for England and Wales in 1971 and, after correction for age and sex differences, found that admission rates for Irish, Polish and Scottish immigrants were higher than that for the English-born. The rates for Indians and Pakistan-born were lower, whilst the rate for Caribbean immigrants was approximately the same as for the English-born. Dean et al.,[62] looking at first-time admissions in South-East England in 1976, found significantly higher admission rates for Afro-Caribbean males and females. This group had the highest admission rates of all his immigrant groups – over one-and-a-half times the expected numbers at age-specific UK-born rates. Dean also distinguished between people born in India, Pakistan and New Commonwealth Africa, the latter being mainly Ugandan Asians. They found that, for males, Indians had significantly higher admission rates than expected, whilst Pakistani men had a significantly lower rate. For females, admission rates were significantly higher for Indians and New Commonwealth Africans and again lower for those born in Pakistan. Both these studies suffered the limitation of using place of birth as the indicator of ethnicity, thus being unable to identify British-born blacks. In fact, very few studies look at ethnic group as opposed to place of birth. In addition, Cochrane did not have information on place of birth for 30 per cent of his sample while Deat *et al.* had missing data on 9 per cent of theirs.

Several smaller studies have looked at place of birth and admission rates.[63] Carpenter and Brockington[64] in a study of first-admissions in Manchester did not distinguish between Indians and Pakistanis and recorded significantly higher rates for the Asian group as a whole, over two-and-a-half times that for the native-born. The rates for the Afro-Caribbean-born were also significantly higher than for the British-born and this was found by Hemsi[65] and Rwgellera too.[66] Hitch[67] in Bradford found significantly higher admission rates for Pakistani women than for British-born but not for Indians.

However, once black people have been admitted to hospital, the situation as regards their diagnosis is clearer. Cochrane[68] found that West Indians, more than any other group, seemed to be diagnosed as schizophrenic. Indians, Pakistanis, Poles and West Indians were all shown to be more than one-and-a-half times as likely to be admitted with a diagnosis of schizophrenia – in the case of West Indians, the rate per 100,000 being 290 compared to that of 87 of those born in England and Wales. Dean *et al.*[69] show that, after acounting for age differences, Indian males are over three times as likely to be diagnosed as schizophrenic, New Commonwealth Africans (mainly Ugandan Asians) four times as likely and Afro-Caribbeans five times as likely than UK-born first admissions. This pattern is repeated in females, the relative rates being similar. Carpenter and Brockington[70] in Manchester also found higher rates of diagnosed schizophrenia in both Asian and Afro-Caribbean groups. Ineichen,[71] reviewing the literature, states that there is widespread evidence that mental illness among ethnic minorities in Britain contains more diagnosed psychosis than among natives. There also seems to be an underrepresentation of psychoneuroses and non-psychotic disorders. The two larger studies confirm this.[72]

Clearly then, blacks tend to be overrepresented at the 'harder' end of the diagnostic spectrum – that is, at the psychotic end. However, diagnosis has often presented psychiatry with problems. Clare[73] discussed the different patterns of diagnosis of schizophrenia in different countries, which lead, for example, to American psychiatrists diagnosing schizophrenia more readily than their British counterparts. Tewfik and Okasha[74] studied 124 West Indian immigrants admitted to hospital and found that, although schizophrenia was a common diagnostic label, only 18 per cent of the sample conformed to the classic description of the diagnosis. The remaining 85 per cent had atypical features which made the diagnostic label somewhat imprecise. Littlewood and Lipsedge[75] were able to reclassify many diagnosed schizophrenics to other diagnostic categories by use of a standardized interview. Given these problems with diagnosis, perhaps Rack's statement in his book, *Race, Culture and Mental Disorder*, that 'the statistics seem to show a high incidence of schizophrenia and paranoid psychoses in the immigrant groups (compensated in some groups by a low incidence of affective disorders and neuroses)'[76] should be seen in the light of the statements by Littlewood and Lipsedge who discuss this under-diagnosis of depressive disorders and go on to say: 'whatever the empirical justification, the frequent diagnosis in black patients of schizophrenia (bizarre, irrational, outside) and the infrequent diagnosis of depression (acceptable, understandable, inside) validates our stereotypes.'[77]

As seen above, the evidence on the mental health of Britain's black population is thin. However mental health issues have been of prominent concern to the black community and psychiatry has been seen by some in that community as a form of social control.[78] To examine this aspect perhaps it is as well to attempt to review the evidence relating to two questions asked by Mercer in his paper 'Black Communities' Experience of Psychiatric Services'.[79] First he posed the question 'how do black people come to the attention of psychiatry?' and second 'what happens to black people in their encounter with psychiatry?'

The evidence relating to both questions is again sparse. There are several routes to psychiatric services, amongst which are GP referrals, hospital referrals, self-referrals, referral by family or friends, or referrals where social workers or police have been involved. Under the Mental Health Act 1959 (and the more recent 1983 Act) patients could come to hospital either voluntarily or, in extreme cases, under a section of the Act where referral agencies have the legal power to enforce admission. Ineichen *et al.*[80] looked at all in-patient admissions throughout the city of Bristol during the period 1978–81. They found that there were high admission rates from the central urban areas of low social class and high black (mainly Afro-Caribbean) concentration. Ineichen also looked closely at the four inner-city wards of Bristol with the highest proportion of black residents. He found that, within these wards, 72 per cent of white UK admissions and 37 per cent of West Indian admissions were on a voluntary basis. The non-white groups together accounted for 36 per cent of compulsory admissions but only 17 per cent of voluntary admissions. Given that the non-white population of these wards was about 17 per cent, Ineichen states that non-whites seemed to be overrepresented among compulsory admissions. In particular, he goes on to state: 'West Indians may be especially over-represented among compulsory admissions and under-represented among voluntary admissions.' Hitch and Clegg[81] looking at first-time admissions in Bradford over a year found that New Commonwealth patients were more likely to reach hospital via the agencies of police or social workers than were UK-born patients. Rwgellera,[82] using the Camberwell Psychiatric Case Register,[83] looked at a group of West Indian and West African patients together with a matched sample of English patients. He found that significantly less black patients were referred by a GP than English ones. He also found that many West Indian patients were brought to psychiatric services by social workers or the police, the rest being self-referred or brought by relatives. In contrast, police or social workers were involved in very few English cases. Pinto[84] also found an excess of compulsory admissions of Asians in a sample drawn from the same source as Rwgellera. Lipsedge and Littlewood,[85] looking at one hospital, found that black patients were twice as likely as whites to be detained under Section 136 of the Mental Health Act (the clause which empowers the police to take people to psychiatric hospital). Black patients were also twice as likely as whites to have been admitted to that particular hospital from prison.

As to Mercer's second question, what happens to black people once they have contacted psychiatry, data on psychiatric treatment is notable for its paucity. Littlewood and Cross[86] looked at 240 adult psychiatric out-patients at an East London general hospital, classifying them as white UK-born, and immigrant and black (West Indian, African or Asian). They found that black patients were more likely to see junior members of staff (who tended to be black). They also found that black patients were more likely to be receiving major tranquillizers than white UK patients with a similar diagnosis. Black and white immigrant patients were more likely to have intra-muscular medication than the equivalent white British-born group and the average dose of medication was greater for black patients than for white patients, though the latter fact seemed to be due to a small group of black patients on exceptionally high doses of medication. Finally, black patients were more likely to receive electroconvulsive-therapy (ECT) without a diagnosis of depression and to receive ECT at least six times.

Bolton[87] examined the case notes of all 92 patients compulsorily detained under the Mental Health Act over a fifteen-month period in a South London psychiatric hospital. This study showed that West Indian and African patients were over four times as likely to be transferred to a high security unit (that is, a locked ward) than were the white English group. In addition, West Indians and Africans were more likely to be described as aggressive (which is associated with being transferred to a secure unit and all non-white groups were more likely to be described as unco-operative. Bolton found that British patients labelled as 'unco-operative' were in the open ward in significant numbers whilst similarly labelled West Indians, Asians and Africans more frequently went to the high security unit.

To summarize, the evidence on whether Britain's black population has a higher admission rate to psychiatric hospital is equivocal. They are more likely to come to hospital on a compulsory admission and police and social workers are more likely to be involved. Once admitted, they are more likely to be diagnosed as psychotic. The little available evidence on treatment shows also that they tend to be on harsher forms of medication than equivalent white groups and seem to be viewed differently once in hospital.

Thus, the overall picture seems grim. Why are black people overrepresented at the psychotic end of the diagnostic spectrum? Why do black people have a greater tendency to come into contact with psychiatric services by way of compulsory admission – and often with the involvement of the police and social work? Why is their treatment different? Such questions have not been answered in the literature. Ineichen[88] suggests that service delivery might be to blame, in the sense that the intervention of medical services comes too late, thus creating an emergency which is followed by compulsory admission. Members of the black community have questioned the role of the police in compulsory admissions[89] and in particular, question marks remain over the deaths of Richard Campbell, Winston Rose, Paul Worrel and Colin Roach.[90] A recent article on the death of Michael Dean Martin in his cell in Broadmoor Special Hospital (a special hospital catering for the 'criminally insane') makes disturbing reading.[91]

Several authors have discussed the possible reasons for any differences in the prevalence of mental illness among different 'immigrant' groups. Lipsedge and Littlewood[92] come to the conclusion that there appears to be no simple explanation for differential rates, although they say that five items contribute to differences in the relative frequency of mental illness, these being lack of community integration, status isolation, experience of discrimination, the under-reporting of illness and the possibility that the immigrants were mentally ill before coming to Britain. On the other hand Rack[93] argues that quantitative comparisons are so problematic and open to misinterpretation that qualitative differences should be concentrated on. However, it is interesting to note that very few authors have attempted to investigate the questions posed in the last paragraph. Indeed, few authors have investigated the role of stress as a causative factor in mental illness and, as a consequence, racism in such areas as employment, housing, education and childcare have not been adequately examined as causatory factors in mental illness.[94]

This section has looked at the most prominent areas of debate on mental health and race. It has omitted discussing areas such as symptomatology in the community,[95] aspects of the family[96-8] and so on. It is clear that, until more work is done in this area to alleviate some of the apparent inequalities in psychiatric care, mental health will be a cause of increasing concern to the black community.

CONCLUSIONS

The Black Report highlighted recent data which shows the gradients in mortality rates between occupational classes for all age groups and both sexes. This gradient is particularly steep in the first year of life, when up to four or five times as many babies die per 1,000 for 'unskilled manual' parents as for parents from the 'professional' classes. This class gradient persists for most causes of death and is particularly steep in the case of diseases of the respiratory system. Moreover, there has been a persistent lack of improvement in the health experience of the unskilled relative to Social Class I throughout the last 20 years. 'Inequalities exist also in the utilisation of health service, particularly and most worryingly of the preventative services. Here severe under-utilisation by the working classes is a complex result of under-provision in working class areas and of costs (financial and psychological) of attendance. . . .' Though working class people make more use of GP services, for themselves if not for their children, 'they may receive less good care. Moreover it is possible that this extra usage does not fully reflect the true differences in need for care . . .'[99] From other chapters of this book it will be clear that many immigrants and black British-born live in poor housing conditions in the inner cities and undertake unskilled or semi-skilled employment. One would thus expect many black Britons to suffer the health disadvantages of the working class. They endure working-class health inequality and then some more. The stillbirth perinatal and infant mortality rates are much higher for blacks than whites – even allowing for maternal age structure and parity and also, from the Birmingham and Northwick Park studies, allowing for social class. Indeed, some of these rates have deteriorated for members of the Pakistani and West Indian communities. The maternal mortality rate in the black population has been three times that in the white. Complications in pregnancy are greater and the incidence of low birthweight, with its implications of aberrant child development, much greater.

For the black population inequality also exists in the utilization of health services, particularly preventative services, and they may well receive less good care. As evidence one can cite the late bookings in pregnancy, fewer antenatal clinic visits and poorer quality of GP obstetric care. In addition, the NHS and government response to specific needs of the black community with respect to sickle cell disease and rickets is either lukewarm or absent. According to Rathwell,[100] the NHS has been slow to recognize that the health care requirements of ethnic minorities are different from those of the white population and that alleviation of these different health problems cannot occur unless there are substantial changes in the present pattern of care: a national policy is required. Many members of the black community see this 'slow recognition' as the inevitable consequence of institutionalized racism in the health services which affects patient care[101] and black employees.[102] This interpretation was supported by the *Guardian* headline 'Race discrimination widespread in NHS'[103] to a report on a preliminary study by the Commission for Racial Equality.

In response to these perceived problems in health care provision, self-help organizations formed by ethnic groups have been proliferating. Wilson[104] reports on groups such as the Black Health Workers and Patients Group, the Sickle Cell Society and the Afro-Caribbean Voluntary Help Association. In addition, many members of the Asian community make use of traditional treatments such as the Ayurvedic and Unani systems.[105]

The need for such groups is indicative of the gap in health care and changes must surely be made in health policy and care provided. Rathwell[106] suggests that administrators in District Health Authorities with sizeable ethnic populations should review service provision according to a number of specific considerations. These include the cultural differences and attitudes towards health and health care, the possible distrust of doctors and hospitals, the stigmas attached by some ethnic groups to certain diseases, the barriers imposed by language and experience of different life styles, the attitudes of those responsible for providing health care to ethnic minorities and the social and psychological stresses in attempting to adapt to the British way of life. McNaught[107] outlines an entire framework for a race relations policy in the NHS.

The NHS was designed to cater for a fairly homogeneous population but, as Mares *et al.* point out, '. . . over the last thirty years the composition of the population in many areas of Britain has changed significantly, and so too have health needs'.[108] In health care, as in other aspects, no civilized society can afford to ignore its ethnic minorities or assume or demand their assimilation into the dominant culture.

Notes

1. P. Townsend, N. Davidson (eds.), *Inequalities in Health*. (The Black Report), Harmondsworth: Penguine Books, 1982, p.58.
2. A. Skrimshire, *Area Disadvantage, Social Class and the Health Service*, Department of Social and Administrative Studies, University of Oxford, 1978.
3. The Black Report, op. cit., p.87.
4. M. Marmot, A. Adelstein and L. Bulusu. 'Immigrant Mortality in England and Wales 1970–78' *Population Trends 33*, OPCS, Autumn 1983; also M. G. Marmot, A. Adelstein, L. Bulusu, *Immigrant Mortality in England and Wales*, Studies in Medical and Population Subjects, no. 47, OPCS, 1984.
5. Marmot *et al.* 'Immigrant Mortality in England and Wales', op. cit.
6. DHSS, *Report on Confidential Enquiries into Maternal Deaths in England and Wales*, Reports on Health and Social Subjects no. 11, 1970–72 (1975); no. 14 1973–75 (1979); no. 26 1976–78 (1982).
7. A. M. Adelstein *et al.*, *Perinatal and Infant Mortality: Social and Biological Factors 1975–77*, Studies on Medical and Population Subjects no. 41, London: HMSO, 1980; OPCS, *Mortality Statistics: Perinatal and Infant: Social and Biological Factors*, Series DH3 no. 7, London: HMSO, 1982; OPCS, *Mortality Statistics: Perinatal and Infant: Social and Biological Factors*, Series DH3 no. 9, London: HMSO, 1983; OPCS, *Mortality Statistics: Perinatal and Infant: Social and Biological Factors*, Series DH3 no. 13, London: HMSO, 1985; OPCS, *Infant and Perinatal Mortality 1983: Birthweight* Monitor, DH3 85/1, London: HMSO, 1985; OPCS, *Infant and Perinatal Mortality 1984: Birthweight* Monitor, DH3 86/1 London: HMSO, 1986.
8. House of Commons Second Report from the Social Services Committee 1979–80, *Perinatal and Neonatal Mortality* (The Short Report), vol I, London: HMSO, 1980.
9. M. Wynn and A. Wynn, *Prevention of Handicap and the Health of Women*, RKP 1979; also M. Wynn and A. Wynn, *The Prevention of Handicap of Early Pregnancy Origin*, FERC, 1981.
10. OPCS Monitor DH3 84/5, *Birthweight Statistics 1983*, London: HMSO, 1984; OPCS Monitor DH3 85/6, *Birthweight Statistics 1984*, London: HMSO, 1985.
11. P. Terry and R. Condie 'Ethnic Differences in Perinatal Mortality', *Postgraduate Medical Journal*, vol 57, 1981, pp. 790–1.
12. P. Terry, R. Condie and R. Settatree, 'Analysis of Ethnic Differences in Perinatal Statistics, *British Medical Journal*, no. 281, 1980, p.1307.
13. R. Settatree, P. Terry, P. Mathew and R. Condie, 'Asian Stillbirths in West Birmingham', *Obstetric Problems of the Asian Community in Britain (OPACB)*, RCOG, 1982.
14. A. Haines *et al.* 'Birthweight and Complications of Pregnancy in an Asian Population', *OPACB*, RCOG, 1982.
15. Ibid., p. 125.

16. R. Barnes, 'Perinatal Mortality and Morbidity Rates in Bradford', *OPACB*, RCOG, 1982.
17. H. Dhariwal, 'Leicestershire – Decline in Perinatal Mortality', *OPACB*, RCOG, 1982.
18. J. Studd *et al.*, 'Labour in Patients of Different Racial Groups', *OPACB*, RCOG, 1982.
19. Barnes op. cit.
20. M. Clarke, 'The Quality and Organisation of Medical Care Provided to Immigrants in Pregnancy in Leicestershire', OPACB, RCOG, 1982.
21. M. Clarke and D. Clayton 'The Quality of Obstetric Care Provided for Asian Immigrants in Leicestershire', *British Medical Journal*, no. 286, 1983, p. 621.
22. Ibid., p. 622.
23. The Black Report, op. cit., p. 123.
24. Community Relations Commission, *Evidence to the Royal Commission on the National Health Service*, London: CRC, 1977.
25. N. Torkington, *The Racial Politics of Health – A Liverpool Profile*, Merseyside Area Profile Group, University of Liverpool, 1983.
26. Ibid., p. 32.
27. P. Roberts *et al.*, 'Vitamin B12 Status in Pregnancy among Immigrants to Britain', *British Medical Journal*, no. 67, 1973, p. 3.
28. P. Clarke and N. Clare, 'Sickle-Cell Anaemia: A Challenge to Health Education', *Health Education Council Journal*, vol. 40, no. 2, 1981, p. 50.
29. Torkington, op. cit., p. 39.
30. Ibid., p. 36.
31. E. Anionwu *et al.*, 'Sickle-Cell Disease in a British Urban Community, *British Medical Journal*, no. 282, 1981, p. 283.
32. S. Tuck, 'Sickle-cell disease and pregnancy', *British Journal of Hospital Medicine*, August 1982, p. 125.
33. Torkington, op. cit.
34. Ibid., p. 43.
35. L. Patterson, 'Vitamin D and the Asian community', *Medicine in Society*, vol. 7, no. 4, p. 27.
36. H. Sheiham and A. Quick, *The Rickets Report*, Haringey CHC, 1982.
37. DHSS, *Rickets and Osteomalacia*, Report of the Working Party on Fortification of Food with Vitamin D; Committee on Medical Aspects of Food Policy (COMA) London: HMSO, 1980.
38. K. Goel *et al.*, 'Florid and Sub Clinical Rickets among Immigrant Children in Glasgow', *Lancet*, no. 1, 1976, p. 1141.
39. J. Ford *et al.*, *Clinical and Sub Clinical Vitamin D Deficiency in Bradford Children*, Archives of Dis. Child., 1976, p. 939.
40. M. Preece *et al.*, 'Studies of Vitamin D Deficiency in Man' *Quarterly Journal of Medicine*, no. 44, 1975, p. 575.
41. T. Stamp, 'Sources of Vitamin D Nutrition', *Lancet*, no. 1, 1980, p. 316.
42. Patterson, op. cit., p. 28.
43. N. Singleton and S. Tucker, 'Vitamin D Status of Asian Infants', *British Medical Journal*, no. 1, 1978, p. 607.
44. Sheiham and Quick, op. cit., p. 15.
45. M. G. Dunnigan, B. M. Glekin, J. B. Henderson, W. B. McIntosh, D. Summer, G. R. Sutherland, 'Prevention of Rickets in Asian Children: An

Assessment of the Glasgow Campaign', *British Medical Journal*, vol. 291, p. 239.

46. COMA, op. cit., p. 44.
47. K. Jones, *Immigrants and Social Services*, London: National Institute of Economic Review, 1967.
48. OPCS and CDSC, *Communicable Disease Statistics 1983: England and Wales*, Series MB2 no. 10, London: HMSO, 1984.
49. J. Darbyshire, 'We don't have tuberculosis in this country any more . . . do we?', *Maternal and Child Health*, vol. 8, no. 5, 1983.
50. MRC, 'National Survey of Tuberculosis Notification in England and Wales 1978–79', *British Medical Journal*, vol. 281, 1980, pp. 895–8.
51. A. Nunn *et al.*, 'Changes in Tuberculosis Notification Rates in the White Ethnic Group in England between 1971 and 1978–79', forthcoming.
52. Darbyshire, op. cit., p. 181.
53. D. Beevers, 'Introduction' to Proceedings of the Conference on Ethnic Differences in Common Disease, *Postgraduate Medical Journal*, vol. 57, 1981, p. 747.
54. P. Sever, 'Racial Differences in Blood Pressure: Genetic and Environmental Factors', *Postgraduate Medical Journal*, vol. 57, 1981, pp. 755–9.
55. D. Beevers and J. Cruickshank, 'Age, Sex, Ethnic Origin and Hospital Admission for Heart Attack and Stroke', *Postgraduate Medical Journal*, vol. 57, 1981, pp. 763–5.
56. S. Jackson *et al.*, 'Ethnic Differences in Respiratory Disease' *Postgraduate Medical Journal*, vol. 57, 1981, pp. 777–8.
57. J. Morrison-Smith and S. Cooper, 'Asthma and Atopic Disease in Immigrants from Asia and the West Indies', *Postgraduate Medical Journal*, vol. 57, 1981, pp. 774–6.
58. L. A. Doyal, 'A Matter of Life and Death: Medicine, Health and Statistics' in J. Miles and J. Evans (eds.), *Demystifying Social Statistics*, London: Pluto Press, 1979.
59. P. Sedgwick, *Psychopolitics*, London: Pluto Press, 1982; Doyal, op. cit., note 51; Black Health Workers and Patients Group, 'Psychiatry and the Corporate State', *Race and Class*, vol. 25, 1983, pp.49–64.
60. P. J. Hitch and P. Clegg, 'Modes of Referral of Overseas Immigrant and Native-born First Admissions to Psychiatric Hospital', *Social Scientific Medicine*, vol. 14A, 1980, pp. 369–74.
61. R. Cochrane, 'Mental Illness in Immigrants to England and Wales: An Analysis of Mental Hospital Admissions 1971', *Social Psychiatry*, vol. 12, 1977, pp. 2–35.
62. G. Dean, D. Walsh, H. Downing and P. Shelley, 'First Admissions of Native-born and Immigrants to Psychiatric Hospitals in South-east England, 1976', *British Journal of Psychiatry*, vol. 139, 1981, pp. 506–12.
63. B. Ineichen, 'Mental Illness among New Commonwealth Migrants to Britain' in A. Boyce (ed.), *Mobility and Migration*, London: Taylor Francis, 1980.
64. L. Carpenter and I. F. Brockington, 'A Study of Mental Illness in Asians, West Indians and Africans Living in Manchester', *British Journal of Psychiatry*, vol. 137, 1980, pp. 201–5.
65. L. K. Hemsi, 'Psychiatric Morbidity of West Indian Immigrants', *Social Psychiatry*, vol. 2, 1967, pp. 95–100.

66.   G. G. C. Rwgellera, 'Psychiatric Morbidity among West Africans and West Indians Living in London', *Psychological Medicine*, vol. 7, 1977, pp. 317–29.

67.   P. Hitch, 'Immigration and Mental Health: Local Research and Social Explanations', *New Community*, vol. 9, 1981, pp. 256–62.

68.   Cochrane op.cit., note 56.

69.   Dean *et al.*, op.cit., note 57.

70.   L. Carpenter and I. F. Brockington, op.cit., note 59.

71.   Ineichen, op.cit., 1980, note 58.

72.   Cochrane, op.cit., note 56; Dean *et al.*, op.cit., note 57.

73.   A. Clare, *Psychiatry in Dissent*, London: Tavistock, 1976.

74.   G. I. Tewfik and A. Okasha, 'Psychosis and Immigration', *Postgraduate Medical Journal*, vol. 41, 1965, pp. 603–12.

75.   R. K. Littlewood and M. Lipsedge, *Aliens and Alienists*, Harmondsworth: Penguin, 1982.

76.   P. Rack, *Race, Culture and Mental Disorder*, London: Tavistock, 1982.

77.   Littlewood and Lipsedge, op.cit., note 71.

78.   Black Health Workers and Patients Group, op. cit., note 54.

79.   K. Mercer, 'Black Communities Experience of Psychiatric Services', *International Journal of Social Psychiatry*, vol. 30, 1984, pp. 22–7.

80.   B. Ineichen, G. Harrison and H. G. Morgan, 'Psychiatric Hospital Admissions in Bristol. Geographical and Ethnic Factors', *British Journal of Psychiatry*, vol. 145, 1984, pp. 600–11.

81.   Hitch and Clegg, op cit., note 55.

82.   G. G, C. Rwgellera, 'Differential use of Psychiatric Services by West Indians, West Africans and English in London', *British Journal of Psychiatry*, vol. 137, 1980, pp. 428–32.

83.   J. K. Wing and A. M. Haile (eds.), *Evaluating a Community Psychiatric Service: The Camberwell Register 1964–1971*, London: Oxford University Press, 1972.

84.   R. T. Pinto, 'A Study of Asians in the Camberwell Area', M. Phil dissertation, University of London, 1970.

85.   M. Lipsedge and R. K. Littlewood, *Compulsory Hospitalisation and Minority Status*, 11th Biennial Conference of the Caribbean Federation for Mental Health, Gosier, Guadeloupe, 1977.

86.   R. K. Littlewood and S. Cross, 'Ethnic Minorities and Psychiatric Services', *Sociology of Health and Illness*, no. 2, 1980, pp. 194–201.

87.   P. Bolton, 'Management of Compulsorily Admitted Patients to a High Security Unit', *International Social Psychiatry*, vol. 30, 1984, pp. 77–84.

88.   Ineichen *et al.*, op. cit., note 77.

89.   Black Health Workers and Patients Group, op.cit., note 54.

90.   Mercer, op.cit., note 75.

91.   E. Frances, 'Death at Broadmoor – The Case of Michael Martin', *Bulletin of the Transcultural Society* (UK) no. 7, 1985, pp. 7–11.

92.   Lipsedge and Littlewood, op.cit., note 71.

93.   Rack, op.cit., note 72.

94.   Mercer, op.cit., note 75.

95.   R. Cochrane and M. Stopes-Roe, 'Psychological Symptom Levels in Indian Immigrants to England – A Comparison with Native English', *Psychological Medicine*, vol. 1, 1981, pp. 319–27; P. E. Bebbington, J. Hurry and C.

Tennant, 'Psychiatric Disorders in Selected Immigrant Groups in Camberwell', *Social Psychiatry*, vol.16, 1981, pp. 43–51.
96. A. W. Burke, 'Attempted Suicide among Asian Immigrants to Birmingham', *British Journal of Psychiatry*, no. 128, 1976, pp. 528–33.
97. A. W. Burke, 'Socio-cultural Determinants of Attempted-Suicide among West Indians in Birmingham: Ethnic Origin and Immigrant Status', *British Journal of Psychiatry*, no. 129, 1976.
98. A. W. Burke, 'Family Stress and the Precipitation of Psychiatric Disorder', *International Journal of Social Psychiatry*, vol. 26, 1980, pp. 35–40.
99. The Black Report, op.cit., p. 206.
100. T. Rathwell, 'Health Planning for Ethnic Minorities: Meeting Needs', *Medicine in Society*, vol. 7, no. 4, pp. 14–15.
101. Brent Community Health Council, *Black People and the Health Service*, Brent CHC, 1981.
102. D. Smith, *Overseas Doctors in the National Health Service*, Heinemann, 1980.
103, *The Guardian* 7 January 1984.
104. M. Wilson, 'Health Care for Ethnic Groups: Networking for Health', *Health and Social Service Journal*, 12 May 1983, pp. 565–7.
105. M. Aslan and M. Healey, 'Present and Future Trends in the Health Care of British-Asian Children', *Nursing Times*, 11 August 1982, pp. 1353–4.
106. Rathwell, op.cit.
107. A. McNaught, *Race and Health Care in the United Kingdom*, Occasional Paper no. 2 Health Education Council, 1985.
108. P. Mares, A. Henley and C. Baxter, *Health Care in Multiracial Britain*, Health Education Council National Extension College, 1985, p. 8.

8

Social Services*

Philip Roys

INTRODUCTION

Writing in 1978, an ADSS/CRE working group concluded that 'the
response of social services departments to the existence of multi-
racial communities has been patchy, piecemeal and lacking in
strategy'.[1]

Almost a decade later this conclusion is still valid and social
services are the subject of criticism, not only from establishment
bodies, but also from members of the black communities, whose
experience of their operation is frequently negative. As Mercer
states:

> Social workers inspect our families, keep them under surveillance
> and at the last resort have the power to take children from their

* This chapter has emerged from my involvement in the Ethnic Study Group at
St George's Hospital, and I am grateful for the stimulation and support of all its
members, but especially Aggrey Burke.

Ashok Bhat provided invaluable criticism and encouragement, and without his
help I doubt that I would have completed the task. I would also like to thank
Sushel Ohri for his comments.

Any errors of fact and judgement are, of course, my responsibility.

parents and into care . . . you dont have to take an anti-social work stance to be aware of how some of the functions of social work reproduce and reinforce institutional racism.[2]

The 1980s have witnessed a higher profile for black politics; uprisings in the inner cities and the entry of a number of black people into the formal political process are leading to a challenge to white-dominated institutions. This has resulted in social services provision for the black population receiving increased attention in professional literature and political debate. But in only a few local authority departments is such attention beginning to be systematically translated into policy and practice; the general picture is of services and institutions failing to offer an adequate response to the needs of the black communities.

One of the consequences of this lack of attention is the relative paucity of hard and reliable research data. In this respect, little seems to have changed since the first edition of this work.[3] In 1983 the CRE, in its evidence to the House of Commons Select Committee, stated 'it is difficult to obtain reliable statistical information about children and adolescents in care'.[4] In other areas of social services provision, the same problem arises.

Thus, although in this chapter reference will be made to formal studies where they exist, given their scarcity, it will also be necessary to rely on the *impressions* of those involved in social services both as workers and consumers. Such impressions, although not an adequate substitute for more rigorous enquiry, can nevertheless provide a valuable supplement to that research which is available.

THE PRESENT POSITION

There is evidence to suggest that black consumers are underrepresented as clients receiving the preventative and supportive elements of social services provision. David Duncan observes, 'Asian communities make up 30% of the population of a typical inner-city area in Birmingham yet comprise only 8% of referrals to social services in an average month'.[5]

A recent investigation into the circumstances of the black communities in Handsworth[6] suggested that:

It is constantly being stated that few black elderly are coming to the notice of Social Services – even when some contact is made various practices and assumptions perpetuate the invisibility of black people. For example, the myth that black elderly are supported by a wide variety of community organisations, and the extended family.[7]

Such *underrepresentation* of black people in the supportive aspects of social services may help to explain *overrepresentation* in those aspects of social services activity which involve overt social control and institutionalization. In childcare for example, in 1982 a study of an area team in a northern city showed that the rates of children in care were 20.16 per 1,000 for white children; 24.32 per 1,000 for Afro-Caribbean children and a staggering 142.24 per 1,000 for children of mixed parentage.[8] In another local authority 54 per cent of its children in care were black, although black children comprised 47 per cent of the child population and blacks only 19 per cent of the population of the authority concerned.[9]

The reasons for this disturbing state of affairs are complex, but it can be argued that black consumers may enter a downward spiral, resulting in statutory intervention which might have been avoided were extensive and effective services available at an earlier stage.

Preventative and supportive measures can obviate the need for formal intervention by social services; the provision of counselling, day care and welfare rights advice may, for example, make it unnecessary to take a child into care. However, it appears that 'although social workers are initially accepted with trust and deference, the experience of social work and social workers which many black clients have are alienating ones'.[10] Relying on studies undertaken by Robinson[11] and Burke,[12] Bagley and Young conclude that the clients of social services 'often emerge from their experience angry and alienated. It appears that many black people have contact with social services only in the most desperate circumstances.'[13]

Given negative experiences of white institutions, black people may prefer not to approach social services except as a last resort. Thus, they may struggle to cope with difficulties with which they might have received help, were social services more responsive. Contact may, however, occur at a later stage, either when the situation is so desperate that help must be sought or when social services intervene to exercise statutory responsibilities (for example to take a child into care). Whether such later contact has been initiated by the client or by social services, the outcome is less likely to be satisfactory than if effective help had been available at an earlier stage.

In the field of metal health, Mercer suggests that:

social workers rather than adopting an imperialist attitude to intervention in the black family are reluctant to intervene until a distressing situation has reached crisis point – the effect of non-intervention is to leave the field open to more repressive agencies as attention for blacks only arrives when the black subject is already on the threshold of criminalisation.[14]

At whatever stage contact takes place, there is evidence that black consumers may not receive an acceptable standard of service from white workers. Not only is there the possibility of overt racism, but also 'liberal overcompensation' may lead to neglect by default. Some white workers may be confused and guilty about the issue of race to the extent that their normal professional capacities are suspended. This can lead to serious consequences. Giving evidence to the inquiry into the death of Jasmine Beckford, Mr Phil Sealy commented '. . . in my view there was an over-compensating approach in order to identify with this black family . . . in certain respects, this involved too liberal a professional outlook'. He believed that if the family had not been black, 'social workers would not have accepted their excuses, or, if there had been black social workers, they would not have accepted them'.[15]

The outcome of such confusion may not always be so tragic, but there are questions about the extent to which white workers are able to offer an effective response to black consumers.[16]

When *services* are provided there is evidence that they may be inadequate or frankly distressing to those receiving them. The Handsworth report suggests that:

. . . there is a general lack of cultural awareness. Asian elderly are not asked whether they want to pray in the afternoon. Not only do they have to put up with the lack of awareness of the

211

staff, but black elderly also have to cope with the attitude of other residents.[17]

The report cites the example of the single black resident of an old people's home who was 'spending his days wandering around the home because white residents kept telling him to go away'.[18]

The practice of transracial adoption has provoked particular criticism.

As the proportion of children in care who were black rose, itself indicating the tremendous socio-economic pressures upon the black family and the stigmatising attitudes of many white-dominated welfare agencies, the black community came to believe that it was a net donor of its most precious assets to white families. The self-respect and sense of self determination of the community has been threatened by a situation whereby most of its children in care were growing up either in white families or in white controlled residential settings.[19]

This chapter seeks to explain why, despite the fact that a substantial black population has been settled in Britain for over 30 years and despite the existence of many liberal-minded practitioners within social services, provision for the black communities give such cause for concern in so many areas.

It is clear that, although the needs of black consumers are receiving increased attention an *assimilationist* perspective still dominates much policy and practice. Where change has occurred this has tended to amount to piecemeal concessions deriving from the model of *cultural diversity*. It will be argued that both these models offer inadequate perspectives from which to approach the needs of black social services consumers and have contributed to the neglect of provision for the black population. It is only when the issue of *race* is taken seriously that there is any real prospect of this neglect being remedied.

Such a perspective, having race as its central concern, not only provides an explanation for the current neglect of the interests of the black communities but identifies key aspects of institutional organization and service delivery which require urgent attention if the neglect of black interests is to be addressed.

ASSIMILATION

A recent newspaper report from Kent explicitly states an attitude which is frequently held, but perhaps only rarely openly stated:

> Gravesham Cllr Thomas [said] 'I am getting fed up with all this talk about ethnic minorities. It is high time people from other countries who come here to live adapted themselves to our laws and did not try to live as separate groups. Integration must come from the minorities who choose to live here'.

The *assimilationist* perspective suggests that existing institutional arrangements and service provision are adequate and do not require any modification and change. Essentially, proponents of this position argue that it is the responsibility of the black communities to make any necessary adjustments in order to accommodate to British society and institutions. It follows that policy-makers and practitioners have no responsibility to examine institutional arrangements or services provided to ensure that they meet the needs of the black population.

A '*colour blind*' approach to service delivery is proposed. Social services are provided for those who are defined to be in need or disadvantage in some way and are organized around categories of need; children at risk, the mentally handicapped and the elderly for example. Members of the black communities who require services would simply be allocated to existing categories of need. The possibility of significant differences between black and white consumers within these categories which may indicate a need for modification or substantial change to the services provided is not recognized, nor is consideration given to the possibility that entirely new services might be necessary.

Given the emphasis on assimilation and the wish to deny differences between black and white, it is not surprising that attempts to argue for modification of services of institutions frequently evoke a defensive response from assimilationists which pejoratively equates differential treatment with apartheid and separate development. Such a response may derive in part from the 'unusual convergence of socialist and liberal thought'[20] referred to by Cheetham.

Socialists tend to argue that poor blacks and whites share the common heritage of the working class and that their problems are best tackled by revolutionary and other means. The achievement of this goal depends on the power of a united working class. Liberals argue that colour, racial and ethnic differences should not be regarded as overriding objects of concern because this denies a common humanity. A colour blind approach is the one most likely to ensure equal treatment.[21]

Such an approach fails to recognize that race has a significance in British society which, to some degree, is independent of social class and denies the different economic and cultural experience of black and white. For example, social deprivation alone cannot account for the disproportionate numbers of black children in care. A study, reported by Ouseley,

> . . . indicated that black families with children in care were different in their economic and housing situations to white families with children in care. Whereas white families in this situation were atypical of most white families in Lambeth, black families were very representative of black families in the borough, covering a wide range of income, employment and housing conditions.[22]

That the assimilationist perspective is the dominant paradigm in most social service departments is underlined by the CRE's submission to the House of Commons Social Services Select Committee Inquiry into children in care.

> It has perhaps been the inability (or unwillingness) of agencies to face up to the diversity that has given an edge to expressions of concern as to the difficulties of social work with ethnic minority clients. Concern about insensitive social work intervention which increases, rather than solves, family problems has led to social services being characterized by the leader of one black organization as a 'bane to the West Indian community'.[23]

They go on to say:

214

The incoherence, absence of strategies and lack of effective concern on the part of social services are particularly worrying, and when considering additional problems faced by many ethnic minority communities in Britain. It is clear from several studies that many Afro-Caribbean and Asian families suffer from the stress caused by racism, both personal and institutional, of contemporary Britain.[24]

Why, given the clear neglect of the black community in its midst and the clamour for change, have social services remained 'colour blind'? One important factor is the lack of blacks in the political, managerial and professional institutions whose activities determine the scope of, and priorities in, social services provision.

However, one also has to see that social services are a part of the state and, as Sivanandan has argued about the Immigration Acts:

They had stemmed from an economic rationale, fashioned in the matrix of colonial-capitalist practices and beliefs. They served to take racial discrimination out of the market-place and institution-alise it – inhere it in the structures of the state, locally and nationally.[25]

Such an anlaysis could equally apply to social services.

In recession, and in a political climate which is unsympathetic to welfare, social services policy-makers are defending the status quo and consequently adopting an assimilationist position by default.

INTEGRATION

An overt or covert assimilationist position may still characterize the practices of many social services agencies. However, perhaps as a result of the challenges to, and questioning of, British institutions by members of the black population and because of the personal and professional experiences of social services practitioners, another perspective is becoming common. According to Denney:

..it was after the riots in the late 1950's that the notion of

215

integration was increasingly heard. This implies that there had to be some attempt on the part of the 'host' community to understand the difficulties faced by black people.[26]

Denney quotes Roy Jenkins, the Home Secretary in 1966, who defined integration 'not as a flattering process of assimilation, but as equal opportunity accompanied by cultural diversity in an atmosphere of mutual tolerance'.[27]

Such a perspective has informed academic aspects of mainstream social policy since the 1960s, but it is only recently that social services institutions have begun to examine the implications of policy and practice for the black population. This approach emphasizes *cultural diversity* and focuses on the relevance of differences in language and culture for service provision, implying the need for changes in services to take account of such differences.

CULTURAL DIVERSITY

To a degree it is not difficult for policy-makers and practitioners to embrace the notion of cultural diversity; it can be viewed as consistent with the tradition in social work which advocates respect for individual differences. Thus, modifications to service delivery which take into account issues of language, diet, religious and cultural belief are at least in principle acceptable to many policy-makers and planners. Indeed, as Denney argues, 'the cultural position . . . crystallised into a powerful current within social work thought.'[28]

Roger Ballard's important paper[29] provides one of the best-argued statements of this position. He criticizes the 'colour blind' approach to practice suggesting that this can mask a form of cultural imperialism with assimilationist implications. Essentially Ballard argues that Britain is a multicultural society and that

. . . a straightforward process of assimilation is not taking place. The 'immigrant' minorities are sustaining culturally destructive patterns of social relations.[30]

. . . it is becoming increasingly evident that distinct and separate

216

patterns of behaviour are being sustained by the second generation minority groups.[31]

For the practitioner the question of whether the minorities ought or ought not to remain ethnically distinct should be irrelevant. The fact is that they are.[32]

Thus, the approach to practice of those that hold this view, is of attempting to overcome the linguistic and cultural barriers which prevent understanding, thereby achieving more sensitive and responsive services.

What then do the proponents of cultural diversity recommend to overcome these problems? Interestingly, their prescriptions are generally vague and unspecific. Ballard urges workers to adopt a stance of 'cultural relativity':

> . . . such a perspective makes it possible to avoid making judgements about the relative merits of cultural systems. It presents a realisation that cultures must be seen as systematic totalities and that an attempt to evaluate single elements in isolation is meaningless.[33]

But, apart from commending a general orientation, Ballard is reluctant to offer more detailed remedies:

> . . . the fact is that information on the values of internal structures of the minorities is still in very short supply, it would be presumptuous, as well as premature, to lay down detailed prescriptions as to how more ethnically sensitive services might be provided.[34]

In practice, the main solutions that cultural diversity has offered are specialist staff recruitment and training.

Section 11 funding

Many authorities have recruited specialist workers under the provisions of Section 11 of the 1966 Local Government Act. This permits the Home Office to fund 75 per cent of a post of which at least 50 per cent is devoted to work with residents who are defined as originating from the 'New Commonwealth'.

Although such posts may help to increase the sensitivity of social services departments to the needs of minority communities, the use of Section 11 funding can be criticized.

There is evidence that such funding has not always been used for the purposes for which it was intended. Inadequate monitoring by central and local government has sometimes led to funds being employed to sustain mainstream provision rather than to improve services for the minority communities.[35] It remains to be seen whether more stringent monitoring procedures recently introduced by central government will reduce or eliminate any further abuse.[36]

Such posts also carry the danger that work with minority communities can become marginalized. Rather than methodically examining the scope and relevance of mainstream provision, authorities may define work with such communities as a specialism which can be left to a few relatively junior specialist workers. The authority can satisfy itself and potential critics that the needs of minority communities are being attended to when, in fact, no thorough attempt has been made to evaluate their needs.

Some workers appointed to Section 11 posts appear to face unreasonable and unrealistic expectations, occupying an uncomfortable position between minority communities requiring more sensitive services and an unresponsive institution. Ballard suggests that

. . . many professionals drawn from the minorities resent being treated as ethnic specialists, feeling that they are being pushed into a kind of ghetto, dealing with second-class cases in a backwater, from which they believe that they would have great difficulty in achieving promotion to more senior posts.[37]

A further problem with Section 11 funding is the notion that the special needs exist because of emigration from the 'New Commonwealth'. While it is true that such emigration can give rise to particular difficulties, there is no reason to suppose that, once communities have become established in Britain, special needs disappear. Increasing numbers of the members of the minority communities have been born in the UK and, as Ballard argues, 'distinct and separate patterns of behaviour are being sustained by

218

the second generation minority groups'.[38] Section 11 funding appears to be based on an assimilationist premise which is likely to become increasingly irrelevant as second-and third-generation minority group members predominate.

Cultural diversity and training

Those who adopt a culturalist perspective also generally place emphasis on the importance of raising the level of cultural awareness amongst workers, both on initial training courses and via in-service training. Such an approach is strongly commended by Ballard.[39] However, while, on superficial examination, such a proposal seems reasonable, closer exploration reveals certain substantial difficulties and dangers. A central problem is what precisely should be taught. Unless enormous resources are spent on linguistic and ethnographic instruction, it is unlikely that the awareness of practitioners can be increased to the extent that they are properly equipped to deal with the whole range of issues and problems they are likely to encounter. Nevertheless, even if such resources were available, ignoring race as a central issue would make such training of limited value.

The typical training event is currently two or three days in length. Unless conducted in a particularly skilled and sensitive fashion such brief courses may give rise to as many difficulties as they attempt to solve. In the first place, there is the danger of disseminating negative stereotypes. According to Shama Ahmed:

> . . . the strengths of black cultures are rarely commented on and all too often subsumed into the 'deficit', the union of many Asian families is criticised for 'male dominance' and the protective support of some Afro-Caribbean mothers viewed as 'too strong'.[40]

This can lead to 'cultural racism' in which cultural constructions are adopted with a negative connotation.

Shama Ahmed suggests that, when working with Asian girls, social workers typically focus narrowly on notions of 'generation gap' and 'family conflict'.

Expressed desire by some Asian girls for freedom on a western model is uncritically accepted. Asian girls are rarely counselled to look critically at their aspirations to reflect whether in rebelling they are adopting a 'white model' strategy to resist racism.[41]

Even if negative stereotyping of cultures is avoided, there is a danger that students will take away cultural constructions which can rapidly become obsolete. Cultures are constantly changing (perhaps particularly so following migration) and such brief training courses may lead to the construction of unhelpful and inaccurate stereotypes.

Although avoiding negative stereotyping is essential there is also the danger of taking students too far in the other direction. Given that an underlying message of such training programmes may be that of respecting the strengths of cultures (cultural relativism), there is the possibility of encouraging an uncritical approach to practice, which assumes cultural strength and ignores the emotional and material factors which may, in certain circumstances, inhibit the capacity of a culture to care for its members and lead them to need social services. The belief that the extended family generally has the material and emotional resources to meet the needs of family members, and that intervention or support from social services are not therefore required, is one not uncommon assumption which can lead to neglect by default.

Finally, underlying the prominence given to training by the advocates of culturalism is the dangerous notion that, by itself, training can ensure the development of services able to meet the needs of the black communities. Contentious questions concerning the recruitment of black staff and the development of substantially modified and new services may be ignored in favour of relatively comfortable forays into social anthropology,

The limitations of cultural diversity

Despite the increasing influence of the culturalist perspective, as far as most authorities are concerned, little impact was seen to be made upon existing policies and practices. In her recent survey of six social services authorities, Connelly reports 'we were not aware of discussions having taken place in any of the six departments about strategy for social services provision to meet the needs of ethnic communities'.[42] She reports examples of the establishment of ethnic playgroups, changes in the diet available at day and residential centres and in the meals on wheels service and the provision of language classes and interpreters. Some attempts had been made to provide a more sensitive service at the time of the possible reception of a child into care: 'practitioners . . . spoke of working longer and harder to avoid taking a child into care – and of increasing flexibility so that, for example, a child might be placed with grandparents'.[43] But 'most of this change has been incremental, a gradual response by individual practitioners to a situation they saw as new and requiring a response somewhat different from that in use'.[44] There is therefore, no evidence of a coherent and systematic attempt to respond to cultural diversity by social services institutions; where the existence of minority communities has been recognized, this seems to have led to confusion, uncertainty and piecemeal change rather than to a systematic evaluation of the relevance of existing provision.

Thus, cultural diversity seems not to have significantly impinged on the assimilationist position. However, were it to do so, there would be obvious major objections to this approach.

The primary objection to cultural diversity as an organizing principle is that it ignores the material and political realities of contemporary Britain. The difficulties faced by the black population are the result not only of migration and differences in culture and language but also of living in a society which is hostile to black people, denies them equal life chances and can expose them to enormous material and psychological pressure. The clients of social services present with not only linguistic and cultural complexities, but also with the profound effects of racism. In order to offer effective help social services institutions must therefore be sensitive not only to language and culture but also to the processes of racism.

The model presented by the proponents of cultural diversity ignores the question of race and adopts a naive belief that minority cultures can be insulated from political and economic realities. Despite the fact that a substantial black population has been settled for over a quarter of a century, there is no evidence to suggest a willingness on the part of the majority population to accommodate cultural differences, especially when these adversely affect their material interests.

Much space has been devoted to the culturalist approach since, at the present time, most of the attempts to challenge the assimilationist position by white bodies come from this perspective. However, it is evident that this approach has failed to achieve even the limited goal of culturally and linguistically sensitive services. To explain this failure it is necessary to understand the social and political context in which this plurality of cultures and social services institutions exist.

RACE AND RACISM

This wider context is focused upon by the perspective of race and racism. This position states that Britain is not a culturally pluralist society but one in which the majority culture, being more powerful, is able to impose its version of reality upon, and advance its material interests against, minority groups. As Shama Ahmed argues, 'In British Society there is a hierarchy of cultures and cultures of racial minority groups are ranked very low indeed.'[45] The long history of denigration of, and discrimination against, minority racial groups has led to contemporary social relations being structured not only by class but also by race.

Relationships between ethnic groups must be seen in the context of the history of colonialism and of the pattern of recent immigration to the UK.

Driven to this country by endemic poverty, black people were actively encouraged to migrate to Britain in order to fill a gap in the British post-war labour market. On arriving they found themselves living in substandard housing, taking the jobs rejected by the white population.[46]

The first generation struggled to build a life in a hostile society but as economic recession replaced boom

. . . a new generation of black people had grown up in the 'colonies' of our inner cities [who] were less willing to be deferential to white society. Between the late 1960's and early 1970's distinct movements of resistance to racism developed, until the recent events in Toxteth, Brixton and other urban centres the lid had been kept on the situation. However, despite various forms of state intervention both coercive and consensual the structural conditions remain . . . [47]

Elsewhere in this volume, reference has been made to the relative material disadvantages of the black communities. Blacks tend to live in poorer quality housing,[48] and to have higher rates of unemployment and for longer periods of time.[49]

Such gross material deprivation gives rise to a disproportionate need for social services, but 'It is not "disadvantage" per se which shapes the black person's experience of life in Britain, but more particularly their awareness that this disadvantage is unjust and racist.'[50] This subjective experience is a central and objective material deprivation when considering the social services needs of the black population.

John Small argues: 'As racial tension increases, the professions must adapt themselves to the prevailing racial climate.'[51] But it is clear that few social services departments have responded positively to this challenge.

The adoption of a perspective which emphasizes race directs attention to the routine practices and procedures in society which result in black people having poorer life chances than do the white majority. This system operates because black people are excluded from the structures of power and influence and its practices may be described by the term 'institutional racism'.

As far as social services are concerned, it is necessary to recognize not only that black consumers are the objects of racism but that the racism in the wider society is reflected in, and reinforced by, racism in social services institutions. Thus, in providing services, practitioners and managers must be sensitive to the dynamics of racism not only as these affect their clients in the wider society but also in their contact with social services.

This analysis has profound implications for social services institutions for it questions not only how individual practitioners relate to their black clients but also how the priorities and policies of the institutions are decided, by whom and in whose interests. Few authorities have made any systematic attempt to consider the implications of race in the delivery of services. The issue raises question which are uncomfortably fundamental and threatens powerful vested interests.

There is however, a duty placed on local authorities by Section 71 of the 1976 Race Relations Act

> to make appropriate arrangements with a view to securing that their various functions are carried out with due regard to the need to eliminate unlawful discrimination and to promote equality of opportunity and good relations between persons of different racial groups.[52]

A handful of authorities have begun to examine the implications of their practices and activities for the black population and some have produced new policies and initiatives in an attempt to improve the quality of service delivered. However, only where there has been strong political direction has this been attempted in any systematic fashion, and the national picture is one of piecemeal activity or no serious activity at all.

Where authorities have begun to explore institutional issues, three areas have received particular attention; staff recruitment, training and ethnic monitoring of services.

Anti-racist employment practices

A few authorities (the most well known being the London Boroughs of Brent, Camden and Hackney) have attempted to recruit a workforce which reflects the racial and ethnic composition of the population which is being served.[53] There is a threefold justification for such a strategy. First, the authority as a major employer has a duty to promote social justice: if it fails to promote equal opportunities it is merely colluding with the racism of the wider society. Secondly, if social services are to become more sensitive and responsive to the needs of the black population, that population must be properly represented within the institution so that a black perspective is brought to bear on its activities. Black staff can contribute not only to the formulation of policy but can also sensitize white staff to the racial and cultural aspects of their practice. Thirdly, if the institution is to gain the confidence of the black community, it must be seen to be promoting racial justice in its employment practice and as

224

able to deliver a relevant and sensitive service. The visible presence of black staff and the contribution they make to the practices of the institution is likely to promote such confidence. However, such a radical approach to recruitment is very uncommon.

A related policy considered by some authorities (Young and Connelly report 10 London boroughs as actively interested in their 1981 survey)[54] is that of monitoring the ethnic origin of their staff. Such an initiative may be linked to an 'Equal Opportunities Policy', a declaration that the authority will not discriminate against minority or disadvantaged groups in employment practices and procedures.

As with all local authority policies the outcome and effect of such procedures depends on whether there is a real commitment at political and managerial levels to its successful implementation. Potentially, such a policy might eliminate much institutional racism in employment but equally, if clumsily implemented, or implemented without any teeth it could become counter-productive, or an empty ritual.

Such measures to eliminate institutional racism in the employment of staff and to attract black staff to work in social services organizations may not be widespread but they have provoked considerable controversy. It can be argued that to appoint black staff to an organization which operates policies and procedures which perpetuate the disadvantages of the black population and whose culture is predominently white Anglo Saxon puts such staff in an exposed position. Despite the fact that such staff (although often employed in relatively junior positions) are frequently recruited in order to bring a black perspective to bear on the activities of the organization, if they challenge institutional arrangements or practices too readily or vociforously they may be regarded as troublesome and either not be taken seriously or perhaps become the subject of disciplinary action. Alternatively, they may become socialized into the culture of the organization, their capacity to make relevant observations thereby being reduced. As David Divine argues:

The recruitment of black social workers often makes only a marginal impact because their effectiveness is curtailed by being co-opted into existing power structures. In winning the battle for individual advancement they lose the war against racism.[55]

Until such time as black staff are adequately represented at all levels in the organization, special measures may be required if black staff recruited into a predominently white organization are to survive while bringing to the service a necessary critical and educative function. David Divine urges such workers to keep contact with their communities: 'Their power base is not within the department, but in the collective powerbase outside.'[56] Aggrey Burke argues that 'the robust workers who seek to change rather than be marginalised into existing power structures are most vulnerable to additional stress'.[57] The establishment of formal and informal groups for black workers, the engagement of independent black workers to act as consultants and the formation of organizational mechanisms through which observations and critiscisms can be channelled, may all be necessary.[58]

Access to social work

The scarcity of qualified black social workers led, in 1981, to CCETSW (the official body which accredits social work courses) to begin monitoring the ethnic origin of applicants to professional social work courses. The results of this exercise show that the percentage of successful applicants from 'ethnic minorities' has increased from 7.9 per cent in 1981 to 11.8 per cent in 1984.[59] However, during the same period, total applications rose by 32 per cent in the ethnic majority group but by 72 per cent in the ethnic minority group, and an average of 29.9 per cent of the majority group applicants were successful compared with 24.4 per cent of minority group applicants.

It might be suggested that this evidence of discrimination against minority applicants could be explained by the majority applicants having better qualifications and more relevant experience. But this does not appear to be the case for 'where minority ethnic group applicant, held similar qualifications to those of the majority group applicants, the latter were more likely to be successful in gaining a place on a course'.[60] Such institutional barriers to the acceptance of black students on social work courses clearly require close scrutiny, and appropriate action will need to be taken if the numbers of qualified black staff are to be substantially increased. There are, however, indications that such issues are beginning to receive some attention. The Polytechnic of the South Bank has produced a policy document considering some of the issues involved[61] and, in a recent curriculum study, CCETSW draws attention to the need to consider carefully the selection and assessment processes if black students are to be properly represented on qualification courses.[62]

But the elimination of institutional racism in the selection of students will not in itself ensure a more sensitive and skilled service for black clients. The content of the courses also requires attention, given that, on many courses, the particular needs of the black population are frequently considered as a subsidiary unit 'and so fail to reach many students, who may well complete their professional education with scarcely any teaching on multi-racial social work'.[63]

The CCETSW document *Teaching Social Work for a Multi-racial Society*[64] lists seven major aims including attention to race and culture in professional education. These range from basic information dissemination on 'the main ethnic minority groups . . . their experience of migration, change and life in contemporary British Society' to 'awareness of minority perspectives' and of students' responses to them, to an examination of 'agency function to ensure that effective service delivery is provided in a racially just manner'.[65] The document also draws attention to the danger that, unless appropriate action is taken, a social work course 'can become a "bleaching" agent by failing to support and enhance the cultural attributes' of black students – 'A critical look at the atmosphere of a course might reveal underlying values which are not relevant or acceptable to minority ethnic group students or clients.'[66]

Clearly, there is a need to address the question of course content to ensure that the circumstances and needs of the black population are properly considered. There are probably a number of ways in which such teaching can be approached, but given that this area is only beginning to be explored there is too little experience for firm conclusions to be drawn about the most effective methods.

Race and in-service training

The failure of professional courses to attend adequately to issues of race has probably contributed to the decision of a number of local authorities to organize their own training programmes in 'Racism Awareness'. Such courses aim 'to develop a set of techniques and methods for changing the behaviour and attitudes which are affected and continue to be affected by racism'.[67] Frequently based on experience in the USA by authors such as Judy Katz,[68] these courses have attracted considerable controversy.[69]

Apart from suspicions that such training (frequently lasting only two or three days) merely serves a 'window dressing' function, giving the appearence of serious commitment to confront racism when in fact no such intent exists, 'Racism Awareness' courses have been criticized for psychologizing issues which are institutional in origin and therefore require institutional intervention if they are to be tackled.

Clearly, individualizing institutional processes carries certain dangers but if institutions are to change, some attention to individual attitudes may be justified, given that to some degree change can be promoted or hampered by those who make up the institution and particularly by those who occupy senior positions. The difficulty appears to be that of achieving an appropriate balance between individual and institutional issues and in creating an atmosphere in which assumptions and values can be explored constructively. Intense emotions can emerge and unless these are dealt with skilfully, destructive consequences may flow from such training.

Race and ethnic monitoring of services

Although the recruitment of black staff and the provision of appropriate training programmes may improve the relevance of services for the black population, managers and policy-makers cannot be sure about this unless there is a mechanism for monitoring the performance of the organization. A few authorities have therefore begun to consider monitoring the users of services in an attempt to establish which groups are using the services provided. 'Ethnic monitoring' of service users is a controversial programme and, according to Young and Connelly,[70] has nowhere been fully implemented. However, providing the practical difficulties can be overcome and the co-operation of staff and service users is forth-coming, information concerning 'under-use', 'over-use' and 'inequity' in use can be gathered.

Such information by itself cannot usually answer all relevant questions, nor does it normally provide clear guidelines for future policy and practice. However, it can provide a basis for further enquiry, sharpening the focus on potential problem areas in the institution.

> . . . if there is apparent 'under use', direct and indirect dicrimi-nation may be operating; needs may be less or may be being met suitably by other means; the service may be inadequate or inappropriate in conception, presentation or content. Similarly, if there is apparent 'over use' of service, direct or indirect discrimination may be operating; there may be special needs within ethnic communities for the service offered, or the service may be particularly appropriate for members of such communities.[71]

It is difficult to plan relevant services without adequate information. In the field of childcare for example, it is important to know:

> . . . whether a disproportionate number of black children are being received into care, where they are being placed, how long they remain in care etc. Many people working in this area will have an idea of the answers to these questions, but in a field where myth and reality can become confused, accurate infor-mation is essential if positive measures are to be implemented.[72]

But formal ethnic record-keeping is only one means of monitoring services and some might suggest that it carries certain dangers. First, however benevolent the intentions of those who initially gather the information, there is always the possibility that a future regime of a different political persuasion might use it against the interests of the black communities. Thus, the local population and the staff concerned may be reluctant to co-operate with such exercises and certainly are likely to require detailed information about the uses to which the information will be put and about the arrangements for confidentiality and security, before they will agree to participate.

Secondly, there is the possibility that, far from leading to progressive changes in service, ethnic monitoring – being a complex and lengthy process – could be used as a device for delaying necessary changes or avoiding dialogue between service users and managers. Authorities might argue that they preferred not to make changes until all the potentially relevant information from the monitoring exercise was available; this could delay obviously necessary changes. They might also be less inclined to meet with, and take seriously the views of, black consumers, preferring to rely instead on information gleaned from monitoring exercises. An approach involving direct dialogue between service organizers and the local population is rare and, as it cuts across the formal political process, raises questions of accountability. However, obtaining the views of the local population and especially of service users seems to be extremely difficult if only the formal political process is relied upon. Given that the black population is generally excluded from this process it seems important to promote opportunities for black people to express their views concerning the scope and quality of social services provision if this is to be made more sensitive and relevant. Ethnic monitoring may provide useful information but it cannot be a satisfactory substitute for direct communication between the local population and those who organize services.

Some authorities are in the process of reorganizing social services on a decentralized basis in an effort to be more responsive to the needs of the local population and to promote community involvement in service provision. This movement for 'patch'-based social work, although partly deriving from the observations of the Barcley Report,[73] has a number of different ideological origins and the impetus for its development is not specifically a response to the needs of the black population. In certain authorities it does seem to indicate a recognition that large and remote bureaucratic organizations can easily become oppressive and unresponsive to the needs of service users. However, it remains to be seen whether decentralized service delivery will result in better links between social services departments and the black communities and whether, as a consequence, services will become more responsive and relevant.

CONCLUSION

Although there is a developing awareness of the particular social services requirements of the black population, the foregoing discussion should not be misunderstood. It is possible to identify some key issues and preoccupations in an ongoing debate but it would be erroneous to conclude that anything other than piecemeal or marginal change has taken place in either service provision or institutional arrangements.

The fact that a debate is occurring at all, and that it is possible to focus some attention upon the needs of a previously neglected group of social services consumers, reflects the growing resistance to exclusion and marginalization by Britain's black population. But although race may be on the agenda of social services, it is unlikely that substantial change will occur in provision unless and until black people occupy positions of power and influence.

Such wider political questions are of fundamental importance not only in achieving better social service provision for black clients but in reducing the numbers of such clients; the achievement of greater political and economic power could lead to an improvement in the life chances of the black population and hence reduce the need for social services.

It is, however, important to keep discussion of the politics of social services in perspective, for the contribution which social services can make to achieving social change may become over valued; social services are in fact relatively marginal and powerless when compared with other social institutions. Furthermore, although the difficulties of many social services clients may have ultimately arisen as a result of structural social processes, this is not true of all clients and, even when it is the case, secondary (and frequently psychological) consequences can follow from structural origins. Thus, interventions other than material and social may be necessary.

To date, relatively little attention has been given to such issues. Of necessity, the major emphasis has been on attempting to achieve institutional change and detailed discussion of the implications of race for service delivery and social work practice (with the notable exception of the question of transracial adoption and fostering) has yet to feature prominently in the debates concerning race and social

231

services. It is, however, important that this imbalance is eventually remedied for it is an improvement in the quality of service received by black consumers which must be the ultimate goal.

This is not, however, to detract from the fundamental importance of black people achieving greater political power and influence, for it is only when this happens that institutional change is likely to take place and the necessary inmprovements in service delivery and social work practice can be achieved.

Notes

1. Association of Directors of Social Services and The Commission for Racial Equality, *Multi-Racial Britain: The Social Services' Response*, London, CRE:p. 14.
2. K. Mercer, 'Black Communities' Experience of Psychiatric Services', *International Journal of Social Psychiatry*, vol. 30, nos. 1 and 2, 1984, p. 24.
3. The Runnymede Trust and the Radical Statistics Race Group, *Britain's Black Population*, London: Heinemann Educational Books, 1980.
4. Commission for Racial Equality, *CRE's Submission to the House of Commons Social Services Select Committee Inquiry into Children in Care*, London: CRE, 1983, p. 4.
5. D. Duncan, 'Eliminate the Negative', *Community Care*, 5 June 1986, pp. 18 –19.
6. West Midlands County Council, *A Different Reality: Report of Review Panel*, p. 48.
7. Ibid.
8. Commission for Racial Equality, op. cit., p. 4.
9. E. Arnold, *'Finding Black Families for Black Children in Britain'* in J. Cheetham, *Social Work and Ethnicity*, London: Allen and Unwin, p. 99.
10. C. Bagley and L. Young (1982), 'Problems of Adoption for Black Children' in J. Cheetham op. cit., p. 84.
11. L. Robinson, 'A Study of Migration and Mental Illness among Asians', MSc Thesis, University of Surrey, 1979.
12. D. Burke, 'A Perspective on Racism', MSc Thesis, University of Surrey, 1980.
13. Bagley and Young, op. cit., p. 84.
14. Mercer, op. cit., p. 24.
15. 'News Reports', *Community Care* 27 June 1985.
16. P. King, 'Racial and Cultural Factors in a Casework Relationship' in J. Cheetham. op. cit.; J. Tien and H. Johnson, 'Black Mental Health Clients Preference for Therapists: A New Look at an Old Issue', *International Journal of Social Psychiatry*, vol. 31, no. 4, 1985, pp. 258–66; A. Kadwhin, 'The Racial Factor in the Interview', *Social Work*, vol. 17, no 3, 1972, pp. 88–97; A. Gitterman and A. Schaeffer, 'The White Professional and Black Client', *Social Casework*, no. 53, 1972.
17. West Midlands County Council, op. cit., p. 48.
18. Ibid., p. 48.

19. Brent Social Services Department, *A Policy Regarding Transracial Adoptions and Foster Care Placements*, Document no. 24685, London, 1985, pp. 6–7.
20. J. Cheetham, 'Positive Discrimination in Social Work', *New Community*, vol. 5, Part I, p. 28.
21. Ibid
22. M. Ouseley *et al.*, *The System*, Runneymede Trust and South London Equal Rights Consultance Publications, p. 72, quoted in Commission for Racial Equality, op. cit., p. 4.
23. Commission for Racial Equality, op. cit., p. 3.
24. Ibid.
25. A. Sivanandan, 'From resistance to rebellion: Asian and Afro-Caribbean struggles in Britain,' *Race and Class*, XXIII, 1981, p. 124.
26. D. Denney, 'Some Dominant Perspectives in the Literature Relating to Multi-Racial Social Work', *British Journal of Social Work*, vol. 13, 1983, p. 150.
27. Roy Jenkins quoted by Denney, op. cit., p. 154.
28. Ibid., p. 162.
29. R. Ballard, 'Ethnic Minorities and the Social Services' in V. Saifullah Khan, *Minority Families in Britain*, London: Macmillan, 1979.
30. Ibid., p. 147.
31. Ibid., p. 152.
32. Ibid., p. 164.
33. Ibid., p. 158.
34. Ibid.
35. H. Sharan, 'Rob the Poor – Give to the Rich?' *Social Work Today*, 11 March 1985.
36. I. Cook, 'Section 11 and Freeze Puts Mars on Ice', *Social Work Today*, 19 May 1986.
37. Ballard, op. cit., p. 160.
38. Ibid., p. 147.
39. Ibid., pp. 159–60.
40. S. Ahmed, quoted by M. Jervis, 'Areas of Racism in Social Work', *Social Work Today*, 2 June 1986, p. 8.
41. Ibid.
42. N. Connelly, *Social Services Provision in Multi-Racial Areas*, London: Policy Studies Institute,1981, p. 39.
43. Ibid., p. 37.
44. Ibid., p. 40.
45. S. Ahmed, 'Blinkered by Background', *Community Care*, 15 October 1983, p. 20.
46. Denney, op. cit., p. 164.
47. Ibid., p. 165.
48. J. Cheetham, 'Positive Discrimination in Social Work' op. cit., p. 32.
49. Commission for Racial Equality, *Half a Chance*, London, CRE, 1981; D. J. Smith, *Unemployment of Racial Minorities*, London: Policy Studies Institute, 1981.
50. Denney, op. cit., p. 166.
51. J. Small, 'The Crisis in Adoption', *International Journal of Social Psychiatry*, vol. 30, nos. 1 and 2, 1984, p. 132.
52. Race Relations Act, 1976, p. 71.

53. L. Eaton, 'Reasons for Untrained Workers', *Social Work Today*, 6 May 1985.
54. K. Young and N. Connelly, *Ethnic Record Keeping in Local Authorities*, London: Policy Studies Institute, 1981, p. 3.
55. D. Divine, quoted by M. Jervis, 'Our Own Race Against Time', *Social Work Today*, 2 June 1986, p. 8.
56. Ibid.
57. Ibid.
58. A few authorities have appointed 'Race Relations Advisors' to Social Services Departments (some with a team of staff) to act as a focus for policy review and development. See 'Report of the Race Relations Adviser' (Social Services) Islington Social Services, Appendix 'A' to Committee Paper *Social Services and Islington's Ethnic Communities*, Agenda item 8(1) Social Services Committee, 10 September 1984.
59. Central Council for Education and Training in Social Work, *Ethnic Minorities and Social Work Training*, London, 1985.
60. Ibid., p. 6.
61. A. Kendall and C. Tegg. 'Race – Some Strategies for Tackling Racism on the Diploma in Applied Social Studies', London: Polytechnic of the South Bank, unpublished paper.
62. CCETSW, *Teaching Social Work for a Multi-Racial Society*, London, 1983, pp. 15–20.
63. Ibid., p. 22.
64. Ibid.
65. Ibid.
66. Ibid., p. 23.
67. Ibid., p. 61.
68. J. Katz, *White Awareness – Handbook of Anti-Racism Training*, Oklahoma, USA: University of Oklahoma Press, 1978.
69. Jervis, op. cit.
70. Young and Connelly, op. cit., p. 13.
71. Ibid., p. 10.
72. Ibid., p. 15.
73. *Social Workers, Their Role and Tasks*, London: Bedford Square Press, 1982.

PART III
RACISM AND THE INDIVIDUAL

9

Identifying Ethnic Origin: The Past, Present and Future of Official Data Production

Heather Booth

INTRODUCTION

Until recently almost all of the data produced[1] on ethnic minorities came from national sources. Local government tended to play a secondary role in such data production, though local authorities use much of the data that national sources make available for their areas. In the late 1970s, many local authorities were looking to the impending census not only for new data but also for guidance on the production of data on ethnic origin. Neither were particularly forthcoming. Many authorities saw this as a handicap to their efforts in the area of race relations, and some sought to remedy the situation by producing their own data.

This chapter is concerned with the production of data on ethnic origin on a national basis. It examines the official justifications for, and popular opposition to, the production of such data, and details the methods of production and sources of data since production began. The benefits of the last 20 years of data production are discussed, not only in terms of the political and technical experience gained, but also in terms of the benefits to ethnic minorities that have resulted specifically from the existence of data. In all cases, it is argued that the benefits are minimal, and existing plans for the future do not suggest that national data sources will bring any greater benefit to those whom they are purported to help.

WHY PRODUCE DATA?

The use of specific questions identifying members of ethnic minorities for national statistical purposes began to increase in significance in the early 1960s. The areas in which such statistics were produced were unemployment and migration, a reflection of the concerns of the day as far as ethnic minorities were involved. In contrast to some of the data production exercises of today, the introduction of these statistics was uneventful, and it was not until 1972 that an official statement appeared concerning the production of (by then) a whole range of statistics concerning ethnic minorities. In terms of presenting a reasoned argument for the collection and use of the statistics, this statement is less than adequate:

> Public policy and public discussion need to be informed by relevant and reliable data on such issues [as immigration]. This means that it is vital to define clearly the population involved. . . . The more detailed treatment (in this statement) accorded to this group [the population of New Commonwealth ethnic origin] reflects public interest focused upon the potential and actual social issues arising from the increase in immigrants of ethnic origins previously represented in this country to only a small extent. These issues relate, among other things, to language difficulties, the concentration of some immigrants within urban areas of decayed housing and the differences in general social and cultural traditions.[2]

It is clear that early production of statistics came about in response to what were perceived as the problems created by the presence of ethnic minorities. It was considered necessary to quantify these problems in the vague belief that policies would follow. What these policies would be was not made clear. They could address the needs of ethnic minorities, but they could equally address the desires of racists. The statistics could serve either purpose. Only occasionally

238

were the needs of ethnic minorities specifically mentioned as a reason for the production of data:

A main purpose of collecting the statistics (of pupils of overseas origin) is that they enable the Department to take account of immigrant needs, for instance, in assessing building and manpower priorities.[3]

Whether these data were actually used for these purposes is doubtful, as will be seen later in this chapter.

This basic approach of quantification had not changed by the late 1970s. In 1978, the proposal to include a direct question on ethnic origin in the 1981 Census was more explicit than the 1972 statement, but its purpose remained essentially the same:

In addition, there is a need for authoritative and reliable information about the main ethnic minorities. In order to help in carrying out their responsibilities under the Race Relations Act, and in developing effective social policies, the Government and local authorities need to know how the family structure, housing, education, employment and unemployment of the ethnic minorities compare with the conditions in the population as a whole. Any study of community relations must start from a knowledge of the demographic, social and economic characteristics of the ethnic minorities and, in particular, from knowledge of changes in their geographical distribution.[4]

Neither of these pronouncements made explicit reference to racial disadvantage or to the measurement of its extent, and it was not until 1981, when the Home Affairs Committee reported on the subject, that the need for such information was raised.[5] The government accepted that there was a need to measure and monitor racial disadvantage,[6] so that this has become the official justification for the production of data on ethnic minorities. In practical terms, however, this represents little, if any, change since 1972. The type of data produced remains essentially the same and there is still no explicit intention to act upon these data.

For the Home Affairs Committee, amongst others, this lack of political will to introduce programmes to combat racial disadvantage and discrimination does not deter them from arguing in support of the production of data on ethnic minorities. Though, in their report on ethnic and racial questions in the census, they stated that:

> We entirely accept that black people are not in themselves a problem: the major problems are that they have some needs that might be neither perceived nor catered for by the Government, that policies do not reach them and that they suffer from racial discrimination.[7]

They do not consider political will to be a necessary precondition for the production of data:

> We believe such a declaration of will, whilst highly desirable, is not essential, since a wide range of existing policies and funding, *already* rely on ethnic data . . . [8]

For the Committee, these existing policies would be made to reach ethnic minorities merely by improving the accuracy of the statistics on which the allocation of funds is based. That this is a wholly fallacious argument is seen in the examination of the use of data in funding allocations in later sections of this chapter.

WHY NOT!

Though there have always been individuals who have opposed the collection of data on ethnic origin, the extent of refusals to co-operate only became significant in the second half of the 1970s. The early opposition was not directed at all national data production exercises, but only at the field tests prior to the 1981 Census. These tests were concerned with how best to present questions on ethnic origin in the Census. At first, the tests were relatively well received though there were technical aspects to improve upon,[9] but the refusal rate soon began to rise. The West Indian community was the first to raise their objections to the question on ethnic origin, but other minority groups soon joined in, resulting in serious statistical problems of non-response.[10]

The reasons for these refusals were varied, but almost without exception stemmed ultimately from government policy. Even the technical aspects of the questions were adversely affected by government decisions: the early tests found that some of the objections to the questions arose from the classifications used and that if some such term as 'black' or 'black British' was employed these objections would be at least partially satisfied. The use of colour as a means of identification in the census was, however, proscribed as a policy decision because of the legal compulsion to complete the form.[11] Other objections were more directly related to legislation and institutionalized racism. The central fear was that the data would be misused, that the names and addresses of members of ethnic minorities would be passed to other government departments, such as the Home Office. This fear was heightened by the fact that the 1981 Nationality Act, which caused a great deal of insecurity and anxiety, was then passing through Parliament.

By the time of the final field test on April Fool's day 1979 in the London Borough of Haringey, a local campaign against the question had been mounted, fuelled by the fact that one of the main party candidates for the area made the question a central issue. In the run-up to the 1979 General Election, the campaign forcefully convinced the government that the question should not be included in the 1981 Census.[12]

Whilst opposition to the question in the census was growing, many national surveys and statistical systems successfully began to include a direct question on ethnic origin in their questionnaires. Such surveys differ from the census in that they are both voluntary and anonymous[13] and this would appear to be an important factor in securing the co-operation of the respondent. But this is probably not the most significant factor. Unlike the census (and at least its final field test), surveys are not usually publicly announced so that the respondent receives no advance warning of the interviewer's visit or of the questions that will be asked. The respondent thus has to decide there and then whether or not to agree to be interviewed. Without knowledge of the questions and without the opportunity to discuss the issue with family and friends, the respondent is probably more likely to consent to an interview. In this situation a refusal to be interviewed would be a personal action. It is significant

241

that the opposition to the 1981 Census question was collective and organized, rather than the sum of isolated and individual refusals.

In monitoring in sensitive areas, visual assessment has been used to try to circumvent respondent non co-operation, It has, however, resulted in further opposition because of the offensive nature of the method. It has been recently and unsuccessfully tried in the monitoring of unemployed people who claim unemployment benefit. In this case, however, opposition to the two schemes involved came not only from ethnic minority communities and claimants but also from servants who were expected to do the monitoring. In the latter case, the relevant unions were involved.[14] Once again it is collective and organized opposition that has been most effective.

PAST AND PRESENT PRACTICES

It was first possible to identify foreigners in official statistics in the 1841 Census, which included a question on place of birth. This question has been included in every census since then and has become more important in recent decades because it identifies people born in the New Commonwealth and Pakistan (NCWP). A question on nationality was introduced into the census in 1851 and remained in use for more than a century until its discontinuation after the 1961 Census when it was not well answered and was, in any event, of reduced usefulness because, by then, many of the 'foreigners' had British passports.

Early migration statistics made no attempt to cover migrants from the colonies because of their British citizenship and right of abode in the UK. Then, as now, these statistics covered only those immigrants (not emigrants) who were subject to immigration control. Today, some migrants from the Commonwealth and those from Ireland are still exempt from control and therefore do not appear in the statistics. These Commonwealth migrants are mostly white by virtue of their patrial status.[15] However, black or ethnic minority migrants from the Commonwealth are almost all non-patrial and as such are subject to control and counted.[16] It is clear that the statistics reflect the legislative situation, which in turn

242

reflects the dominant racist concern in British society to reduce black immigration to even less than the current tiny flow.

Other migration information comes from the International Passenger Survey which began in 1964[17] to measure migration both to and from the UK, collecting information on citizenship (defined as the nationality of the migrant's passport), country of birth, and country of previous (for immigrants) or next (for emigrants) residence. None of these classifications is now very effective at identifying ethnic minority migrants, and in any event the sample size is too small to produce very reliable statistics.[18]

For most purposes, country of birth provided adequate identification of ethnic minority groups in the early 1960s. Unemployment was one of the early areas of debate for which information was required. In 1963, the Department of Employment began to record the country of birth of adult immigrants from the Commonwealth who were registered as unemployed. Though only totals were produced on a monthly basis, quarterly analysis divided these totals into three groups of birthplaces: Australia, Canada and New Zealand; Cyprus, Gibraltar and Malta; Africa, India, Pakistan (including present day Bangladesh), West Indies and All Other Commonwealth Territories.[19]

For the children of immigrants, country of birth was not adequate and other means of identification were needed. In 1966, the Department of Education and Science (DES) introduced the production of statistics on schoolchildren belonging to ethnic minorities.[20] For those born with parents abroad, their country of birth was recorded; and for those born in the British Isles whose parents had lived in the British Isles for less than 10 years, the country of origin of the family was recorded. The production of these statistics ceased in 1973 after they were deemed unsatisfactory by the Select Committee on Race Relations and Immigration,[21] and they have not been replaced despite recommendations to the contrary.[22]

Public interest and debate began to centre on fertility, resulting in further data. Following the use of country of birth in the census, vital events were classified in the same way. In April 1969, birthplace was added to the information collected at the registration of births and deaths, though not of marriages. In the case of birth registration the birthplace of the mother and of the father (where known) are recorded; for death registration the birthplace of the deceased is recorded.[23] In both cases, this information is only partial since birth and deaths also occur to members of ethnic minorities who were born in the UK.

Health also became an area of concern. In 1969, the Hospital-In-Patient Enquiry[24] began to obtain information on the place of birth of patients and, in the following year, the same question was introduced into the Mental Health Enquiry for England.[25] Both enquiries continue to obtain these data. Prior to this concern with the health of ethnic minorities, the Department of Health and Social Security (DHSS) had long been monitoring its workforce. Data have been produced on the place of birth of medical staff for over 25 years, and country of birth of trainee nursing staff is also recorded. In addition, the nationality, country of birth and last address abroad are recorded for people entering national insurance from abroad.[26]

In November 1970, the Department of Employment changed from monitoring immigrant unemployment to 'coloured' unemployment, because there had been little demand for data on white unemployed immigrants. This was achieved by the introduction for the first time of visual assessment: only those assessed by employment exchange staff as 'coloured' were asked questions on country of birth. In addition to the existing question on own country of birth, a question on each parent's country of birth was introduced. It was thus possible to identify various ethnic minority groups consisting of those coloured people born in the Commonwealth or whose parent or parents were born in the Commonwealth. Data for seven groups were available: East Africa; Other African Countries; West Indies; India; Pakistan; Bangladesh (after 1973); Other Commonwealth Countries. In May 1971, coverage was extended to include unemployed youths aged under 18.[27] These data were collected for more than a decade but were discontinued in September 1982[28] when registration at job centres became voluntary and the production of unemployment statistics was transferred from job centres to unemployment benefit offices.

The 1971 Census included questions on place of birth and on parent's place of birth, thus identifying immigrants and their children. At that time this was an adequate means of identifying the ethnic minority populations because there were very few members whose parents were born in the UK. About 35 per cent of the 1971

244

population of NCWP ethnic origin was born in the UK, and it was not long before some of these were old enough to have children of their own. Birthplace of parent was thus to be a short-lived means of identification. It was nevertheless introduced into several sources of statistics in the early 1970s.

Questions on birthplace and each parent's birthplace have been used since January 1971 in the then newly launched General Hospital Survey (GHS) which is still continuing. However, data on place of birth from GHS are not used to identify groups by ethnic origin for cross-tabulation with other variables. For these purposes, the variable 'colour' is used: a person is classified as 'white' or 'coloured', the latter category including all non-whites such as people of African descent and of Asian descent including the Chinese and Japanese. This variable is not obtained from questions asked of the respondent, but from the interviewer's visual assessment of colour.[29]

In 1973, the first Labour Force Survey (LFS) was conducted in Britain as part of the EEC statistical programme. This is a biennial survey, and those conducted in 1973, 1975 and 1977 recorded information on nationality and country of birth.[30] The inclusion of a question on nationality, despite its not having appeared in a British survey or census for more than a decade, was due to the need for a comparison with other EEC countries and to interest in the movement of EEC nations between member states. The question on country of birth was also aimed at identifying migrant labour rather than entire minority populations. In terms of identifying the population of NCWP ethnic origin, the LFS was a backward step.

By the mid-1970s plans were in hand to explore the possibility of including a direct question on ethnic origin in the next census. Fieldwork began in 1975, testing the first of a series of possible questions, and further tests were undertaken in 1976 and September-October 1977.[31] As a result of these tests, the best compromise question recommended for use in the 1981 Census consisted of the following categories: White; West Indian; African; Indian; Pakistan; Bangladeshi; Arab; Turkish; Chinese; Other or Mixed (specify).[32] The exact form of this question was never actually field-tested, however, nor used in the census.

The technical experience gained from these tests was by no means wasted since other surveys were able to draw upon it. The first phase of the National Dwelling and Housing Survey which began in October 1977 employed a form of question similar to the above recommendation. This was, in fact, the first direct question on ethnic origin to be included in a major official survey. The categories employed were White; West Indian; Indian; Pakistani; Bangladeshi; Chinese; Turkish; Other Asian; African; Arab; Other (specify); Mixed (specify).[33] The same categories were again employed in the second and third phases of the survey conducted in 1978 and 1979.[34] The question was reported as being well received and respondents showed no difficulty in answering it.

Meanwhile, further testing continued on the proposed question for the 1981 Census. The 1978 test sought to determine whether certain European groups could be distinguished: notably Italians, Greeks, Turks and Poles, avoiding the term 'white' altogether. It also tested the possibility of asking the question of certain 'ethnic' groups only (including some Europeans), because, in earlier tests, many white indigenous people had failed to complete the question, not recognizing themselves as Europeans. By then, however, public opinion to the question was gaining strength, and the test suffered seriously from non-response.[35]

After the proscription of colour as a means of identification in the census, it was necessary to modify the compromise question already reached by replacing the category 'White', and two categories, 'English, Welsh, Scottish or Irish' and 'Other European' were chosen. In addition, the category 'Turkish' was omitted, so that the final test version was: English, Welsh, Scottish or Irish; Other European; West Indian or Guyanese; African; Indian; Pakistani; Bangladeshi; Arab; Chinese; Other or Mixed (specify). For comparison, the test also covered the question on parent's country of birth used in the 1971 Census. It also included a question on nationality, though with the Nationality Bill passing through Parliament, the word itself was avoided. This information on nationality was in fact required in order that Britain should comply with the EEC agreement to harmonize census data and had already been tested in 1976.[36] Its inclusion was thus a political decision and took no account of the situation within Britain regarding the fears of ethnic minorities. It was this final test that met with the organized campaign of opposition which resulted in its failure[37] and the abandonment of questions on both ethnic origin and nationality.

Despite this opposition to the proposed census question, the direct question used in the 1979 Labour Force Survey[38] met with no opposition and only 1 per cent of overseas-born respondents did not reply to it. This question was additional to the existing questions in the LFS on nationality and country of birth and was introduced to obtain coverage of the whole ethnic minority population including those born in the UK. The categories used did not include 'White' because it would not have allowed comparison with the census, should the proposed census question have gone ahead. The version used was: English, Welsh, Scottish or Irish; Polish; Italian; Other European; West Indian or Guyanese; African; Indian; Pakistani; Bangladeshi; Arab; Chinese; Other or Mixed. Though well received, the question was sometimes 'misunderstood'. The question asked respondents from which ethnic group they were descended, causing some West Indians to classify themselves as of African descent. In addition, many Asians who came from Africa classified themselves as African, and some West Indians classified their UK born children as English, Welsh, Scottish or Irish. Finally, the omission of any request to specify those in the residual category 'Other or Mixed' meant that this large group of people was of unknown composition.

In March 1980, the first survey of the Youth Opportunities Programme (YOP) of the Manpower Services Commission (MSC) was undertaken. As in unemployment, visual assessment was used, though in this case no supplementary questions were asked. The categories used were: Asian origin; Black (West Indian/African origin); White.[39] In 1981 a similar survey was undertaken using the categories: Asian origin; West Indian/African origin; White; 'Other' ethnic origin.[40] In both cases the sample, which covered 1–2 per cent of all trainees, was too small to be useful regarding ethnic minorities.

With the decision to exclude a question on ethnic origin from the 1981 Census, the LFS became free to adopt the use of the category 'white' as in the original form of question recommended for the census. In addition, the notion of descent was replaced by that of belonging to an ethnic group and the category 'African' was moved to appear much further down the list so as to elicit 'better' responses from West Indians and Asians. The 1981 LFS version was thus: White; West Indian or Guyanese; Indian; Pakistani;

Bangladeshi; Chinese; African; Arab; Mixed (specify); Other (specify).[41] The separation of the residual category into two categories and the addition of requests to specify ethnic origin for these categories allowed the examination of their composition, in particular of the group of people of mixed ethnic origin.[42] In the 1983 LFS the version used was the same as in 1981.

In 1982, the Home Office undertook the first round of the British Crime Survey.[43] This obtained information on the ethnic origin of both the respondent and, where known, their assailant. In both cases the information was visual assessment: for respondents, the interviewer's assessment was recorded, and for assailants, the respondent's assessment was obtained. The main categories used in both cases were: White; Black, that is West Indian or African; Indian, Pakistani or Bangladeshi. For the respondent's ethnic origin, two residual categories were used: 'Other Non-white' and 'Mixed or Uncertain'. For the assailant's ethnic origin, an open-ended residual category was used. The second round of the survey, undertaken in 1984, used the same methods and categories.

The Home Office also began in 1982 to collect data on the ethnic origins of people entering prisons. For these purposes, a self-classification question was employed, using the same form of question as that used in the 1981 LFS. This data production exercise was neither well received nor working satisfactorily,[44] however, probably because of the sensitivity of the area involved.

With the transfer of the production of unemployment statistics to unemployment benefit offices in 1982, the previous statistics of 'coloured' Commonwealth unemployed people were discontinued. Attempts to monitor the same group by essentially the same means were unsuccessful due to the opposition already mentioned, and the matter is still unresolved.

From January 1983, the General Household Survey has included a direct question on ethnic origin. This is additional to, rather than instead of, the questions already asked on country of birth and parent's country of birth and the interviewer's assessment of colour. It will thus allow analysis of the relationship between ethnic origin as determined by the respondent's, own and parent's countries of birth, and colour as assessed by the interviewer. The categories used in 1983 and continuing in use in 1984 are: White; West Indian or Guyanese; Indian; Pakistani; Bangladeshi; Chinese; African;

Arab; Mixed (specify); Other (specify). This is the same form of question as that used in the 1981 and 1983 rounds of the Labour Force Survey, as well as for the prison population, and as such has come closest to being the standard question used for self-assessment.

Finally, the MSC decided in April 1983 to obtain information on the ethnic origin of young people entering Youth Training Schemes (YTS) which replaced YOP and which became operational in late 1983. The categories used are: White/European; African/West Indian; Asian; Other.[45] In practice, these data are far from complete and reliable because of opposition to their production. In the first place, a minority of scheme managers refuse to obtain this information from the trainee and since some of these managers are local authorities, the number of trainees involved is substantial. Secondly, it has been found that the 'Other' category includes a significant proportion of people of West Indian, African or Asian origin who for a variety of reasons have not been classified as such.[46] A further feature of this data production exercise is its uncertain method of assessment: the scheme managers decide how entry forms are completed such that, in some areas, the data on ethnic origin is obtained by self-assessment on the part of the entrant whilst, in other areas, visual assessment is used, and in many cases visual assessment is used to supplement self-assessment.

BENEFITS OF EXPERIENCE?

From the last 20 years of experience, it would appear that in some respects very little has been learned about the production of data on ethnic minorities. Visual assessment is still being proposed as a method of obtaining data in areas where it ought to be possible to use direct questions, such as in monitoring unemployment. The method is used mainly in sensitive areas, either as a means of identifying members of ethnic minorities for questioning on their ethnic origin, or as a means of monitoring itself. By its nature it is subjective, for which it is criticized both politically and technically, but the main objection to the method is its offensiveness in that it uses colour (or whatever criteria the assessor uses to assess ethnicity) to single out members of ethnic minorities for monitoring, usually without their knowledge. Thus, in 1970, when the method was first introduced, visual assessment was used to identify 'coloured' unemployed people for monitoring by birthplace when no such monitoring of white people took place:

> Real interest centres on statistics of unemployed coloured workers and it was decided that the least objectional [sic] way to collect these statistics was to base them on the country of birth of the individual or his [sic] parent or parents. The method of collection of these statistics relies on the visual identifications by employment exchange staff of coloured persons on the register. Extra information is then sought from such individuals on their country of birth and that of their parents.[47]

Clearly, though monitoring by ethnic origin was seen to be a sensitive and potentially objectionable issue. the use of clandestine visual assessment was condoned. As if to make the point that colour was not in fact the variable of interest, however, the Department of Employment went so far as to exclude from the published statistics the tiny group of UK-born coloured unemployed people whose parents were also born in the UK.[48].

Visual assessment has been used in several other situations. In the General Household Survey, it was originally used to assess the accuracy of country of birth data in identifying ethnic minority populations, and thus provided some information on the likely accuracy of the 1971 Census data.[49] This statistical consistency on the data and the publication of tables by colour still continue, but it is highly questionable whether these justify the use of visual assessment.

Other uses are perhaps more justifiable. The visual asessment of pupils by their teachers in the 1978 and 1979 rounds of the School Leavers Survey was used by the Rampton Committee to investigate the educational attainment of children of West Indian origin.[50] This was probably the most effective method of monitoring children. First, it is very doubtful, but not condonable, that pupils would have been able to refuse to be monitored by ethnic origin whatever method was employed. Secondly, only broad categories were used, leaving little room for error; and thirdly, the teachers' assessment would have been based on a knowledge of their pupils rather than merely on visual assessment.

In the case of the British Crime Survey, visual assessment is clearly a necessity if an assessment of assailants is to be made at all (given that most crimes are not solved). It is not necessary, however, for the victim's ethnic origin to be visually assessed by the interviewer. Undoubtedly the method is employed because of the sensitivity of the subject, but it is precisely that sensitivity that heightens the offensiveness of the method.

More than a decade after its first introduction in monitoring the unemployed, it is the visual assessment of the unemployed that has finally become the target of opposition to the method. Whether used as a method of monitoring in itself, with or without notices warning of its use, or as a means of identifying members of ethnic minorities for special questioning on ethnic origin, the method is opposed as racist. That this opposition involves both members of ethnic minorities and of the white population, and both assessors and assessed can only be welcomed. If monitoring is to take place, it must be with the knowledge of those who are being monitored and done in such a way that their co-operation is secured.

Though little seems to have been gained politically from the experience of the last 20 years, several technical points have been learned. First, it would appear that the question wording is quite important in determining the response. Questions asking about descent tend to elicit responses about descent. Historically aware West Indians, for example, quite legitimately claim to be of African descent. The use of descent is adequate where the broad grouping Afro-Caribbean is of interest, but it should be avoided if Africans are to be categorized separately from West Indians.

The order in which categories appear on the questionnaire also affects the response. The LFS found that the category 'African' was particularly ambiguous and problematic. Not only do West Indians classify themselves as Africans, but many Asians who have lived in Africa also do so. The frequency with which this occurs is greater if 'African' appears early in the list, as it did in the 1979 LFS, indicating that it is probably an error on the part of people of an Asian origin. It is thus technically preferable to place the category 'African' further down the list than 'West Indian'; 'Indian'; 'Pakistani'; and 'Bangladeshi'.

These technical problems arise, of course, from the inadequacies of the categories used to classify people.[51] In this respect, there are theoretical objections to the use of 'white' in conjunction with such terms as 'West Indian' or 'Pakistani'. The term 'white' has been used extensively to classify those members of the population who are indigenous to the UK or who are of European origin, and has been found to have several practical advantages over other classifications. First, it is a convenient collective term which avoids the need to list a variety of ethnic origins (or nationalities). Secondly, it is much better understood than the alternative collective term 'European'. which, for xenophobic reasons, the indigenous population fail to recognize as describing themselves. Thirdly, it prevents most members of ethnic minorities from 'erroneously' classifying themselves as, for example, 'British' or 'English'. In practical terms, 'white' is a useful classification though its usefulness clearly stems from the racism of those identifying with it.

If, then, 'white' is the most practicable classification for the indigenous or European population, what of the use of 'black' or other terms of colour for the ethnic minority populations. The use of the term 'black' has been shown in tests prior to the 1981 Census to be preferred by many West Indians especially those who wish to classify their children as 'black' or 'black British'.[52] From both a theoretical and practical point of view, the use of 'black' may be preferable, but it either makes no provision for those of the various Asian ethnic origins, or if they are to be included, it results in a very broad and therefore not very useful category for the identification of ethnic origin. In fact, the census tests showed that many Asians preferred to be classified according to their country of origin and according to their religion.[53] Here, theoretical and practical considerations diverge.

In terms of the 1981 Census, there were conflicting political considerations about the categories to be used. The preferences for 'black' as expressed by West Indians and for country of origin and religion as expressed by Asians are political decisions. So too is the indigenous population's preference for 'white', though this may not be overtly recognized as such. In the usual course of events, these political decisions are translated into technical detail of question design. In the case of the proposed question in the 1981 Census, however, an overriding political decision by the government prevented the use of the term 'black'. As a corollary of this decision, the indigenous population were not to be classified as 'white'. In addition, a much longer tradition dictated that religion should not be asked, since it is regarded as too sensitive for censuses of mainland Britain, though it does feature regularly as a voluntary question in the census of Northern Ireland. If future censuses are to include questions on ethnic origin that are acceptable to those at whom they are aimed, these conflicting political factors must be resolved. It remains to be seen whether government is prepared to change its policies on these issues.

BENEFITS OF DATA?

Almost all of the data produced in these various national data production exercises are an end in themselves rather than means to an end. They describe, and quantify the situation that prevails; they measure and monitor racial disadvantage. They continue to add to and update the existing wealth of information that clearly demonstrates the existence and extent of discrimination and disadvantage. But having added their weight to this evidence, no further use is made of the majority of the data that arc produced. Most data are not used directly as indices for the provision of funding and other measures. Indeed, in education (where statistics were justified in terms of need) this disregard of the data has been most blatant: in 1973, Margaret Thatcher, then Secretary of State for Education and Science announced:

> My department makes no use of them [the statistics on schoolchildren belonging to ethnic minorities] whatsoever except to publish them. They do not form the basis of any grant from my department . . . none of our grant formulae are on the basis of immigrants. . . . [54]

Nor are the data used indirectly by central government in the policy-making process, as is evident from the absence of national policies and measures committed to equal opportunities or affirmative action.

There are several exceptions to this limited descriptive role of the data. Section 11 of the Local Government Act 1966 allows central funds to be used by local authorities, based on a measure of the ethnic minority population. Until the beginning of 1983, local authorities qualified for grant aid if they had more than 2 per cent of their school age population with parents who were born in the NCWP and who had arrived in the UK in the preceding 10 years. Additionally, until 31 March 1984, local authorities could obtain 'formula payments' from central funds according to, for example, the proportion of children in care belonging to ethnic minorities or the population using local authority day nurseries. Though these formula payments were based on local authority data, the school population statistics were obtained from DES data on children in schools. Even here, however, the direct use of data was severely curtailed when DES ceased to produce the required statistics in 1973, justified by Margaret Thatcher in the above quote. The allocation of Section 11 funds thus continued on the basis of out-of-date information or on that collected by the local authorities themselves. In 1982, new guidelines were issued concerning the qualification for grant aid: the 2 per cent and 10 year criteria were abolished and replaced in 1983 with the nebulous criterion of 'substantial numbers' of 'Commonwealth immigrants'.[55] This criteria is deliberately not defined so that local authorities with less than 2 per cent of their population of minority ethnic origins may apply for funds, and to enable the Home Office to exercise maximum flexibility. Nevertheless an authority's eligibility still depends 'largely' on the relative size of its 'Commonwealth immigrant population'[56] and data from the 1981 Census on birthplace of head of household are now used to estimate the proportion of the population of ethnic minority origin. Thus, though data still provide a guide for funding allocations, they are less important now than previously.

The rate support grant also uses data on ethnic origin to calculate indicators of need or grant-related expenditure assessments (GREA) in education, personal social services, environmental health and housing. In education the size of the local authority's ethnic minority population is one of six factors used to determine the grant, and is given double weighting so that its weight is two-sevenths of 28.6 per cent. This weight does not represent the proportion of grant-related expenditure distributed on the basis of ethnic origin, however: this proportion is not available.[57] In other areas, the use of data on ethnic origin is less important. In aggregate terms, areas with a large ethnic minority population receive 2–3 per cent of their GREA on the basis of the ethnic origin factor.[58] The data on which estimates of ethnic minority populations are based are now 1981 Census data, though the NDHS was used previously.

A third area in which data on ethnic origin are used for purposes other than description is in the Urban Programme. The proportion of the population that is 'non-white' is one of nine (formerly eight) variables used to determine special status. Until recently, the NDHS provided the requisite proportion, but the 1981 Census was used for 1983–84. The amount of funding received by an area is not directly related to the non-white population size, however. The Urban Programme is intended to improve conditions generally, and ethnic minorities benefit only in so far as they suffer economic and social disadvantages.

In relative terms, the amount of funding allocated on the basis, albeit partial, of data on the size of the ethnic minority population is small. Section 11 funding in 1982–83 amounted to £87.5 million, 75 per cent of which is paid from central funds. About 80 per cent is spent on education, the remaining 20 per cent being spent on liaison officers, interpreters and the social services. There is no statutory limit to the amount of money available, but, in practice, an internal limit is imposed by the requirements that the local authority meet 25 per cent of the costs.

The rate support grant system currently pays out a total of £9,000 million per year in block grants in education, personal social services, environmental health and housing. The amount of money distributed according to GREAs in education is larger than in the other areas, so that the actual effect of the ethnic factor in these other areas is small.[59] In education, money is distributed on the basis of indicators containing additional educational needs factors such as ethnic origin. In the case of Manchester, £15,8 million was distributed in 1982–83. This is about 8 per cent of the total GREA for education in an area where about a third of their children have additional educational needs.[60]

Spending on the Urban Programme is much lower than on the

rate support grant. The amount for both 1983–84 and 1984–85 is £348 million, more than half of which is paid to the seven inner-city partnership authorities. It is impossible to determine how much of this money is allocated as a result of the size of the minority population since the link between the two is very indirect.

In both the Urban Programme and the rate support grant it is clear that although data on the ethnic minority population size are used to enable local authorities to qualify for central funds, those funds are not allocated to specific areas or services nor are they allocated to provision for the ethnic minority population. Indeed, in the case of the rate support grant, although the size of the grant is determined as the aggregate of assessments in separate areas – such as education and personal social services – there is no statutory requirement that the grant be spent in proportion to those separate assessments. Thus, though ethnic origin received double weighting in education, the money received may be spent in other areas, or equally money obtained as a result of assessments in other areas may be spent on education. In any event, funds obtained as a result, however indirect, of the presence of an ethnic minority population are not required to be spent on services for that population.

The ditribution within local authorities of Section 11 funding is also open to abuse. Although these funds are allocated to authorities on the basis of the size of the ethnic minority population, and although the funds are specifically intended to meet the special needs of ethnic minorities, they are in fact often used for general purposes:

> Taking two obvious examples (Section 11 and Urban Aid) the misuse of the former by local authorities the length and breadth of the UK is legendary.[61]

Thus:

> It is common knowledge that these funds which central government makes available to local authorities in which there is a black presence have been claimed and used to supplement mainstream spending.[62]

But this is not the only way in which data on ethnic origin are in fact ignored. Even where there is a clear statistical case for funding, funds may not be obtained because there is no statutory requirement to apply for funding:

> In other situations where particular needs of black people falling within the terms of Section 11 funding have been identified, local authorities have simply not bothered to address themselves to this source of funding. The recent review of Section 11 and the new guidelines which have been proposed have simply side-stepped these issues, since local authorities are only accountable in statutory terms to government functionaires within the Home Office, who are in no position to identify and assess the particular needs of local communities.[63]

In most cases, then, data are used to describe racial disadvantage, and in the few cases where data are used to obtain funds, they play an indirect role. Even then, these funds may be misappropriated because of the lack of statutory control over their use. The role of data on ethnic origin is thus very minor indeed in terms of the benefit that they bring to ethnic minorities. Any improvements in the accuracy of the data would thus make virtually no difference to the existing situation.

THE FUTURE CENSUS

The absence of a direct question on ethnic origin from the 1981 Census was a significant omission. The strength of opposition to the question was largely unexpected, and it made clear the fact that the issue was primarily political rather than a technical matter of question design. With the possibility of a quinquennial census in 1986, the issue of the inclusion of a direct question arose again, but the matter was taken out of the hands of government statisticians and placed into those of politicians. The Home Affairs Committee recommended that a question should be included in the next census, which will be in 1991 at the earliest. This recommendation was based on the Committee's prior support for a question,[64] on the experience in the USA and Canada, and on evidence submitted to the Committee.[65]

The central argument of the Committee in favour of a direct question on ethnic origin in the census was that this would provide 'definitive' data rather than the existing estimates based either on surrogates for ethnic origin in the census or on sample surveys. Indeed, in addressing the question 'what if any effect the absence of definitive Census-based data on ethnic origin (has) on racial disadvantage programmes,'[66] the Committee imply that the existence of definitive data is the norm or ideal, and that their absence has if anything a negative effect.

A second implication of the above question is that explicitly *racial* disadvantage programmes already exist in Britain. On a national basis, this is an overstatement of the truth. The three sources of funding which might loosely be regarded as addressing social disadvantage have already been discussed. In practice, there are no statutory programmes dealing with racial disadvantage. Despite this fact, the Home Affairs Committee argued that, within the existing arrangements for funding, ethnic minority communities would benefit if better, definitive data were available on which to base the allocation of funds. That this is not necessarily true has been argued elsewhere;[67] in brief, the potentially high level of under-reporting and the fact that present estimates include some white people mean that definitive data would not necessarily lead to a more advantageous distribution of funds for all ethnic minority groups. But these considerations are insignificant compared to the unequal take-up of funds by local authorities and the fact that funds may not reach the minorities for whom they are intended: definitive data would make no difference in these respects.

Recognizing the limited use of data in present funding arrangements, the Committee argued in support of their descriptive and quantifying function. With definitive data, they argued, campaigns against discrimination and for new policies would be much more effective:

By accurately delineating disadvantage ethnic data could be used to great effect by elected representatives and ethnic minority people to put pressure on employers, service-providers and others not to discriminate and to adjust policies to take account of unmet needs shown up by the data.[68]

The fact that existing data delineate disadvantage and discrimination sufficiently adequately for campaigning purposes is overlooked by the Committee. So too is the fact that campaigns are generally ignored by government. Indeed, the Committee does not even include the government amongst those on whom pressure is to be brought to bear. Finally, it should not be forgotten that the Committee is addressing the issue of data from the census, a source which is not suited to investigations of discrimination and of the details necessary for policy adjustment.

Mindful of the opposition already shown towards the inclusion of a direct question on ethnic origin in the census, the Committee made recommendations on how to gain the confidence of the ethnic minority community so that accurate data could be produced. These involved American-style publicity and persuasion,[69] but also include a recommended form of question, shown in Figure 9.1. Though technically poor,[70] this question raises some interesting aspects which differ from existing forms of the question.

In the first place, the question is headed by the words 'RACIAL DISCRIMINIATION AND DISADVANTAGE' rather than headings such as 'RACE OR ETHNIC GROUP' or no heading at all. This is clearly aimed at reassuring the respondent as to why the question is being asked, but it is factually incorrect: the question asks for ethnic origin, not for information about racial discrimination or disadvantage. It is doubtful whether this heading would make any difference to the acceptability of the question; it is a mere trimming and the substance of the question is not masked by it.

Of more significance in affecting the question's acceptability is the note explaining the purpose of the question,. This is something that has not appeared before on census[71] and national survey forms, though it has appeared in local authority data production exercises where it serves not only to explain the purposes of the question but in doing so also encourages the respondent to respond. In normal census situation this latter function would be only marginally relevant because of the legal obligation to complete the form, but after the opposition to this question in the test prior to the 1981

RACIAL DISCRIMINATION AND DISADVANTAGE

The answers to these questions will help Governments, local authorities and other organisations to identify racial descrimination and disadvantage, to develop more effective policies against them, and monitor the progress of these policies.

a.   Are you white?   Yes/No
b.   Are you black?   Yes/No
     If you are black, are you   ☐ British
                                                       ☐ West Indian
                                                       ☐ African
     Tick as many boxes as apply   ☐ Other
c   Are you of Asian origin?   Yes/No
     If yes, are you   ☐ British
                                                       ☐ Indian
                                                       ☐ Pakistani
                                                       ☐ Bangladeshi
                                                       ☐ West Indian
                                                       ☐ Chinese
                                                       ☐ Vietnamese
     Tick as many boxes as apply   ☐ Other
4.   Other groups
     Are you   ☐ Mixed race
                                                       ☐ Arab
                                                       ☐ Greek Cypriot
                                                       ☐ Turkish Cypriot
     Tick one box   ☐ None of these

Source: Home Affairs Committee, *Ethnic and Racial Questions in the Cenus*, vol 1, London: HMSO, 1983, p. xxxii.

Fig. 9.1   Form of question recommended by the Home Affairs Committee

Census, it is an important element. Statements of this sort are, in general, to be welcomed in that they inform the respondent of the rationale behind the question and of the uses to which the data will be put. Without statutory backing, however, there remains the issue of whether those who currently oppose the question will be swayed by statements on census forms, even if they are accompanied by the recommended publicity campaigns and other measures seeking to ensure acceptability.

The use of the category 'British' in the context of ethnic origin is also a new departure. Its introduction would certainly improve the response rate amongst those who wish to be categorized as 'black British' and indeed it seems that its recommendation is influenced more by considerations of acceptability than accuracy. The Committee only hints at the possibility that this information would not in fact be coded,[72] but in multiple-tick cases, as recommended here, it seems the most likely category to be ignored. Conversely, in cases where the respondent has ticked only the category 'British' (whether in section b or c), such data would provide sufficient detail to determine her ethnic origin. A 'British' category would thus not necessarily produce more accurate data. The category would also be open to problems of reduced acceptability if it were linked by the respondent with nationality, an issue that is still controversial and on which the Committee recommends there should be no direct question.[73]

The use of colour is also influenced by considerations of the acceptability of the question to the respondent, rather than the accuracy of the data. As already mentioned, its use would require a change in the policy that prevailed at the time of the tests prior to the 1981 Census. With the Committee's recomendation, however, it would seem that this policy has already been changed.

AN UNCERTAIN FUTURE

Recent years have witnessed a significant increase in the production of data on ethnic origin, so that by now there is a considerable volume of data available. As descriptive material these data are of use to local authorities, pressure groups and researchers, but there is very little evidence that they are used in a direct way by government departments to reduce social disadvantage. Indeed, there has never been any suggestion by government that this should be their purpose: official justification for the production of these data stops short of stating how they will be used. This lack of commitment to the use of the data was a contributory factor to the failure of the Haringey test: the Office of Population Censuses and Surveys found that they did not have a positive case to put[74] concerning the question on ethnic origin and that 'it was not possible to say how the information would be used . . . because nobody at the time was prepared to say how it would be used; they had not decided how to use it'.[75] In short, government departments were not actively interested in ethnic minorities, and this is still the case today.

If the production of data has increased, so too has the opposition to the methods of production and to the production of data per se. These issues are becoming increasingly a matter of public concern. Opposition to the Haringey test received considerable attention and the issue was even taken up by a main-party candidate in the run-up to the 1979 General Election. Civil service unions are currently involved in the opposition to the methods of monitoring the unemployed. And the Home Affairs Committee formally recognized the political nature of the issue in inquiring into the census question.

Despite this move towards the public and political arena, the central issue of data production and racial disadvantage continues to be masked by attention to detail. Thus, we have seen 20 years of surveys, monitoring and censuses from which the only lessons learnt have been technical improvements in question design. Even after the defeat of the government by popular opposition on the issue of the question in the 1981 Census, the Home Affairs Committee failed adequately to address the central issue, choosing instead to concentrate on the benefits which they saw in having definitive data. The crux of the matter lies not with data production however. It is the absence of political will on the part of the government to act upon data that is the major stumbling block in the fight against racial disadvantage and discrimination. No amount of data, no matter how accurate and comprehensive, will change the situation if there is no appropriate legislation and insufficient funding to bring about that change.

It is often claimed that legislation cannot be formulated until the facts of racial discrimination are known; until new and better data are available. Such sentiments are no more than a delaying tactic. The data that already exist show that disadvantage and discrimination are part of the everyday lives of ethnic minority people. This message has been clear for many years. In the formulation of legislation, therefore, there is no need to wait for more information. Indeed, it might be argued that there is no point in producing more data until such legislation exists or at least until there is an expression of political will. Furthermore, given the misappropriation of funds acquired by local authorities ostensibly for the benefit of ethnic minorities, it might also be argued that data production should cease since they serve no useful purpose. Data have not been instrumental in reducing racial disadvantage.

These arguments directly confront the issue of data production on ethnic origin. They are not new arguments; indeed they have been widely side-stepped for a long time. The lack of political will on the part of government has long been accepted as the framework within which the race relations industry operates and within which data are produced. But by working within this framework, the effects of ethnic minority people to challenge the lack of political will are continually undermined. The real need is thus not for better definitive data but for a new framework of political will aimed at reducing and eradicating racial disadvantage and discrimination. It is only within this context that appropriate data can be instrumental in reaching that aim. Until such a framework exists, data on ethnic origin will continue to serve nothing more than a descriptive role.

Notes

1. On data *production*, as opposed to data collection, see John Irvine, Ian Miles and Jeff Evans, 'Introduction: Demystifying Social Statistics' in J. Irving, I. Miles and J. Evans (eds.), *Demystifying Social Statistics*, London: Pluto Press, 1979.
2. C. A. Moser, 'Statistics about Immigrants: Objectives, Sources, Methods and Problems', *Social Trends*, no. 3, 1972, p. 20.
3. Ibid, p. 29.
4. White Paper on the 1981 Census, Cmnd 7146, London: HMSO, 1978, para. 24.
5. Home Affairs Committee, *Racial Disadvantage*, vol.1, London: HMSO, 1981, para. 8.
6. The government's reply to the fifth report from the Home Affairs Committee (ibid.), Cmnd 8476, London: HMSO.
7. Home Affairs Committee, *Ethnic and Racial Questions in the Census*, vol.1, London: HMSO, 1983, para. 11.
8. Ibid., para. 106.
9. Ken Sillitoe, *Ethnic Origins, 1,2 and 3*, Office of Population Censuses and Surveys Occasional Papers, 8,9 and 10 respectively, London: HMSO, 1978.
10. Ken Sillitoe, *Ethnic Origins, 4*, Office of Population Censuses and Surveys Occasional Paper, 24, London: HMSO, 1981.
11. Ibid., p. 34.
12. The government's decision to exclude the question was announced on 20 March 1980. For details, see Office of Population Censuses and Surveys Monitor CEN 80/3, *Government Decision on an Ethnic Question in the 1981 Census*, London: HMSO, 2 April 1980.
13. Few surveys are truly anonymous because of the practice of numbering

respondents for call back purposes. Even if the respondent's name is unknown, the address is known to the interviewer.

14. See Heather Booth, 'Which "Ethnic Question"? The development of questions identifying ethnic origin in official statistics', *Sociological Review*, vol. 33, no.2, May 1985, pp. 254–74.

15. A patrial is a person who has a right to live in the UK, by virtue of close connection with the UK.

16. See Home Office, *Control of Immigration Statistics, United Kingdom*, London: HMSO,annual.

17. Office of Population Censuses and Surveys, *International Migration*, Series MN, London: HMSO, annual.

18. See Dave Drew, 'The Politics of Statistics' in Runnymede Trust and Radical Statistics Race Group. *Britain's Black Population*, London: Heinemann Educational Books, 1980.

19. The monthly totals by region were not published until July 1971, but the quarterly data were made available on request. See Department of Employment, *Employment Gazette*, vol. 79, no. 7, London: HMSO, July 1971.

20. Department of Education and Science, *Statistics of Education, Vol.1, Schools*, London: HMSO, annual (1967–74).

21. Select Committee on Race Relations and Immigration, *Education*, vol. 1, London: HMSO, 1973.

22. Select Committee on Race Relations and Immigration, *The West Indian Community*, London: HMSO, 1977; Department of Education and Science, *Education in Schools, A Consultative Document*, London: HMSO, 1977; Committee of Inquiry into the Education of Children from Ethnic Minority Groups (The Rampton Committee), *West Indian Children in our Schools*, Interim Report, Cmnd 8273, London: HMSO, 1981; Home Affairs Committee, *Ethnic and Racial Questions in the Census*, vol. I, op.cit. in note 7, para. 31. See also Home Affairs Committee, *Ethnic and Racial Questions in the Census*, vol. II, London: HMSO, 1983, qu. II 764–94.

23. Office of Population Censuses and Surveys, Monitor Series FMI, *Births by Birthplace of Parents*, London: HMSO; Office of Population Censuses and Surveys, Monitor Series DHI, *Deaths by Birthplace of Deceased*, London: HMSO.

24. Department of Health and Social Security, *Hospital In-Patient Enquiry*, London: HMSO, annual. Place of birth within the UK is also collected; religion is an optional question collected in some areas.

25. Department of Health and Social Security, *Inpatient Statistics from the Mental Health Enquiry*, London: HMSO, annual. Place of birth within the UK is also collected.

26. See DHSS, *Health and Personal Social Services Statistics for England*, London: HMSO, annual; and Welsh Office, *Health and Personal Social Services Statistics for Wales*, Cardiff: HMSO, annual.

27. C. A. Moser, op.cit. p. 28.

28. Department of Employment, *Employment Gazette*, London: HMSO, monthly. See vol. 90, no. 9, Table 2.17 for latest data.

29. Office of Population Censuses and Surveys, *The General Household Survey, Introductory Report*, London: HMSO, 1973.

30. Office of Population Censuses and Surveys, *Labour Force Survey 1973, 1975 and 1977*, London: HMSO, 1980.

31. Sillitoe, op.cit., 1978.
32. Ken Sillitoe, 'Ethnic Origin: The search for a Question', *Population Trends*, no. 13, 1978.
33. Department of the Environment, *National Dwelling and Housing Survey*, London: HMSO, 1978.
34. Department of the Environment, *National Dwelling and Housing Survey, Phases II and III*, London: HMSO, 1980.
35. Sillitoe, op.cit., 1981.
36. See Sillitoe, *Ethnic Origins 2*, op.cit., 1978.
37. Office of Population Censuses and Surveys Monitor CEN 80/2, *Tests of an Ethnic Question*, London: HMSO, 20 March 1980.
38. Office of Population Censuses and Surveys, *Labour Force Survey 1979*, London: HMSO, 1982.
39. Trevor Bedeman and Juliet Harvey, *Young People on YOP*, Research and Development Series no. 3, Sheffield: Manpower Services Commission, 1981.
40. Trevor Bedeman and Gill Courtenay, *One in Three: The Second National Survey of Young People on YOP*, Research and Development Series no. 13, Sheffield: Manpower Services Commission, 1983.
41. Office of Population Censuses and Surveys, *Labour Force Survey 1981*, London: HMSO, 1982, Chapter 5 in particular.
42. Office of Population Censuses and Surveys Monitor LFS 83/1 and PP1 83/1, *Labour Force Survey 1981: Country of Birth and Ethnic Origin*, London: HMSO, 22 February 1983.
43. Mike Hough and Pat Mayhew, *The British Crime Survey*, Home Office Research Study no. 76, London: HMSO, 1983.
44. Home Office Statistical Department, 'Sources of Statistics on the Ethnic Minorities – Non-Demographic Data', *Home Office Statistical Bulletin*, no. 24/82, para. 18.
45. Manpower Services Commission, Youth Training Board, *Ethnic Minority Participation in YTS*, MSC Ref. YTB/84/N1.
46. Steve Fenton *et al.*, *Ethnic Minorities and the YTS*, Appendix: Summary of the main report and recommendations. Presented at workshop on Equal Opportunities and YTS, ESRC Research Unit on Ethnic Relations, Birmingham, June 1984.
47. C. A. Moser, op.cit., p.28.
48. Ibid.
49. Office of Population Censuses and Surveys, *The General Houshold Survey*, op.cit. Tables showing the relationship between country of birth and colour appear in the annual reports of the GHS, the earlier volumes of which also show parent's country of birth by colour.
50. Committee of Inquiry into Education of Children from Ethnic Minority Groups (The Rampton Report), op.cit.
51. See R. M. White, 'What's in a Name? Problems in Official and Legal Usages of "Race" ', *New Community*, vol. VII, no. 3, 1979, pp. 333–49; and also *New Community*, vol. VIII, nos. 1–2, 1980.
52. Sillitoe, op.cit., 1981. p. 33.
53. Home Affairs Committee, *Ethnic and Racial Questions in the Census*, op.cit., para. 87.
54. Quoted in Shan Nicholas, 'Education' in Runnymede Trust and Radical Statistics Race Group, op.cit. See also this edition, Chapter 6, note 8.

55. Home Office Circular no. 97/1982. 'Commonwealth immigrants' are now defined as those born in the Commonwelath and in Pakistan prior to her leaving the Commonwealth, and their children aged 20 or less. In practice, 'Commonwealth' means New Commonwealth, and 'immigrant' means member of ethnic minority.

56. Ibid. para. 4.

57. Home Affairs Committee, *Ethnic and Racial Questions in the Census*, op.cit., vol. II, qu. 556.

58. Ibid. vol. I, para. 20.

59. Ibid. vol. II, qu. 581.

60. Ibid. vol. II, qu. 575.

61. Memorandum submitted by Walsall Council for Community Relations, in Home Affairs Committee, *Ethnic Racial Questions in the Census*, op.cit., vol. II, p. 336.

62. Ibid., p. 337.

63. Ibid.

64. Home Affairs Committee, *Racial Disadvantage*, op.cit.

65. Home Affairs Committee, *Ethnic and Racial Questions in the Census*, op.cit., vols. II and III.

66. Ibid., para. 2.

67. Heather Booth, 'Ethnic and Racial Questions in the Census: The Home Affairs Committee Report'. *New Community*, vol. XI, nos. 1–2, 1983, pp. 83–91.

68. Home Affairs Committee, *Ethnic and Racial Questions in the Census*, op.cit., para. 107.

69. Ibid., paras. 96–104 and Annex 2.

70. Heather Booth 'Which Ethnic Question?' op.cit., 1985.

71. Census forms are accompanied by an information leaflet, and enumerators also answer queries.

72. Home Affairs Committee, *Ethnic and Racial Questions in the Census*, op.cit., para. 74.

73. Ibid., para. 77.

74. Ibid., vol. II, qu. 306.

75. Ibid., vol. I, para. 34.

10

White Attitudes: The Rhetoric and the Reality

Pam Nanda

INTRODUCTION

The previous chapters in this volume have examined the position of Britain's black population and found, whether it be in employment, housing, education, social services or health, that they are disadvantaged relative to Britain's white population. This chapter examines the context of this disadvantage, both with respect to how some white institutions collude to maintain this inequality, and how black people themselves have attempted to respond to the position they find themselves in. In particular, the chapter draws attention to the situation in South Africa today and highlights the links between the British government's attitude to the plight of South African blacks and the experiences of the black people in this country.

THE CONTEXT

A major proportion of the earth's population is now classified and referred to, by those in the West, as the 'Third World'. Synonymous with this term, and implicit in this classification, is the notion that 'Third World' countries and their population are backward and still in the process of development. This classification has its roots in the dual forces of imperialism and racism, which permitted and justified the plundering of the material and cultural riches of 'Third World' countries, whilst concealing essential facts and truths relating to their history, civilization, and culture, and which left them as the arenas of continuing neocolonialist struggles.

These struggles continue to be waged on all fronts – economic, political, educational, social and cultural – and they utilize all the forces which neocolonialism can muster. The natural resources of the 'Third World' remain very largely in the hands of imperialists. Giant multinational corporations continue to pump out of these lands whatever sources of profit they have to offer. The vast majority of their people still suffer from poverty, disease and oppression, and every day are forced to watch the riches of their lands, the very earth upon which they walk and which is their birthright, being sucked dry in order that wealth can accumulate, at any expense, in almost unimaginable amounts, in the hands of that infinitesimal white-majority which wields economic power.

All this has not gone on unresisted. 'Third World' peoples – men, women and children – have continued to struggle against those forces which attempt to deprive them of their right to human existence. Time and time again they have risen up in revolt to overthrow their oppressors. Nowhere has this been more apparent than in South Africa, where the infamous system of apartheid embodies racism in its crudest and most reprehensible form.

The whites in South Africa, mainly of Dutch, German and British origin (many of whom sympathized with the Nazis in the last war), comprise only 15 per cent of the country's total population. This notwithstanding, they control the entire country, its political institutions, its economy and its wealth, and occupy 87 per cent of all its land. The majority, black Africans, who make up 85 per cent of the population, are confined to 13 per cent of the land – the vast majority of which is infertile, incapable of sustaining even subsistence farming, and lacking in mineral wealth.

This pernicious system is actively upheld by Britain. It has been supported diplomatically, politically, militarily and morally by successive British governments, irrespective of party colours. It is true that, over the last decade, South Africa's regime of apartheid has been the subject of numerous international conferences. It is also true that resolution after resolution has been passed condemning both the ideology and the practice of apartheid.

Overall, however, the outcome of such conferences and resolutions has amounted to little more than a few cosmetic reforms. Through her presence at these international conferences, and through her frequently uttered platitudes, Britain has hoped to encourage a view of the British people, its government and its industry as individually and collectively caring, decent and law-abiding. For Britain to admit that her involvement in South Africa is motivated by greed, by a desire to maximize profits, in disregard to the murders committed in the process, or of the imposition of oppressive regimes along the way, is inconceivable. Indeed, the standard arguments put forward by British governments and corporations is that if they were to break off diplomatic relations with South Africa, or disinvest in the South African economy, it would be the blacks of South Africa who would suffer the most.

In effect, Britain would have those same black people whom she both directly and indirectly exploits and oppresses believe that she is their liberator. At home she seeks to nurture the belief that Britain is unsupportive of the system of apartheid, philanthropic in their attitudes to black South Africans, and committed to working for the relief of the oppressed. Equally, she is at pains to promote an image of Britain as a society which is based on justice and racial equality.

It is the gap between Britain's *official* position on apartheid in South Africa and on institutionalized racism at home, and her *actual* and active collusion with both – (that is, the gap between rhetoric and the reality) – which is the subject of this chapter. Its aim is to highlight the links between racism in Britain and apartheid in South Africa; to examine some of the institutions, systems and practices, particularly the immigration laws and the media, which have played and continue to play a direct role in the promotion of white supremacy and British racism; and to outline some responses to them from the black communities in Britain – responses which often pass unrecognized, unmentioned and unheeded by government, by policy-makers and by Britain's white population alike.

IMMIGRATION

In Britain the most brutal and wide ranging racism which occurs
day after day is not the work of fascist minority parties but of
Her Majesty's Government.[1]

Amrit Wilson's quote above refers to Britain's immigration laws,
for the strongest influence in government policy in the field of race
relations has been fear of white racism and its main instrument,
that of immigration control.

The history of immigration control has been well documented
from its early beginnings in 1905 – when the Aliens Act, 1905 was
introduced to control the flow of Jewish migrants into Britain – to
1983, when the government attempted to exempt immigration
control from the new data protection laws.[2]

Britain is the only country in the world to refuse entry to its own
nationals to the national territory.[3] Though race is not mentioned
in the Nationality Acts or Immigration Acts, it is clear that they
are intended to be racist. The effect of the laws on speeches in
Parliament made clear their intent to restrict blacks.

The most recent Act, the 1981 British Nationality Act, epitomizes
the nature of these laws. For example, Section 39 of the Act gives
several million (almost all white) existing 'partial' government citizens the same right of abode in the UK that British citizens are to
have. At the same time, British dependent territories' citizens,
British overseas citizens, British protected persons and British
subjects without citizenship of any Commonwealth country are to
have no right of abode under the Act. The vast majority of people
in these categories are of Indian, Chinese, Afro-Caribbean or other
non-European descent.[4]

Under the current law there are also wide discretionary powers
for officials: to enter premises without a warrant if they suspect an
illegal immigrant is being harboured there; to impound and read
the private correspondence of an applicant for entry; and to impose
medical tests. (The 'virginity' tests and x-raying of children used
both to be carried out under these powers.) There have been a
number of 'passport raids' on homes, workplaces and, in 1980, on
a supermarket, where a number of shoppers, as well as employees,

were apparently detained at random.[5] It is not difficult to see in these actions the operation of a covert pass law.

The latest Act creates a situation where thousands of parents will be uncertain whether or not their children born here are aliens (the Act withdrew the principle of *ius joli*.

The Immigration Act also allows the Home Office to declare that persons who were once legally admitted to the Home Office's satisfaction can be regarded as illegal entrants on the basis of subsequent allegations that they failed to disclose some 'material fact' – even if not asked previously about such a fact.

Under Schedule 2 of the Immigration Act 1971, a person whom the Home Office suspects of being an illegal entrant can be detained in prison indefinitely without a hearing, and removed from the country without a hearing. If such a person applies for a writ of *habeas corpus*, the courts have ruled that the burden of proof is on that person to show he is being unjustly detained, and not on the Home Office to say why it is detaining him. As the Home Office is not bound to produce evidence, the person has no effective way of establishing a case.[6] Such is the fairness of British law.

This section looks at a number of crucial factors in the development of immigration controls (both external and internal) in Britain, and at some of the effects which immigration control has had on the black community, both in terms of experience and response.

In the post-war reconstruction period, Britain, like all European powers, was desperate for labour. It sought this labour from the black Commonwealth. As Sivanandan states:

> . . . in the sphere of employment, where too many jobs were seeking too few workers – as the state itself had acknowledged in the Nationality Act of 1948 – racialism did not debar black people from work per se. It operated instead to deskill them, to keep their wages down and to segregate them in dirty, ill-paid jobs that white workers did not want – not on the basis of an avowed racialism but in the habit of an acceptable exploitation.[7]

As the demand for jobs dried up there was a corresponding increase in the calls for immigration control. Effective controls on the immigration of people from the Commonwealth began in 1962. The

271

policies which were developed at this time were based very much on what has come to be known as the 'numbers game'. Essentially, the 'numbers game' works on the premise that the fewer black people live in Britain, the better race relations will be. Implicit in this theory is the belief that black people, and not the response of white people to black people, are the source of race conflict. Robert Moore has rightly argued:

> Once the debate is about numbers there are no issues of principle to be discussed, only how many? . . . The argument about numbers is unwinnable because however many you decide upon there will always be someone to campaign for less and others for whom one is too many. Since you have admitted that black people are a problem in themselves, it is impossible to resist the argument for less of them.[8]

Nowhere was this view encapsulated so succinctly as in the Enoch Powell speeches of the 1960s.

The year 1968 brought the Commonwealth Immigrants Act into effect. On the face of it, the Act merely applied a familiar set of qualifications for the acquisition of citizenship to immigration law. The real purpose of this provision, however, was to deprive British Asians of their right to entry to the UK on the grounds of their colour and race. UK passport holders who could not demonstrate so-called 'close connection' were placed in the same legal category as those Commonwealth citizens who were already subject to strict entry control. In addition, a voucher system was introduced. Possession of a voucher entitled a UK passport holder and his close dependents to enter and settle in Britain.

In the early months of 1968, Powell consistently returned to the Kenyan Asians, and it was partly his continued pressure that induced the government to introduce a panic Bill in the House of Commons. The Bill was passed in a matter of 24 hours and the voucher system for the Kenyan Asians was introduced. Powell himself must have been surprised at the speed and success of his campaign on this issue, which gave him (one of) the greatest public support/responses of his career. It was Powell's speech of 20 April 1968, which transformed immigration from just another political issue to *the* issue which dominated both politics and the media. In this speech he took a stance which allowed him to justify his cause as the defender of the native English people and culture who:

> found themselves made strangers in their own country. They found their wives unable to find hospital beds in childbirth, their children unable to find school places, their homes and neighbourhoods changed beyond recognition, their plans and prospects for the future defeated.[9]

Powell's speech, although officially condemned by the Conservative Party leadership, served to underline just how powerful anti-immigration feeling was, both within the Conservative Party and among the general white public.

In December 1968, Conservative Political Centre analysts stared in disbelief at the result of a confidential survey which they had designed to establish the views of 412 constituency groups

> 327 wanted all immigration stopped indefinitely. A further 55 wanted 'strictly limited' input of dependants of people already in Britain, combined with a five year halt on immigration. Some suggested special housing areas on an apartheid system, and one even talked of permanent camps in which immigrants could be placed.[10]

It was a salutory lesson for the Conservative Party, and it was their realization of the extent of support for Powell that led them to stiffen their own position on immigration. In Powell's terms, however, the Party had not gone far enough, for he not only wanted the 'numbers game' to be enacted through legislation, but also favoured the establishment of a Ministry of Repatriation to assist and encourage a massive, albeit voluntary, repatriation. Powell's one reservation was that he would not propose compulsory repatriation – perhaps the only respect in which his views differed from those of the National Front.

It is ironic that 1968 also saw the introduction of the 1968 Race Relations Act, aimed at dealing with discrimination on grounds of 'colour, race or ethnic or national origin' in employment, housing, the provision of goods, facilities of services to the public and the publication of or display of discriminatory advertisements or notices.

This Act, along with the Race Relations Acts of 1965 and 1976, represented a radical departure from the tradition of the British legal system, for it was an attempt to influence behaviour and attitudes through legislation which declared that everyone in Britain was henceforth to be treated on the basis of individual merit, regardless of race and colour. At the same time, the government was steadily endorsing the act of discrimination through its own immigration legislation. This dichotomy is perhaps best represented in the fact that Britain stands alone among Western societies in having no Bill of Rights or written constitution to guarantee equal protection of citizens under the law.

In 1971, the Conservative Government of the day endorsed some of Powell's requests by passing the 1971 Immigration Act, which provided assistance for immigrants who wished to return home and which virtually ended black 'primary' immigration, thus largely restricting future immigration to the dependants of those already settled in Britain. However, and perhaps predictably, this innovation did not end the 'immigration debate'. Instead, it encouraged those who wished to see the numbers of black people reduced even more by virtually any means available.

The Act was followed by a resurgence of openly fascist right-wing movements, whose organizational basis was – and remains – anti-black racism, and whose main policy was an end to immigration and the repatriation, by force if necessary, of all black people in the UK. The most openly fascist right-wing group is, perhaps, the National Front, who throughout this period were putting forward candidates in local elections; organizing demonstrations at Gatwick and Heathrow airports as the first Asian exiles began to arrive from Malawi; and demonstrating through the immigrant heartland of Bradford's Lumb Lane, etc.

The National Front's approach was well suited to the waves of racial tension being engendered in Britain and was aided by the BBC, for in 1976, the BBC decided to screen an anti-immigrant message from the British Campaign to Stop Immigration on its public access programme. This programme, whatever the rationale behind the decision to show it, merely added to the respectability of the 'stop immigration' forces. Other media forces, such as the

Daily Mail, Daily Mirror, the *Daily Telegraph*, the *Daily Express* and the *Guardian*, also supported the NF view by publishing a wave of articles which clearly inflamed the already sensitive issue of race relations and for which the British press and media must bear a crucial responsibility.

Nor was Enoch Powell silent during this period. In May 1976, the *Daily Mail* splashed the announcement in the Commons by Enoch Powell of a confidential report on Asian immigration. The report, at the time Powell quoted from it, was unpublished, and documented a visit to the Indian sub-continent by D. F. Hawley, a senior Foreign Office official. Hawley had been asked by the government to examine immigration procedures in the sub-continent, particularly the methods of screening dependants.

It revealed that, whilst dependants were being treated by immigration authorities as satisfactorily as possible, an increasing number were gaining entry fraudulently through both abuse of the system and through forging papers required to enter Britain. The speech from Powell on the Hawley report heralded yet another wave of racist media reporting and the political temperatures in the area of race relations rose several degrees.

In Southall, a young man, Gurdin Singh Chagger, was stabbed to death outside a pub; in East London, Mohammed Riaz Khan was charged with the murder of a white boy, Chris Adamson whilst Adamson's three brothers sat in the same court charged with making an affray. In Blackburn, local community relations officers presented documentation describing 30 or more attacks upon Asians in ten days. In East London, among the Bengali community, defence patrols of young Asians were formed to patrol the streets at night, and in Southall, Leicester, Bradford, Birmingham and Hackney, immigrant groups responded.

Groups aimed at defending themselves and their communities were a response to racist attacks and police inability or unwillingness to take action against the perpetrators of the violence.

The Labour Government of the day offered little hope of solving the increasing racism in Britain. In fact, it offered no answers at all, except the old remedy of toughening the Race Relations Laws, while simultaneously tightening the controls on immigrants. The Labour Government then, like the Conservative Party today, did not agree that legislation, despite its wider power, cannot succeed

275

in a vacuum. Inevitably, the success of any law depends upon factors such as minority and majority attitudes, political will, government leadership and backing, judicial and skilful enforcement, critical and far-reaching court decisions, linked with severe penalties for offenders.

The black population of this country does not need to ask why government immigration legislation works 'so well' and the Race Relations Act does not. It knows.

In the first month of 1978 came the notorious Margaret Thatcher speech in which she claimed that the British people were afraid that they might be 'rather swamped by people with a different culture'. The Conservative Party was clearly looking to an end to immigration. It set up a Parliamentary Select Committee on Race Relations and Immigration. Their recommendations about immigration controls *after* entry within the UK were draconian:

> The Committee had said not only that the police and the immigration services should be given more resources to deal with breaches of immigration law, and that sanctions should be enforced against businesses which employed people who were illegal immigrants or not entitled to work, but also that the government should establish an inquiry to consider a fully fledged system of internal controls within the UK. The Committee did not spell out what such a system would involve, but it was clear that it would be similar to other European systems and would require everyone or at least those subject to control. to produce an identity card if required by a police officer or other state official.[11]

In the end, the inquiry did not take place on account of some weak objections by the Labour Party, nor perhaps does it need to happen, for as many black people will witness, internal controls are already a fact of life. In 1978, the *Financial Times*, 'a newspaper not noted for hysterical reaction, commented on new British immigration proposals by asking, "How far is it from there to the pass laws?" '[12]

Now that a system of internal controls has been developed *unofficially*, one asks why the British white press do not ask the same question, for it is a question and issue that is consistently raised by organizations such as the Joint Council for the Welfare of Immigrants, the No Pass Laws Here Group, and the numerous deportation campaigns across the country.

Black groups have campaigned long and hard against virginity tests, deportations, the increase in internal controls and passport checking, not only in an attempt to alleviate injustices against individuals but to widen the understanding of the issues related to the nature of immigration controls. It is little wonder that so few of the deportation campaigns and attacks on the black community reach the white public. It is not in the interest of either the government or the white majority to acknowledge it. Indeed, the enforcement of immigration laws has spread into all areas of life – employers, government departments, health service officials, local government officers, and so on, now regularly take it upon themselves to carry out their own checks on immigration status.

This ethos in white British society, however, does not just affect the unfortunate 'illegal' immigrant but all black people – for who are the people being checked on? Many are people born in Britain or who have a right to be here but just happen to be black, and it is their blackness that makes them 'immigrants' and subject to continual harassment.

THE MEDIA

In South Africa, the government spends more per annum on information propaganda than it spends on black children's education. Britain has actively participated in South African propaganda, the aim of which is to deceive the world by camouflaging the inhuman apartheid system, by describing it in 'acceptable' terms such as 'separate development', 'plural democracy' and 'good neighbourliness'. If British governments, British corporations and the British public believe that South Africa deserves a dialogue with those decent-minded countries which are opposed to racism and apartheid, then they have simply fallen for the propaganda churned out by the Pretoria regime.

Yet this is not surprising, for Britain, too, has its propaganda machinery, it is called the media. Nowhere is the perpetuation of myths about black people more apparent than in the television, radio, films, books and newspapers, for the media is not only a key

277

barometer in measuring the level of racism that is acceptable in all areas of British society, but also an effective means of promoting and reinforcing racist attitudes and reproducing dominant racist ideologies. Images of black people as illegal immigrants, as alien, as criminal and as a problem, are continually projected, while at the same time the views of black people continue to be ignored.

Such processes are best described with reference to specific examples. On 11 March 1982, the *Daily Telegraph* reported:

Over the 200 years, up to 1945, Britain became so settled in internal peace that many came to believe that respect for the person and property of fellow citizens was something which existed naturally in all but a few. A glance at less fortunate countries might have reminded us that such respect scarcely exists unless law is above the power of the tribe, or money, or the gun. But we did not look; we let in people from the countries we did not look at, and only now do we begin to see the result. Many young West Indians in Britain, and, by a connected process, growing numbers of young whites, have no sense that the nation in which they live is part of them. So its citizens become to them mere objects of violent exploitation. People who think this way cannot be placated by judicial sympathy because to them the judgement of society is meaningless. They refuse to live within the law and figures suggest they have discovered how to live above it: if the law is to survive, the police must be allowed to ensure that offenders are made to live beneath it.

What we see in this article is merely the reworking of an old myth – an ideology, in which cruder, historically specific notions of black inferiority and lack of civilization are replaced by feelings of cultural differences, of 'Britishness', of 'whiteness', and which have been embodied in certain political and cultural traditions. In the terms of the article, cultural supremacy is being threatened 'on the streets' of Britain as it was in former colonies. The black youth in this case is defined as 'alien'; a threat to 'Britishness'; a person with no right to be here who is threatening the very fabric of British society and influencing white British youths. An examination of the press ten years previously demonstrates how views of black people as 'alien' and 'criminal' were institutionalized in a term now often used synonymously with black youth – 'mugger'.

On 5 November 1972, Mr Robert Keenan was 'mugged' on the way home from a pub by three youths. On 19 March 1973, three young men were charged with attempted murder, robbery and wounding with intent to grievous bodily harm. They were sentenced as follows: Paul Storey, 20 years; James Duigan, 10 years; and Mustafa Tuat, 10 years. All three youths were from Handsworth, Birmingham, an area known for its large black population, poor housing and high unemployment rate.

The Handsworth case prompted intensive press coverage, and its handling exemplifies the media approach to 'black' stories. It must be remembered that it is not so much the content of news coverage features but their implied ideologies which we must focus on, for:

. . . ideologies are not simply sets of ideas and beliefs about the world hanging loose in people's heads. They are made active and realised in concrete practices and apparatuses – for example, the practices and apparatuses of news construction.[13]

Prior to the Paul Storey cases, the press had covered a number of 'muggings' in the USA. Much of this coverage was both exaggerated and sensationalized. Since the principle venues of such 'muggings' were the 'black ghettos', mugging was thus linked to a whole set of complex social themes: the involvement of blacks in violent crime; the expansion of black ghettos; black unemployment and general social disorganization.

Consequently, long before 'muggings' appeared in a British setting, the general white public already had a frightening picture of 'mugging' as defined in the American context. The British public had been warned that, at home, inner-city areas were expanding and deteriorating; unemployment rates were rising. At the same time the criminal activities of black youths had been brought into the public focus.[14]

By the time that the Paul Storey case surfaced, the image of the 'mugger' as an undisciplined violent youth, was fully developed. Newspaper headlines read:

20 YEARS FOR BOY, 16, WHO WENT MUGGING FOR FUN
(*Daily Mail*, 20 March 1973)

20YEARS FOR 16 YEAR OLD MUGGER – five cigarettes and 30p from VICTIM
(*Daily Telegraph*, 20 March 1973)

GANGS SEEM TO REGARD MUGGING AS A SPORT
(*Police Federation*, 1973)

The headlines were dramatic not merely because of the nature of the crime committed, but because for many, violence represents a fundamental breakdown in social order, which can and does evoke intense feelings of antagonism against the offender. Added to these headlines were features on Paul Storey and his associates. Attempts were made to typify them and to look for the 'cause' which led them to their 'criminal careers'. In the absence of specific signs of personality disorders, the press looked to other signs: separated parents; unemployment; petty street crimes; poor environment; schooling and family breakdown. The search for such causes carried the implicit suggestion that disadvantages can lead to deviance, and equally, that a 'good' family, employment, 'decent' housing, 'sound' education, law and order, and the like keep the rest of society 'on the right road'.

Yet there was a further and more ambiguous way in which these youths were differentiated from the rest of society – namely, through the index of race. Stuart Hall *et al.*[15] point out that both the *Daily Mail* and the *Daily Express* introduced the fact that Storey had a 'West Indian father' and reported his racial resentment. The *Daily Mail* went further by underlining the 'otherness' of his 'alien' cultural background with reference to his home where 'the walls are hung with Oriental mats'.

Most newspapers, however, concentrated on the general problem of the poor environment of Handsworth, whose essential characteristics were documented as 'crime, race and poverty'. There was a continuous circle of association in which race and crime defined the 'ghetto' and in turn were defined by it; yet nowhere was there any indication of, or explanation for the possible mediations between

280

other factors, such as racism, or government policy. Equally important, the papers did not stress that violent crimes of the Storey type were not common. Though they did and do occur, the police spend much of their time dealing with petty crimes, such as driving offences, petty theft.[16]

In summary, what was presented by the newpapers was a description of associations – race, crime, housing, unemployment. Out of this emerged the image of anti-social black youth of which Storey was a prime example. The *Daily Mail* successfully summarized the familiar themes of race and crime:

All the sentenced youths are either coloured or immigrants and live in one of Birmingham's major problem areas. Police and social workers have been battling for five years to solve community problems in Handsworth, where juvenile crime steadily rises and there are continuous complaints about the relationships between police and the predominantly coloured population. (*Daily Mail*, 20 March 1973)

In so doing, it submits a powerful image of decay, race and crime, yet gives no explanation; thus the white stereotype of the black population is once again reinforced, and white images and ideologies are cemented in the pages of the newspaper propaganda they read.

In 1985, the response from the media to the most recent rebellion in Handsworth had not radically altered:

These are sensless occasions, completely without reason. (Mr Douglas Hurd, The *Guardian*, 11 September 1985)

Either they forego the anarchic luxury of these orgies of arson, looting and murderous assaults against the men and women whose task it is to uphold the laws of this land, or they will provoke a parliamentary reaction unknown to mainland Britain. (*Daily Mail*, 8 October 1985)

'They' in this case referred largely to black people, but as *A Different Reality* points out:

281

Who were the 'black lawless' rebels? Variously they were described as: 'Knots of West Indian youths', 'bitter Asians hating Blacks', 'rastafarians', 'immigrants', 'ethnics', 'criminals', 'looters', 'arsonists', 'ghetto youths', 'unstable', 'dim', 'jealous Blacks', 'drug barons', 'muggers', 'disaffected West Indians', 'tribal', and 'community leaders'. These are the plethora of terms used in the media to describe those people involved in the urban rebellions. In actual fact, those people involved in the rebellion were British, mostly born here, and they would describe themselves as white, black, Asian and black Afro-Caribbean. The urban rebellions involved both black and white people and equally those people who lost property and businesses during the rebellion were of Afro-Caribbean and Asian origins as well as white.[17]

It will not surprise you that *A Different Reality* was sponsored as an independent black view documenting the voices and interests of the local black community in Birmingham. It comprises a description of the black experience in Britain today, and locates it in a Birmingham context, but rarely can the analysis or the voices of black people be heard in the white mass media.

The fact that black people are disillusioned with their treatment at the hands of the media is evidenced by the growth of black and ethnic minority newspapers and an increasing number of initiatives aimed at establishing alternative radio stations to cater for black people's needs and news.

A major factor in the recent shelving of plans to establish community radio stations was the government's fear of ethnic minorities having their own radio stations. On television, Channel 4 has opened the door to *Black on Black* and *Eastern Eye*, Indian films, and so forth. and at times there are comedy programmes such as *No Problem* or Eastern cookery classes aimed at teaching the masses how to cook a curry – but as Sivanandan rightly states:

These programmes merely replicate white media, even Black plays and comedies. 'No Problem' is a problem; we are laughing at ourselves. The system wants that kind of replication. What we want on 'Black on Black' and 'Eastern Eye' is an unbalanced view. The whole society is unbalanced against us . . . [18]

It is the unbalanced view that perhaps marks out certain sections of the black press, journals, books and newsletters, from the mainstream white mass media. For the black media recognizes the importance of the media of communication and information, especially in societies in which racist oppression exists. Perhaps the parent of the black press was when the *West Indian Gazette*, in 1958, became the first major black newspaper. The *West Indian Gazette* stood for an independent and united West Indies; justice for black people in Britain, and world peace:

> For the first time in the history of blacks there developed a campaigning and a popular newspaper with the concerns being the conditions of Blacks in Britain and the Caribbean, and the liberation of all peoples everywhere.[19]

The *Gazette* campaigned vigorously on all issues – riots, immigration control, housing, unemployment, police frame-ups, and so on, and on the role of the black press in campaigns Scobie comments: 'Most bitter and outspoken against immigration controls were the black publications. Among those foremost in fighting the Act were the West Indian Gazette and Flamingo – both published in London.'[20]

It is hardly surprising that black publications are still the only ones to argue systematically against immigration controls, to report on racial attacks, to cover police frame-ups, and to outline and analyse the racist inner-city policies of the government. The white press have not yet opened their minds to the need for an anti-racist media and will continue to do little unless strong government leadership by example indicates otherwise.

BRITAIN'S LINKS WITH SOUTH AFRICA

British racist ideology can be most clearly seen in the British state's complicity with apartheid despite its diplomatic protestations to the contrary.

The International and Defence Aid Fund identified between 2,000 and 25,000 transnational corporations as having subsidiaries or associated companies, or other investments in South Africa. 'In

1980, Britain was at the top of the list and continues to be one of the largest investors in South Africa.'[21] This is illustrated clearly in Table 10.1.

Table 10.1
Number of companies in South Africa based in other countries, 1980

Britain	1,200	Australia	35	Spain	6
W. Germany	350	Belgium	20	Canada	5
USA	340	Italy	20		
France	50	Switzerland	12		
Netherlands	50	Sweden	10		

Source: 'Apartheid and Business', *Business International Multi-client Survey.*

It is hardly surprising, therefore, that Britain has always argued against imposing sanctions against South Africa on the grounds that they will not work. This stance insults the oppressed blacks of South Africa.

They are in effect saying to the blacks that they are stupid and incapable of differentiating between their long-term interests and self-destruction. They pretend they are unaware of the fact that the blacks of South Africa want the multi-national corporations, which they regard as monsters, out of South Africa.[22]

In contrast, when Britain has been encouraged to impose sanctions against Iran or Poland, she seems to have had no such qualms! If British governments and corporations invest in South Africa because of their missionary, philanthropic zeal, why do they not show their concern for the black citizens of their own country? There are perhaps not many differences between the thoughts of Cecil Rhodes who, as he walked across the South African veld, said:

As I walked, I looked up at the sky and down to the earth and I said to myself this should be British. And it came to me in that fine, exhilarating air that the British were the best race to rule the world.[23]

and the words of Margaret Thatcher in her now notorious 'swamping of the culture speech' which succeeded so well in whipping up feelings and fears against black people in Britain.

Inherent in Britain's imperialistic history, in the apartheid system and in racism in Britain today, is the innate belief in the superiority of the white race and hence in the 'white man's burden'. A burden which allows the oppression of black people across the world whilst projecting a paternalistic, missionary and philanthropic attitude which belies its true motives. It is therefore hardly surprising that the major institutions and organizations – from churches, to the media, to parliament – are unwilling to ask:

'How do we ensure human rights for all human beings?'

'How do we need to understand and act upon our complicity in the racist structure of South Africa, through the economic involvement of Britain and her institutions?'

'How do we become sensitive to the insidious way in which racism so often becomes excused in the name of white superiority, economic interest, religion, justice, etc.?'

'How do we dismantle racism, which is the most pernicious tool in Britain used by those holding power to maintain their privileged position?'

In South Africa, rigid theological and political conditioning of white South Africans perpetuates apartheid. The tactics used to perpetuate apartheid and the maintenance of white supremacy differ only in their delivery. In Britain from the year that history first documented the presence of black people, the notion of white supremacy has abounded and with it the dehumanizing of black people into, at worst, sub-humans more akin to animals, and at best, children who need to be taught what only the 'master race' can offer.

In the nineteenth century, British writer Winwoode Reade wrote:

285

The typical negro, unrestrained by moral laws, spends his days in sloth, his nights in debauchery. He smokes haschisch till he stupifies his senses, or falls into convulsions; he drinks palm wine till he brings on a loathsome disease; he abuses children; stabs the poor brute of a woman whose hands keeps him from starvation; and makes a trade of his own offspring. He swallows up his youth in premature vice; he lingers through a manhood of disease; and his tardy death is hastened by those who no longer care to find him food. Such are the 'men and brothers' for whom their friends claim not protection but equality! They do not merit to be called our Brothers; but let us call them our Children.[24]

This statement is typical of many to be found throughout history and which persist in Britain today. The language may have altered but the myths have been perpetuated and continue to ensure that black people are always seen as unequal to whites.

The racism and discrimination expressed by black people in relation to housing, employment, education, immigration laws, police, racial attacks, politics, social services, involvement in decision-making – in fact in any area of life – receive insignificant coverage in mainstream media or government policy. Racism in Britain or Britain's attitude and actions in South Africa will not be solved until central government leads by example. Whilst it fails to do so, blacks in South Africa and black people in Britain will be touched by racism in every aspect of their daily lives.

CONCLUSION

In 1977, following the Grunwick dispute where Asian workers were fighting for union recognition against exploitative, adamant management, Tyndall, a member of the National Front, stated:

Equip the police with water cannon, tear gas, and rubber bullets, with full authority to use those implements as the situation requires. . . . When we obtain the mandate to govern this country as one day we will, we will take all measures necessary to restore the rule of laws to our streets and places of work, learning and leisure.[25]

Now the rhetoric and reality in this case are one. (Only the distinction in party title is different.)

This chapter has sought to show that the British government's inaction towards the racist regime in South Africa is not an isolated act, but part of an historical and structural situation which pervades the lives of contemporary black Britons.

In Birmingham, black youths voice the opinion of black people across the country.

We just want to be ourselves.
We want to do our own thing.
We don't want no harassment.
We don't want no discrimination.
That's not a lot to ask for – its very basic – but we can't get it![26]

The rhetoric as been the same for many decades, it is just the reality that has changed. The message has always been clear, but the agenda has always been set by both government and the media.

Notes

1. Amrit Wilson, *Finding a Voice*, London: Virago, 1978, p. 72. Asian women in Britain.
2. For example see J. Garrard, *The English and Immigration: A Comparative Study of Jewish Influx, 1881–1910*, Institute of Race Relations and Oxford University Press, 1971; R. Moore and T. Wallace, *Slamming the Door*, London: Martin Robertson, 1975; C. Peach, *West Indian Migration to Britain*, London: Oxford University Press, 1968.
3. Action Group on Immigration and Nationality (AGIN), *Background Briefing on Reform of Nationality and Immigration Laws*, London: AGIN, n.d., p. 2.
4. Ibid., p. 3.
5. Ibid., p. 4.
6. Ibid., p. 3.
7. A. Sivananandan, 'From Resistance to Rebellion: Asian and Afro-Caribbean Struggles in Britain,' *Race and Class*, vol. 23, 1982, p. 112.
8. Paul Gordon, *Policing Immigration*, London: Pluto Press, 1985, p. 37. Britain's internal controls.
9. Martin Walker, *The National Front*, London: 1977. p. 109.
10. Ibid., p. 111.
11. Gordon, op.cit., p. 1.
12. Ibid.
13. Stuart Hall, *et al.*, *Policing the Crisis*, London, Macmillan, 1978, p. 83. Mugging, the state, and law and order.
14. For more detailed discussion see 'Blacks, Police and Crime', Chapter 3 in this volume.

15. Hall, op.cit., note 13.
16. See chapter 3 in this volume.
17. West Midlands County Council, *A Different Reality*, Report of the Review Panel into the Handsworth rebellions of 1985, 1986, p. 12.
18. *Black Trade Unionist*, January-June 1984, p. 5.
19. Buzz Johnson, *I Think of My Mother*, Ilinois: Karia Press, 1984. p. 82.
20. Ibid., p.83.
21. International Defence and Aid Fund (IDAF) *Apartheid, The Facts*, London: International Defence and Aid Fund for South Africa in co-operation with the UN Centre Against Apartheid, 1983, p. 82.
22. Sipo E, Mzimela, *Apartheid – South African Naziism*, New York, 1983, p. 181.
23. Ibid.
24. Peter Fryer, *Staying Power*, London: Pluto Press, 1984. p. 188.
25. Walker, op.cit., p. 231.
26. West Midlands County Council, op.cit., p. 61.

Subject Index

Author Index